THE RACE TO 270

THE RACE TO

270

THE ELECTORAL COLLEGE AND THE
CAMPAIGN STRATEGIES OF 2000 AND 2004

DARON R. SHAW

THE UNIVERSITY OF CHICAGO PRESS

Chicago and London

DARON R. SHAW is associate professor in the Department of Government at the University of Texas at Austin and coeditor of *Communication in U.S. Elections: New Agendas* (2001, with Roderick Hart).

The University of Chicago Press, Chicago 60637
The University of Chicago Press, Ltd., London
© 2006 by The University of Chicago
All rights reserved. Published 2006
Printed in the United States of America

15 14 13 12 11 10 09 08 07 06   1 2 3 4 5

ISBN-13: 978-0-226-75133-7 (cloth)
ISBN-13: 978-0-226-75134-4 (paper)
ISBN-10: 0-226-75133-3 (cloth)
ISBN-10: 0-226-75134-1 (paper)

Library of Congress Cataloging-in-Publication Data

Shaw, Daron R., 1966–
    The race to 270 : the Electoral College and the campaign strategies of 2000 and 2004 / Daron R. Shaw.
        p.   cm.
    . Includes bibliographical references and index.
    ISBN-13: 978-0-226-75133-7 (cloth : alk. paper)
    ISBN-13: 978-0-226-75134-4 (pbk. : alk. paper)
    ISBN-10: 0-226-75133-3 (cloth : alk. paper)
    ISBN-10: 0-226-75134-1 (pbk. : alk. paper)
    1. Political campaigns—United States. 2. Electoral college—United States.
3. Advertising, Political—United States. 4. Communication in politics—United States. 5. Presidents—United States—Election—2000. 6. Presidents—United States—Election—2004. I. Title. II. Title: Electoral college and the campaign strategies of 2000 and 2004.
    JK1976.S53   2007
    324.973'0929—dc22

                                                              2006011428

To Shelly, my inspiration

CONTENTS

TABLES AND FIGURES

TABLES

ACKNOWLEDGMENTS

This book would not have been possible without the cooperation and assistance of many colleagues, coworkers, friends, and family members. First, I wish to acknowledge members of the Bush-Cheney 2000 and 2004 campaigns whose professionalism and friendship made this project not only possible but enjoyable: Joe Albaugh, Stacey Carlson, Maria Cino, Scott Douglas, Michael Ellis, John David Estes, Don Evans, Denise Gitsam, Adrian Gray, Chris Henick, Israel Hernandez, Emily House, Coddy Johnson, Melissa Langsam, Mark McKinnon, Ken Mehlman, Kristen Palasciano, Anthony Ryba, Michael Shannon, Kevin Shuvalov, Sara Taylor, Meredith Terpeluk, Chris Turner, Erin Vargo, and Neal Zimmerman. Two people from the Bush campaigns merit special thanks: Karl Rove and Matthew Dowd. Without their help and encouragement, this project would not have come into being. I also wish to acknowledge the invaluable time and assistance I received from members of the Gore and Kerry campaigns. Most notably, I acknowledge the contributions of Carter Eskew, Stanley Greenberg, Bill Knapp, and Robert Shrum.

Second, I wish to thank colleagues whose advice, comments, and criticism helped improve the conceptualization and execution of this project: James Campbell, Thomas Holbrook, Sunshine Hillygus, Shanto Iyengar, Kathleen Hall Jamieson, Karen Kaufmann, Robert Luskin, Scott McClurg, John Petrocik, Sam Popkin, Brian Roberts, and John Sides.

Third, I wish to acknowledge the assistance of a number of people at the University of Texas at Austin and at the University of Chicago Press. At UT-Austin, I thank Ernest McGowen, Jeremy Teigen, and Michael Unger for their dedicated and expert work on data analysis and background research. At Chicago, I thank Leslie Keros, Lori Meek Schuldt, Rodney Powell, and John Tryneski for helping me make this book all that I wanted it to be.

Last but not least, I wish to thank my family. The debt I owe to my dad, Robert, and my mom, Cynthia (who died in 1979), is beyond my ability to calculate. My wife, Shelly, and children, Jack, Kelly, and Kyle, bore the direct brunt of this project. They were with me every step of the way through the long hours of the campaign and the arduous task of preparing this manuscript. Shelly also served as my primary editor, sounding board, and cheerleader. It is to her that I dedicate this book.

1

BRIDGING THE GREAT DIVIDE

We knew this would be a tough fight, but the important thing right now is confidence in who we are and all that we have done up to this point. Trust the candidate. Trust the campaign.

KARL ROVE, to the Bush campaign staff the morning after the 2000 New Hampshire primary

This is a different kind of book. It is neither wholly academic nor journalistic. It draws heavily on my education and experience as a social scientist as well as on observations gleaned from my involvement in presidential campaigns. At its core, it is a book that attempts to bridge the gap between those who *study* campaigns and those who *do* campaigns. The perspectives of both academics and practitioners are called upon to shed light on two particular topics: the intent and the effect of presidential campaigns. The central argument is that campaigns affect voters and electorates. Documenting and characterizing these effects, however, requires greater strategic insight and better empirical data than have heretofore been brought to bear.

Both professional and personal factors drive this effort. Professionally, I have noticed a recent shift in the attitudes of campaign consultants and political scientists toward each other. Do not read too much into this observation. Consultants still profess disdain for academics. A Democratic friend of mine told me that James Carville once said to him, "There isn't one idea from political science that has ever been of use in a real political campaign."[1] Setting aside the Carvillian hyperbole of this statement—I assume it means that median voter theory, party identification, and retrospective voting are either irrelevant or so obvious that political science gets no credit for discovering them—it effectively captures the traditional belief among people practicing politics that academicians tend to focus on esoteric concerns. Practitioners often believe that most political scientists have no sense of what campaigns do and therefore are in no position to judge their impact. This opinion is, in a sense, analogous to the disdain many athletes feel for reporters who have never "played the game."

But consultants increasingly monitor, and even read, the top political science journals and university presses. Bush senior adviser Karl Rove freely extols the virtues of Thomas Patterson's analysis of the media in *Out of Order* (1993) and has several copies of Samuel Popkin's book *The Reasoning Voter* (1991) in his office in the West Wing of the White House. Across the partisan aisle, Democratic pollster Stanley Greenberg was an assistant professor at Yale University and often references realignment theory in analyzing trends in contemporary survey data. More generally, in the 2000 and 2004 election campaigns, top-level strategists from both parties were well aware of what political science had to say about primary fights, convention bounces, debate effects, negative advertisements, television ad watches, and (of course) election forecasting models.

On the other side of the divide, political scientists have become increasingly interested in presidential campaigns. I describe the origins of our historical lack of interest in chapter 2, but for the present discussion suffice it to say that for years there has been a consensus that presidential campaigns are primarily the means by which we arrive at predictable outcomes. Jimmy Carter's ouster in 1980 and Ronald Reagan's landslide victory in 1984 reinforced this consensus. Despite the success of presidential election forecasting models in 1988, however, I believe the Bush-Dukakis race sowed the seeds of discontent with the conventional perspective. In particular, many political scientists believe that George H. W. Bush outmaneuvered Michael Dukakis for the presidency, largely by waging a trivial and negative campaign. There is, of course, a fascinating irony here: scholarly interest rose dramatically in the wake of what was to many a disappointing and distasteful presidential campaign.

This increased academic interest is manifest in the emergence of several cottage industries within the study of American elections. Most notably, there has been a surge in research on negative advertising, news media coverage, get-out-the-vote efforts, and aggregate- and individual-level movement in the presidential preference polls. We have also seen a number of political scientists serve in presidential campaigns, bringing back a range of unique and interesting data on candidate and campaign activities as well as on voters' preferences.[2] There appears to be an academic market for the kinds of expertise that campaign consultants have and the sort of data to which they have access.

This confluence of interest and circumstance brings me to my reason for writing this book. I want to describe what it is that presidential campaigns actually do and how well their strategies and activities work toward their goal of winning the election. Of course, it would be a monumental (and foolhardy) task to set out to decide, once and for all, whether campaigns matter.[3] I am not so ambitious. I do believe, however, that I can advance the debate by joining detailed descriptive knowledge of how campaigns operate with high-level analyses of their influence. Perhaps most important, I believe that understanding American campaigns is crucial to understanding the nature of democracy in the United States. Campaigns are the connective tissue between elected officials and citizens. The notion that campaigns are irrelevant, or even mechanistic, calls into question much of what we think we know about politics in the United States. If elections are predictable referenda based on some combination of the performance of officeholders and the underlying distribution of party identification, it doesn't much matter what challengers propose during the campaign; they win or lose based on exogenous factors. Should they be advantaged by conditions and win, it would mean they should not feel constrained by the promises or proposals they made during the campaign when they take office, as voters will judge them solely on results. Nor should they feel compelled to represent particular interests, as party and performance will determine whether or not groups give their support. A truly savvy candidate would therefore care only about creating a favorable environment and then activating latent predispositions. There is, in short, little deliberation, little representation, and only a gross sort of accountability. If even partially accurate, this is a profoundly different type of democracy than the framers of the Constitution had in mind and ought to command the attention of all Americans.

There are, of course, other reasons for caring about campaigns and their effects. Political campaigns around the globe, but especially in the United States, cost a great deal of money. Individuals, corporations, labor unions, and ideological organizations of all stripes contribute money to campaigns, and it would be quite interesting if one were to empirically establish that all of this cash does nothing to affect the outcomes of elections. The prospect of the irrelevant campaign is even more intriguing given (1) the recent increase in free and fair democratic elections around the world, particularly since the fall of the Soviet Union, and (2) the increased prominence of American-style electioneering within these democracies. This first point is particularly unnerving: What if the data show that American election outcomes are as predictable as those in the USSR under Stalin (with incumbent job approval and party identification replacing the secret police as the determinative force)? As for the second point, recent examples of American consultants advising Tony Blair in Great Britain, Vicente Fox in Mexico, Ehud Barak in Israel, and Boris Yeltsin in Russia can be seen as a harbinger of things to come, but only if foreign clients are convinced that these campaign professionals are worth their cost in electoral gold.

As I stated at the outset, the core thesis of this book is that presidential campaigns affect voters and electorates. The particular arguments I advance are simple. First, presidential campaigns see the world in terms of amassing 270 electoral votes, which requires identifying, persuading, and/or mobilizing a requisite number of voters in battleground states. In short, they make plans. Campaigns do not seek to talk to everyone, and if they can avoid "wasted effort," they will. Furthermore, resources are allocated roughly according to the campaign's plan, although the activities of the opposition and the broader strategic concerns of the party force deviations.

Second, although state outcomes ultimately decide the election, paid and free media dictate that media markets also constitute an important level of analysis. Television ads occur at the media market level, and candidate appearances attempt to drive local news media coverage. We run the risk of mismeasurement if we ignore the point at which aggregate political communication occurs.

Third, because it is difficult to attain campaigning advantages in the most significant electoral battlegrounds, favorable movement in voters' preferences is neither easy nor especially common. In fact, perhaps my strongest empirical finding is that one needs to account for the weekly ebb and flow of campaigning to uncover the nature and magnitude of campaign effects. Cross-sectional analyses rarely show campaign effects because they are insensitive to this dynamic strategic reality. This is something campaign veterans know instinctively, but it has never been established empirically.

Fourth, campaigns usually attempt to affect voters' perceptions of candidates, which they presume leads to a positive shift in the vote. In other words, campaigns seek to improve the net favorability of their candidate while eroding their opponent's. Such shifts in net favorability subsequently drive the minor vote shifts we typically see over the fall campaign.

Over the course of my three empirical chapters, I test a variety of subtle twists on each of the main claims, which creates a more detailed picture of the underlying dynamic of presidential campaigns. But these simple arguments anchor the analysis.

The 2000 and 2004 presidential election campaigns provide a unique and serendipitous opportunity to enhance our understanding of what presidential campaigns actually do and how effective their efforts are. Some appreciable portion of this serendipity is personal. In 1999 and 2000, as I was teaching classes and conducting research as an assistant professor at the University of Texas at Austin, I was also serving as the director of election studies for the Bush (and, later, the Bush-Cheney) campaign. In addition to aging considerably during this time, I had an opportunity to see a presidential campaign from the inside. Initially, I had four tasks: (1) developing county- and media-market-level vote targets for the Republican primaries, (2) redeveloping these targets for the general election, (3) developing and maintaining an Electoral College model for rank-ordering states according to Republican potential, and (4) participating in a working group on the Catholic vote. Outside of running a few numbers and writing a memo or two, I did nothing on the fourth task. The other three, however, presented an enormous research agenda.[4]

Not only did I witness the formulation and execution of presidential campaign strategy but the relatively small general staff also made the process more interpretable than might be the case for, say, an incumbent seeking reelection. For example, at its most expansive, the Bush campaign's Strategy Department included only fourteen full-time people: Karl Rove (chief strategist), Matthew Dowd (director of polling), Chris Henick (deputy chief strategist), myself, Israel Hernandez (deputy assistant), Bill Rice (director of computer and IT [information technology]), Kristen Palasciano (administrative assistant to Rove), and interns John David Estes, Josh Ginsberg, Denise Gitsam, Emily House, Michael Shannon, Meredith Terpeluk, and Neil Zimmerman. Moreover, the main office in Austin had approximately 120 people, counting volunteers, throughout the summer of 2000. It was, in short, an opportunity to observe a presidential campaign that many political scientists would kill for.

Following Bush's controversial triumph in 2000, I maintained close ties with the people who would form the nucleus of the Bush-Cheney 2004 reelection effort. Although I did not move to Alexandria, Virginia, to work on the reelection campaign, I served as a consultant for Bush-Cheney '04 and the Republican National Committee. This role afforded me an opportunity to engage in some of the planning and analysis for 2004; ultimately, I helped set state, county, and precinct vote targets. It also allowed me to again witness—though from afar—the development and execution of the campaign strategy. Again, the experience was extraordinarily informative for a researcher whose core interest is election campaigns.

I mention all of this for two reasons. First, I have developed empathy for how political scientists view campaign consultants and how consultants view political scientists. Not just sympathy, but empathy. For example, I understand political scientists who think that campaign personnel can be enormously egocentric in their causal assessments of the political world. Oftentimes, they do not value the necessity of creating and maintaining databases, nor do they appreciate some of the core canons of social science research. Perhaps most annoying is that their interest in broad, theoretical issues tends to dry up and blow away as the leaves begin to turn in autumn of election years.

But I also understand political consultants who think academics sometimes mistake broad tendencies for absolute laws and blur the lines between suggestive correlation and causal argumentation. Furthermore, they often fail to dig deeply into phenomena that are at the core of democratic processes because their preferred theories have not been falsified. Perhaps most annoying is that more than a few scholars fail to employ the "giggle test" when considering the plausibility of their explanations and political insights.

Still, while both sides have their faults, each has an enormous cache of knowledge to share. The exchange of this knowledge has begun and could lead to both significantly improved analyses and more fruitful theoretical complexity. I want to explicitly acknowledge and comment on this interchange throughout this book.

My second reason for spelling out my involvement in the 2000 and 2004 elections is intellectual honesty. Much of what I have to say, including occasional assertions that "this is the way things were," is based on daily observations of (and conversations with) people in the Bush campaign. I do not wish to exclude this experience as some sort of pretense to intellectual objectivity because much of what I experienced is germane to the important arguments I wish to make and the broader questions at hand. Indeed, these experiences breathe life into the data I present here. And I would feel like a phony disguising these experiences as interviews or secondhand conversations (which, by and large, they were not).

The downside is that people may have concerns about the objectivity of my analysis. That is a trade-off I am willing to accept. The questions that motivate this work center on the nature and effects of presidential campaigns, and I do not think I have any particular interest (surely not a partisan one) in arguing that campaigns do or do not matter. One might argue that my history predisposes me to believe that campaigns matter, and I would agree. My conclusions on this matter, however, are more ambivalent than one might assume.

JOURNALISTIC NARRATIVE AS THE DOMINANT APPROACH TO STUDYING CAMPAIGNS

Setting aside for the moment the debates and trends within political science and professional politics, one might reasonably ask: how does this book differ from the scores of presidential campaign books that dot the popular-literature landscape? Answering this question requires a brief overview of the masterworks of the genre. Let me begin at the obvious point of origin: journalistic narratives have dominated the study of presidential campaigns since Theodore White's *The Making of the President, 1960* (1961), the wonderful and evocative account of the presidential race between John F. Kennedy and Richard Nixon.[5] While White's books remain in a class by themselves, a number of other efforts have had both commercial success and an influence on our understanding of specific elections. From 1980 to 1992, Jack Germond and Jules Witcover, two respected political journalists, wrote a series of well-received presidential campaign narratives based on their personal observations and interviews with major players (Germond and Witcover 1981; 1985; 1989; 1993). They stopped after their treatment of the 1992 election, and Germond recently observed, "There is no demand anymore for those campaign books."[6] Similarly, *Newsweek,* which assigns half a dozen or more reporters to presidential campaigns, has published several books in its *Quest for the Presidency* series. These volumes are the product of what newsmagazines call "group" journalism, in which campaign correspondents are asked to "weave their discoveries and insights into a coherent whole and to set it in the context of its time" (Goldman et al. 1994, x). In their 1992 narrative, the authors write,

> This is a work of journalism, not of scholarship, or of political theory, or of public policy. Readers will search it in vain for detailed analysis of the various "plans" offered by the candidates or for a moral commentary on the state of our society and its institutions and processes of self-government. This is, rather, a book about what has come to be called practical politics—the inside story of how presidents are made, (and) broken, in the late twentieth century. (Goldman et al. 1994, x)

Note the candid indifference to both normative and broader theoretical concerns.

Not all journalistic accounts have been straightforward linear narratives, however. In 1992, Richard Ben Cramer's *What It Takes* hit the bookshelves—a 1,047-page tome on six contenders for the White House in 1988. Cramer's book hopscotched from candidate to candidate, simultaneously careening between the here and now of the campaign and the candidates' biographies. Even more off the beaten path is Joe Klein's *Primary Colors* (1996), a fictitious but eerily familiar story of a talented but flawed candidate for the Democratic presidential nomination. The Clintonesque tale mixed the basic story line from the 1992 campaign with exaggerated personalities and drama.

More distantly, there are the seminal books from the 1972 presidential campaign: Hunter S. Thompson's *Fear and Loathing on the Campaign Trail '72* (1973) and Timothy Crouse's *The Boys on the Bus* (1974). *Fear and Loathing* is Thompson's prototype of the reporter-as-participant style known as *gonzo* journalism. In it, the campaign provides a cast of colorful characters (mostly reporters) and a coherent narrative to a story that is otherwise distinguished by episodes of drinking and drugs. Crouse's book also focuses on reporters rather than candidates, but the anecdotes and observations are then used to identify a series of principles about the nature of American campaign reporting. It is Crouse who lays the groundwork for subsequent, more formal conceptualizations of "momentum candidates," "media feeding frenzies," and "gotcha journalism."

As an avid reader of political history and current events, I have devoured these and many other books in this genre. As a political scientist and someone who pores over the latest journals and university press offerings, I occasionally feel a little guilty about enjoying these books. For starters, there is rarely any compelling theory or argument. Campaigns are assumed to be inherently interesting, so there is no effort to say why a particular race deserves our attention. In the parlance of political science, little effort is made to address the "So what?" question. Such is not always the case—for example, *Quest for the Presidency, 1992* offers a detailed argument that the 1992 campaign was a watershed—but more often than not, the narrative is implicitly justified by its entertainment value or by the vague notion that the significance of campaigns is self-evident.

Beyond the frequent absence of a broader theoretical rationale, oftentimes campaign narratives lack even a narrow argument. How was Reagan able to crack open a close race in 1980? How was third-party candidate Ross Perot able to capture one out of five voters in 1992? Was Dukakis's demise in 1988 the inevitable consequence of a decent economy and a popular incumbent? These are the sorts of things that political junkies, as well as political scientists, want to know. Unfortunately, campaign narratives tend not to build a case for a particular interpretation of how events came to pass. Rather, they simply detail the events themselves, occasionally emphasizing some over others as a backhanded way of making an argument.

Perhaps the most difficult thing about campaign narratives is that even when arguments are made, they rely on scant, impressionistic evidence. Secondhand opinions, in particular, are often featured. Did the revelation of George W. Bush's drunk-driving arrest in Maine cost him votes and allow Al Gore to win the popular vote in the 2000 election? Well, according to Gore's campaign manager, it was actually the Democrats' Social Security ads. But a Bush strategist says the incident cost Bush five days of press in New England and ultimately gave Gore the state of Maine. Journalists are not trained to be analysts (just as political scientists are barely trained to be writers), but there is something unsatisfying about allowing the participants to offer competing versions of cause and effect without an independent examination of empirical evidence.

A DIFFERENT APPROACH TO STUDYING CAMPAIGNS

This book focuses on a few "big" questions concerning what a presidential campaign does and how much influence it has on voters and election results. In engaging these questions, I take a perspective similar to that advanced by King, Keohane, and Verba's *Designing Social Inquiry* (1994): To understand a phenomenon, it is appropriate first to identify it, to describe it and all of its constituent parts, and then to analyze its occurrence and effects. What I wish to accomplish is thus one part definitional, one part descriptive, and one part analytic. The relative weight given the parts is not proportional, however, and my predilection is to give greater weight to the third, analytic part.

In fact, the initial definitional component of the book can be dealt with both immediately and parsimoniously. I will concern myself with only the most overt and outward expressions of presidential campaigning: television advertising and candidate appearances. This approach excludes a wide array of campaign activity that is of general interest (such as news media coverage, organization, fund-raising, and opposition research) and some activities that might be of particular interest in 2000 and 2004 (grassroots organization, personal contacting, direct mail, and phone messaging). But it encompasses the most obvious means by which candidates communicate with voters and articulate issues, themes, and agendas. My assumption is that we can learn much about campaigns and their effects by studying the "high-end" manifestations of electioneering. They are not the entirety of campaigning but constitute an important slice of the whole.

The descriptive and analytic parts of the book require more time and energy. After a delineation of the political science literature on campaigns in chapter 2—a detailed examination of what we know and don't know about presidential campaigns—the body of the book contains three empirical chapters. Chapter 3 begins this trilogy by asking what an Electoral College strategy looks like. I offer several possible orienting principles, most gleaned from the 1988 through 1996 presidential election campaigns, and then test them against the actual strategies employed by the campaigns in 2000 and 2004. In describing these strategies, I rely on data and illustrative examples from both Republican and Democratic campaigns. More specifically, I look at their respective methods for identifying battleground states, their targeting criteria within those states, and their processes for updating strategies. The discussion of Republican plans is based on memorandums and conversations occurring during my time as an analyst with (and consultant for) the Bush-Cheney campaigns. The Gore and Kerry plans are deduced from formal presentations and informal discussions involving key players from the Democratic campaigns.[7]

Chapter 4 hones in on the allocation of television advertising and candidate appearances. The fundamental premise of the chapter is that descriptions of the distribution of the volume of campaigning are useful, in fact *vital*, to assessing campaign strategies and their influence on voters' preferences. The most striking feature of this analysis is the availability of detailed data on (1) the presidential (and vice presidential) candidates' campaign appearances, and (2) the candidates' (and parties') television advertising expenditures. Both statewide appearance and TV ad data are charted on a weekly basis from Labor Day to Election Day in 2000 and 2004. These numbers are also presented by media market, arguably the most appropriate unit of analysis, over the same time period. In describing the allocation of these resources by the Republican and Democratic campaigns, I note the significant overall edge in party and candidate resources brought to bear by the Republicans (an edge that was offset by Democratic-leaning interest group activities in 2004). In addition, I test several hypotheses about overall and over-time variations in resource allocations. These tests reveal strategic gambles by the campaigns that may have affected the election outcomes.

Chapter 5 examines the influence of campaigning on voters' preferences. My goal here is to consider campaigning effects from a variety of perspectives. First, I examine impact across states and then across media markets. Second, I consider the influence of campaigning on not only candidate support but also voters' favorability ratings of the candidates. Third, I estimate mobilization and persuasion effects through the use of control and interactive variables in multivariate models. Fourth and finally, I use pooled time series data to construct a more dynamic (and realistic) picture of campaign effects. At first glance, the data seem to demonstrate that campaigning advantages accrued over the fall do not consistently or significantly affect either vote choice or candidate favorability advantages. Upon closer inspection, however, it becomes clear that this is because both sides expend sufficient resources to get their messages out and because it is rare that one side allows the other to sustain a campaigning advantage in a competitive state. This interpretation is most clearly borne out by the pooled time series analysis, which provides evidence that short-term campaigning advantages produce support gains.

Chapter 6 briefly reviews the main results of the empirical chapters and then returns to the curious relationship between academics and consultants. Initially, I consider the "mistakes" made by the campaigns and by political scientists in 2000 and 2004. Ostensibly, this exercise refocuses attention on the different perspectives of practitioners and scholars, highlighting the shortcomings of both. I must admit another motivation, however: it is fun to point out the mistakes of very smart people. Having acknowledged this motivation, I strive to be as generous and constructive as possible. In fact, it is in my own interest to do so since I helped make these mistakes at both levels and will probably be implicated by my academic and practitioner colleagues if I do not do so myself. I conclude with a broader discussion of what the future may hold, with respect to both trends in campaigning and scholarly analyses of these campaigns.

WHY THE BUSH ELECTIONS?

There is some risk, of course, in focusing on only two election campaigns. Invariably questions arise about whether the cases under scrutiny are representative and the lessons learned generalizable. Although I am sympathetic to these concerns, alternative strategies have significant drawbacks. For example, one could analyze and compare several campaigns, with an eye toward developing a broader conceptualization of presidential electioneering. When it comes to the American presidential campaign, however, it is not clear that comparing multiple cases is a wise strategy. For starters, the technical innovations occurring between 1988 and 2004—the Internet, e-mail, cell phones, and the like—are staggering. Campaigning simply looks different today than it did as recently as a decade ago. More-over, relevant data (such as data on television ad buys) are often unavail-able for all but the most recent elections. Another alternative would be to identify a "typical" presidential election and focus on drawing lessons from that campaign. But this strategy is a nonstarter. Setting aside the problem of developing a suitable criterion for "typical," such a campaign would probably be too distant to be of much use for understanding future campaigns.

My selection is not, however, a matter of choosing the lesser of evils. In fact, I believe there is a strong, affirmative case to be made in favor of studying the Bush-Gore and Bush-Kerry campaigns. More specifically, there are four reasons to think these campaigns constitute appropriate case studies. First, the competitiveness of these races means that cam-paign moves were made with precious little room for error. This lack of wiggle room created a greater incentive for purely strategic maneuvering, making it easier to study and assess the contours and effects of strategy.[8]

Second, while these elections were close, they were not unusually vola-tile.[9] Instead, candidate preferences moved incrementally at a few critical junctures, occasionally transforming the nature of these races. Chapter 5, in fact, offers a brief review of voters' preferences across 2000 and 2004 and provides some evidence for this assertion. We are therefore not at all sure that campaigning over the entirety of the 2000 and 2004 elections had much of an impact.

Third, there were a large number of battleground states in both 2000 and 2004. Depending on who does the counting, there were as many as twenty-four states "in play" during 2000 and twenty during 2004. In contrast, seventeen and nineteen states were widely viewed as "in play" during 1996 and 1992, respectively.[10] This means that 2000 and 2004 saw more potential venues for campaigning, which increases the number of cases available for scrutiny.

Fourth, and perhaps most important, extraordinary data are available from the 2000 and 2004 races. Through my involvement with the Bush campaigns and from my contacts with the Gore and Kerry campaigns, I can bring to bear information on the candidates' strategies, their me-dia buys, and their tracking and brushfire polls from battleground states. With each cycle, it seems that scholars are increasingly successful at pry-ing loose appropriate and accurate contextual data from campaigns. For 2000 and 2004, besides the unique and original data from the campaigns themselves, there are also complementary data, which can be used for the generation of hypotheses and for validation. For example, researchers at the University of Pennsylvania's Annenberg School for Communication conducted rolling cross-sectional surveys in each year, interviewing more than two hundred thousand registered voters as the campaigns unfolded. Similarly, there is Knowledge Networks' Internet panel survey, which provided thousands of Americans with computers and Internet access in exchange for these participants agreeing to complete surveys throughout 2000 and 2004. There is also the Campaign Media Analysis Group, which estimated campaign expenditures in most of the nation's top media markets.

To be sure, there are potential pitfalls. For example, some critics might say that using these presidential campaigns to investigate effects is like shooting fish in a barrel. The closeness of the races could be seen as making every aspect of the campaign significant, since events or stratagems worth 537 votes in Florida (in 2000) or 118,600 votes in Ohio (in 2004) are enough to have altered the outcomes. This criticism strikes me as a something of a canard, however. It is certainly possible to judge the magnitude of campaigning's impact with some indifference to the razor-thin outcome. An event that moves the vote by tenths of a percentage point might win an election but should still be judged as only marginally salient for voters.

Others who are especially skeptical about 2000 as a case study might also point to the suggestive evidence from the political science forecasting models, which predicted a substantial Gore victory. From table 1.1, we see that the mean margin of seven prominent forecasting models was 12.0 points (56 percent for Gore, 44 percent for Bush). The mean forecast error for each point estimate in 2000 was thus double that of 1996 and triple that of 1992 (5.6 points compared to 2.1 and 1.5 points, respectively).

TABLE 1.1   Presidential Election Forecasting Models: Predicted Incumbent Party Share of Two-Party Vote

	2004	2000	1996	1992
Forecast model				
Campbell	53.8	52.8	58.1	47.1
Abramowitz	53.7	53.2	56.8	46.7
Norpoth	54.7	55.0	57.1	—
Welzien and Erikson	51.7	55.2	56.0	46.8
Lewis-Beck and Tiena[a]	49.9	55.4	54.8	51.5
Holbrook	55.8	60.3	57.2	—
Lockerbie	—	60.3	57.6	—
Mean forecast	54.9	56.0	56.8	48.0
Actual	51.2	50.4	54.7	46.5
Deviation	−3.7	−5.6	−2.1	−1.5

[a]In 1992, Lewis-Beck and Rice estimated the model.

One might reasonably ask if these errors don't show that the 2000 election is an outlying case.

This claim is dubious, though, since the forecasting models are based on such a small subset of presidential elections. Indeed, with only fourteen elections since the widespread advent of public opinion polling, 2000 may or may not be an unusual election. More generally, I think it is perfectly legitimate to focus on presidential elections at variance with the forecasting models. These are precisely the cases in which much remains to be explained and campaigns are the most obvious explanation for this residual variance.

But the contention that 2000 falls outside the circle of "typical" election campaigns is heard in more casual contexts as well. A friend and colleague of mine confided after the election that he thought 2000 was going to be the campaign that exonerated Michael Dukakis. If Gore could have come back and defeated Bush, it would have showed once and for all (my friend argued) that Dukakis's demise in 1988 had been ordained by the relatively robust state of the economy and the popularity of the outgoing incumbent, not by an incompetent campaign. This interpretation was not simply partisan spin—many reporters and pundits also espoused it. And to some appreciable degree it *did* materialize, with Gore surging to the lead in early September. That Gore fumbled away his lead makes 2000 something of an aberration to many political scientists and (I'm sure) Democratic consultants. I would simply question why one should dismiss the events of October 2000 as any more aberrant than Dukakis's inability to head off George H. W. Bush's attacks in late August 1988.

From my perspective, a more troubling issue with relying on 2000 alone is that presidential election campaigns without an incumbent, known as *open-seat races,* might be more prone to volatility. This is, of course, an empirical question, and it is not clear that they are. Since 1950, we have had open-seat races in 1952, 1960, 1968, 1988, and 2000; preferences in the latter three were somewhat volatile, lending some credence to the claim. But we also saw enormous volatility in 1976, 1980, and 1992, all years in which incumbent presidents ran. That is why the inclusion of 2004, with the incumbent George W. Bush running for reelection, is a particularly important component of the research design.

Taken as a whole, these points suggest I should not engage in any *grand* generalizations based solely on these elections. I do not, however, think that they undermine the relevance and significance of these most recent elections for shedding light on larger questions of campaign strategy and influence.

On the other side of the ledger, the attraction of focusing on the 2000 and 2004 elections is obvious. The 2000 election was the closest presidential election since 1960 and probably one of the four most competitive national elections in American history.[11] Moreover, those of us who study elections for a living did not see it coming. The 2004 election was also close; in fact, it was the closest contest involving an incumbent seeking reelection since 1888. In addition, neither the 2000 nor the 2004 outcome was clear to poll watchers or forecasters until Election Day (or later).[12] Finally, there were also interesting innovations and developments in these campaigns that have yet to be fully digested by either political scientists or practitioners. All things considered, I think it would be folly not to take advantage of the lingering interest in, and data from, these races.

To be sure, care is of the essence. My proposed tack is to (1) be modest in extrapolating from 2000 and 2004; (2) identify context and circumstances, and discuss how they might have influenced what I found in the 2000 and 2004 analyses; and (3) reference research covering the races from 1988 through 1996 whenever possible when considering broader claims. Beyond these objectives, I intend to exploit to the fullest the theoretical and analytic possibilities connected to these most curious of elections. In so doing, I intend to bring the smoke-filled room a bit closer to the ivory tower (and vice versa).

2

WHAT WE KNOW (AND DON'T KNOW) ABOUT PRESIDENTIAL CAMPAIGNS

Even a cursory glance at voting studies over the past half century demonstrates that political scientists have long been ambivalent about the effects of presidential campaigns. In fact, the origins and nature of this ambivalence are standard fare in the opening paragraphs of almost every recent work on the effects of electioneering. Furthermore, recent scholarship has been consistent in its characterization of the partisans in this debate over campaigns: typically, the "minimal effects" scholars are pitted against the "campaign effects" scholars. Not surprisingly, this simple conceptualization sets some academicians' teeth on edge. Indeed, it has produced something of a backlash in the past few years. For example, Lynn Vavreck, an election campaigns scholar at UCLA, has referred to the minimal effects thesis as a "straw man." She argues that some use it as a device to present any presidential campaign effect as a significant contribution to the academy's understanding. And she is not alone in this view. At a recent political science conference, I twice heard the presidential campaign effects debate referred to as "hackneyed." These references were accompanied by impassioned pleas to "move beyond" the minimal effects thesis.[1]

Personally, I am of two minds with respect to the usefulness of framing research in terms of "minimal" versus "significant" presidential campaign effects. As someone who has used this conceptualization in the past, I agree that it can lead to an oversimplified presentation of existing research. Almost no one has argued that campaigns are irrelevant. Moreover, such mischaracterizations can distract from both common ground and remaining puzzles that might otherwise be gleaned from a more nuanced reading of the extant literature.

I would also admit that it was a problem in some of my own earlier work. After chairing a panel on which I had presented a campaign effects paper, Warren Miller—a true pioneer in the fields of political behavior and survey research—pulled my dissertation adviser aside and told him, "that boy needs to go back and reread *The American Voter*." I find this approbation validating in retrospect, but the particular charge levied was on the mark. To set the stage for my discussion of campaign effects, I had presented a caricature of the perspective on presidential campaigns manifest in such seminal works as *Voting* and *The American Voter*.

Still, I disagree with the increasingly prevalent belief that the debate on presidential campaign effects is contrived. Consider the presidential election forecasting models. It isn't so much that there were at least seven presidential election models for 2000. Rather, it is the distinct way in which the various modelers approached, presented, and defended their forecasts.[2] After the election, some modelers pointed to campaign factors to explain the anomalous outcome. In particular, they agued that Gore had failed to prime voters on the strength of the economy and (in the same vein) had failed to deploy President Clinton effectively as his main advocate (see Holbrook 2001; Wlezien 2001). Other modelers, however, suggested that their predictions had been correct (Gore had won the popular vote, hadn't he?) and that whatever "mispredictions" there were could be laid at the doorstep of "measurement error" (especially errors in measuring the perceived state of the economy).[3] These reactions reflect a real fault line: some scholars think presidential campaigns can have independent, significant effects on elections while others do not. And while there is a fair amount of consensus on some aspects of presidential campaigning, the existing scholarship has neither identified the exact points of congruence nor moved appreciably toward the reconciliation of the important remaining differences.

In this chapter, I offer my own review of the classic literature on campaigns, elections, and voting behavior. This review consciously attempts to recognize subtle and complex arguments on presidential campaign effects. I will then discuss the sources of renewed interest in campaign effects, before moving to a delineation of the most recent findings produced by this renaissance. Finally, I close the chapter by identifying common ground and consensus, as well as gaps in our understanding—gaps I hope this book will address.

CAMPAIGN EFFECTS IN THE CLASSICS

It is not surprising that early empirical analyses of public opinion and voting behavior emphasized the ignorance and indifference of the American electorate toward politics. At the high end, a functioning democracy presumes voters have enough information on the parties' positions to vote for the one closest to their own position on issues that matter (e.g., Downs 1957; Enelow and Hinich 1984). More realistically, a functioning democracy presumes voters have enough information to reward successful officeholders or to punish unsuccessful ones (e.g., Fiorina 1981; Key 1966). The initial work of the Columbia and Michigan schools cast doubt on even this low-level rationality, and the empirical findings underpinning this doubt became the focus of subsequent scholarship. This focus is understandable. The finding that voters may not have the requisite information to hold public officials accountable for performance in office creates a profound disconnect: If people are so ignorant, why are presidents who preside over economic recessions or unpopular wars or political scandals voted out of office? Why does the system appear to function rationally in the aggregate if there is, in fact, no individual-level rationality?

But the singular finding that voters do not follow politics has also been critical in shifting our attention away from campaigns. It is therefore worth plumbing the depths of these seminal texts for their specific comments on campaigns to better understand the current contours of the minimal effects debate. Let us begin with the two pillars of the Columbia school's sociological analysis of voting in the United States.

Voting, written by Bernard Berelson, Paul Lazarsfeld, and William McPhee, was published in 1954. It employed a panel study to examine the political opinions, attitudes, and candidate preferences of residents of Elmira, New York, during the 1948 presidential election campaign. The broad argument—that voters tend to get their preferences from contact with "opinion leaders" within their social groups—is familiar to any college student who has taken a course on public opinion and voting behavior. What is less well known is that the authors explicitly acknowledge the fact that political campaigns can have an effect on both individual voters and aggregate outcomes.

For example, the authors estimate that 16 percent of their sample "wavered" between the parties during the campaign, while an additional 13 percent "wavered" between a party and neutrality. The shifts were particularly evident among Elmira's small Democratic population, with 36 percent of these voters wavering between the parties and another 14 percent wavering between the Democrats and neutrality (Berelson, Lazarsfeld, and McPhee 1954, 16–18). More to the point, the whole of *Voting*'s chapter 12 analyzes the trend toward Truman that developed late in the 1948 campaign, arguing that the Democratic rally was due to previously disaffected Democrats (and Democratic-leaning groups) responding to the class issues emphasized by Truman's Fair Deal campaign. The passage on page 270 is particularly illustrative: "It seems clear that impending defeat for the Democratic Party was staved off by a refocusing of attention on socio-economic concerns which had originally played such a large role in building that party's majority in the 1930s."

This perspective is previewed in *The People's Choice*, a precursor to *Voting* penned by Paul Lazarsfeld, Bernard Berelson, and Helen Gaudet (1948). This panel study of Erie County, Ohio, residents during the Roosevelt-Wilkie campaign of 1940 focused on the role of newspapers and radio in the campaign. The main finding was that media effects were not impressive. The study, however, concluded with a sharp recognition of the importance of voters' influences on one another and pointed to the unresolved question of the role of political issues in campaigns.

A decade later, survey researchers in Ann Arbor also acknowledged the potential for campaign effects. The Michigan school was, in many ways, a reaction to the absence of any overtly psychological or political dynamic in the Columbia scholarship. *The American Voter*, coauthored by Angus Campbell, Philip Converse, Warren Miller, and Donald Stokes and published in 1960, offers a seminal analysis of voting behavior during the Eisenhower-Stevenson elections of 1952 and 1956. Furthermore, it remains the bible for students of political behavior. It is in *The American Voter*, for example, where we first see the theoretically complete delineation of "party identification" and such attendant conceptual gems as the "funnel of causality." It is also true that the explanatory power of party identification has led many observers to conclude that the Michigan scholarship does not believe presidential campaigns are significant. But to draw such a conclusion is to ignore the actual argument of the text. In chapter 19 of *The American Voter*, the authors contend that party identification is one of *several* factors that determine vote choice, stating that even though "the distribution of party identification in that year favored Democrats by about 3:2 . . . We know that the actual components of the 1952 vote were more pro-Republican than pro-Democrat" (A. Campbell et al. 1960, 529). Their specific argument is that attitudes toward the candidates, domestic issues, foreign policy issues, parties as managers of government, and group-related attitudes *drive* votes, with party therefore serving as a critical but nonomnipotent conditioning variable (531). The potential significance of campaigns is even apparent in the funnel of causality, in which party identification screens the acquisition and acceptance of political information. In their schematic, Campbell and his colleagues place factors other than party identification, including issues and candidate perceptions, closer to the bottom of the funnel, suggesting that political context is a critical variable for understanding voting.

In addition to his work in *The American Voter*, Philip Converse's subsequent research (most notably, his essay "The Nature of Belief Systems in Mass Publics" [Converse 1964]) significantly shaped our understanding of public opinion campaigns. Admittedly, Converse's later work does not directly engage the issue of campaign effects. But he describes the American public as largely uninformed and unengaged, and he uses this description as the basis for arguing that persuasive information—a category into which campaign messages most certainly fall—faces significant partisan resistance (at the level of the ideologue) or falls on deaf ears (at most other levels of sophistication). Zaller's *The Nature and Origins of Mass Opinion* (1992) demonstrates, however, that a sophisticated reading of Converse does not necessarily lead to a minimal effects perspective. Zaller, in fact, uses Senate election data to suggest that voters with "middle level" awareness may be quite susceptible to information flows. So while Zaller himself is agnostic as to whether there are significant persuasive campaign effects in presidential elections (at least in this study), it is certainly a possibility given his interpretation of Converse.

DEFINING AND REFINING THE MINIMAL EFFECTS THESIS

One of the main consequences of the early empirical works on presidential campaign effects was that subsequent research into voting behavior diversified. Instead of focusing on campaigns, political scientists examined the influence of economic evaluations, partisanship, shortcuts and heuristics, presidential approval, and a variety of other factors on voting. It would be inaccurate to contend that campaigns were neglected. There were, for instance, studies of presidential candidate activities (e.g., Kelley 1961, 1966, 1983) and media influence (e.g., Iyengar 1991; Iyengar and Kinder 1987; Patterson 1980; Patterson and McClure 1976). But because the Columbia and Michigan schools estimated that only 10 to 15 percent of voters were persuadable—with net effects thus constrained to a few points—political scientists looked for subtle, less-direct campaign effects, as well as for other causal explanations of variance in voting behavior.

As suggested earlier, alternative explanations were readily identified. The activation of party identification was developed as a dynamic explanation for aggregate- and individual-level movement over the course of a presidential campaign. Campaigns, the argument goes, are the means by which partisan identities are reactivated and linked to vote choice. Gelman and King (1993) observe that shifts in the fortunes of candidates over the campaign largely involve uneven sequences of partisan activation. Persuasion is confined to independents and some weaker identifiers, and it tends to be driven by conditional and objective circumstances, such as the state of the economy and presidential job approval. Party identification thus determines the base vote a candidate can expect, with genuine (but limited) potential existing for significant improvement (Iyengar and Petrocik 2000).

Aside from party identification, the role of economic variables in shaping candidate preferences became a consistent theme in the voting literature. In the 1970s, political economists began to model presidential elections as a function of macroeconomic factors such as economic growth and unemployment rates (see Fair 1978; Tufte 1978). They found that, by and large, presidents running for reelection win, so long as the economic growth rate exceeds 1.5 percentage points. Political economists also tested the influence of personal economic circumstances on voting behavior but found that this so-called pocketbook voting failed to explain nearly as much of the variance in elections as aggregate, national economic appraisals (Kinder and Kiewiet 1981).

From this set of observations grew a set of studies that combined economic indicators with a few political, contextual variables to predict presidential election outcomes. In addition to Tufte's and Fair's work, Steven Rosenstone's 1983 book, *Forecasting Presidential Elections*, used economic variables, presidential approval, and past voting history to model state-level outcomes and predict electoral vote totals. Also notable in this genre is Michael Lewis-Beck's work (especially Lewis-Beck and Rice 1992), which extended the scope of election forecasting to include congressional elections.

What is interesting is that the forecasting models do not specifically posit that presidential voting behavior is unaffected by campaigns. Most of them, for example, offer presidential job approval as a predictor of the vote, noting that approval rates could clearly be affected by the campaign. Moreover, a few models rely on past vote totals to predict the upcoming race, leaving open the possibility that past campaigns might affect current elections. Even forecasters with no endogenous (or lagged endogenous) variables in their models often admit that campaigns are necessary to educate voters about the external reality upon which their predictions are based.

Besides party identification and economic variables, political scientists have continued to develop the sociological framework established by the Columbia school to explain elections and voting (Katz and Lazarsfeld 1955). Specifically, both political communication and political psychology scholarship have explored the interpersonal networks through which people acquire their political information (Huckfeldt et al. 1995; Huckfeldt and Sprague 1992; Kenny 1992; Knoke 1990; Leighley 1990; McClurg 2004; Mutz 2002; Verba, Schlozman, and Brady 1995). The idea is that voter mobilization is the key to understanding election outcomes, so it is important to know how different groups pass partisan information along to their members (Rosenstone and Hansen 1993). Moreover, it is particularly important to know how these social network processes are changing over time (Putnam 2000). The noteworthy findings from this literature are that (1) opinion leaders exist and are critical to informing the less-aware members of a group (Converse 1964; Zaller 1992), (2) communication differences between and among groups appear to be a function of the distribution of political awareness throughout these groups (Zaller 1992), and (3) interpersonal communication remains vital, even as television has come to dominate the broader dissemination of information (Huckfeldt et al. 1995; Johnson and Huckfeldt 2001; McClurg 2004; Mutz 2002).

The upshot of these studies is that understanding elections and voting does not require an understanding of campaigns. Though not irrelevant, presidential campaigns are epiphenomenal. The minimal effects perspective is therefore not a direct attack on campaigns. Rather, it is an inferred perspective; an attributed position based on its emphasis of noncampaign factors in studies of voting and elections.

Interestingly, there have been no scholarly analyses suggesting that campaigning does not influence voters in congressional or local elections. In fact, the ability to raise and spend funds is a large part of the explanation for incumbency advantages in U.S. House and Senate elections (Jacobson 1983, 1990; Mayhew 1974). The minimal effects inference is thus confined to research on presidential voting, where there are particular circumstances surrounding the presidential election that make it unlikely that a campaign will be decisive.

To be more precise, there are at least four reasons why presidential elections are expected to be relatively impervious to campaign effects. First, federal election law imposes spending limits on the candidates' campaigns in exchange for public funding. In 2000 and 2004, George W. Bush declined matching funds for the primary elections, as did John Kerry in 2004. But Bush, Gore, and Kerry took public money for the general election campaigns (as has every major party presidential candidate since

1976). This public funding supposedly puts the major party candidates on roughly equal footing—certainly in the aggregate—and makes it difficult to achieve an advantage in terms of campaign volume in a given state or locale. Sometimes this equality is "rougher" than not, as we shall see in 2000 and 2004, but it holds as a general condition. Moreover, money is hardly equal in state or other federal elections, where enormous spending advantages often exist. No one would argue with a straight face that money does not matter in American politics, but in presidential elections both sides are guaranteed enough to compete.

Second, the proliferation of polling and focus group technologies makes it unlikely that either campaign will achieve an advantage with respect to strategic information. Both campaigns employ multiple pollsters, the vast majority of whom share professional norms and practices. It is possible that one side will enjoy a technical advantage of some sort for a brief period of time or that one side will simply invest more heavily in detailed public opinion and political behavior research. But these advantages are not likely to be great, nor are they likely to directly translate into distinct resource allocation patterns.

The third reason for expecting minimal presidential campaign effects is that both candidates bring an equal amount of expertise to the table in a given election. The presidential election is, in the words of Republican media consultant Stuart Stevens, the "big enchilada." Although the parties' strategists change over time, minimal effects scholars would point out that the best are almost always involved in the decision-making processes for the presidential candidates. And, contrary to popular opinion, neither the Republicans nor the Democrats enjoy any consistent edge when it comes to strategic thinking.

Fourth and finally, we assume presidential campaigns often produce tit-for-tat resource allocation patterns. For example, we believe campaigns buy television time where their opponents are on the air and at about the same level of intensity. Similarly, candidates stalk each other around the country, in effect canceling out whatever bounce occurs when one of them visits a particular city. This behavior represents a low-risk strategy that could, if taken to the logical extreme, save a great deal of thought; don't bother devising your own travel and television strategy—just follow your opponent.

The minimal effects perspective is thus, as noted at the outset of this chapter, more subtle and challenging than many have suggested. For the reasons outlined earlier, the argument centers exclusively on presidential elections. In these contests, macrofactors, such as the state of the economy and presidential approval, are thought to determine the distribution of

aggregate preferences. Meanwhile, microfactors, such as party identification and sociodemographic characteristics, are thought to determine
the nature of individual preferences. Furthermore, the minimal effects
scholarship does not contend that no one is persuaded by the presidential
campaign but rather that the net effect is typically incidental to the election outcome.

Again, the broader theoretical point of the minimal effects perspective
should not be misconstrued. Most scholars writing from this point of view
seem to believe that campaigns *are* important. First, they see presidential
campaigns as important political institutions. They serve as exemplars
for citizen responsibility and control over political power in the United
States. Second, and more pragmatically, they believe campaigns mobilize
support for the two major-party candidates. Indeed, this mobilization
process might *not* occur without prompting by the parties. In addition,
the way in which campaigns mobilize voters (the particular appeals, the
commitments made, the understanding of their own coalition) could be
a critical factor for comprehending subsequent governance and public
policy decisions. Third, they acknowledge that campaigns can produce
slightly asymmetrical mobilization or persuasion and might thus tip a
close election. Still, scholars who emphasize noncampaign factors hold
that differential mobilization or persuasion effects between the parties
tend to be minimal, which severely limits the chance that campaigns will
determine who wins the presidency.

Despite its reasonableness and scholarly foundations, political pundits
and casual observers of politics—both of whom often see presidential
campaigns as decisive—disagree with this view. Perhaps more interestingly, political communication scholars are also somewhat perplexed by
this perspective because a slightly different minimal effects debate has
already been resolved in their field.

As with the initial empirical studies of election campaigns, early analyses of news media had a difficult time finding effects. McCombs and
Shaw (1972), for example, point out that voluminous research up to that
time revealed precious little correlation between the tone and content of
reportage on a given subject and the attendant nature of public opinion.
The suspicion that news media effects exist persisted, however, and led
political communication scholars to posit and investigate more subtle
influences. McCombs and Shaw presented persuasive evidence that the
media's influence is not in telling people what to think but rather what to
think about. The idea that media effects occur primarily through "agenda-
setting" turned the minimal effects perspective upside down and paved
the way for innovative understandings of impact. Fifteen years later, Iyen-

gar and Kinder (1987) used extensive empirical evidence of public opinion and news media coverage surrounding the Iran-contra affair to contend that the media "prime" citizens to use certain criteria when evaluating a particular figure or issue.[4] Subsequently, Iyengar (1991) posited that the "frame" used by the news media to present a given story can create politically significant connections in voters' minds. Obviously, this research tends to be dominated by experiments, which allow greater control over stimuli and effects. In addition, this work has transformed the nature of the debate on media effects and leaves many political communication scholars wondering what all the fuss is about when it comes to campaign effects. Surely the debates among campaign scholars could be resolved by a more sophisticated conceptualization of effects, coupled with more advanced research designs.

While preexisting attachments (i.e., party identification) somewhat muddy the application of agenda-setting and priming theories, there is something to this line of thought. An overwhelming majority of campaign studies rely only on vote choice (or change in vote choice) as the barometer of campaign influence and make no effort to detect changes in underlying political perceptions. Furthermore, measurement of the campaign and its potential conditional and interactive effects has tended to be imprecise compared to what we see in the experimental designs that dominate media studies.

WHY THE CONTEMPORARY INTEREST?

The implicit and explicit criticisms made by political communication scholars played a small part in jump-starting the new wave of campaign research. I would not, however, focus on ivory tower conflicts alone when explaining the origins of renewed interest. Rather, I believe academics have also reacted to real-world developments and stimuli.

As mentioned earlier, the 1988 election stirred interest in campaigns by tapping into political scientists' normative concerns about the legitimacy and consequences of negative electioneering. Practitioners were also interested in the consequences of negative advertising and, more specifically, the failing to respond to attack ads. Both groups appear to share the conventional view of the 1988 campaign: the Republican candidate, Vice President George H. W. Bush, was able to erase Democratic nominee Michael Dukakis's double-digit lead in the polls by painting Dukakis as unpatriotic (Dukakis opposed a constitutional ban on flag burning) and weak on crime (Dukakis, who was governor of Massachusetts, presided over his state's controversial prison-furlough program, which became infamous with the "Willie Horton" ad).[5] Moreover, many scholars and practitioners also believe that Bush's victory was driven by a campaign that was explicitly disingenuous and implicitly racist (see Mendelberg 2001 for an analysis of "the race card" in the 1988 campaign) and by a Dukakis campaign too inept to rebut these attacks.

Democratic consultants were especially affected by 1988. In particular, they were adamant about not being "Dukakisized" in subsequent elections. For example, in the award-winning documentary *The War Room*, Clinton campaign consultant James Carville delivers an impassioned speech to campaign staff and volunteers in the days before the 1992 New Hampshire primary. Reacting to the rash of news media stories about Clinton's alleged marital infidelities and evasion of the Vietnam draft, Carville claimed that Republican media consultant Roger Ailes (who produced many of the Bush ads in 1988) was responsible for the allegations. He went on to argue that unless Clinton was elected, Republicans would do it "again and again" and that you would never see a strong Democrat "with real ideas" willing to run for high office. This assertion is not only gripping cinema verité but also an insightful representation of the sentiment that pervaded Democratic circles on the heels of 1988.

Tactically, Democratic campaigns institutionalized rapid-response teams responsible for making sure Republican charges were answered within the same news cycle. They also beefed up their opposition-research staffs so that attacks could be responded to in kind. And the content of their direct mail and phone contacting became more aggressive, especially in the last days of the campaign when it becomes more difficult to respond to attacks. Republicans, of course, developed their campaigns on these fronts as well, but by 2000 it would be difficult to prove either side was more capable when it came to bare-knuckle campaigning.

The 1988 election, in and of itself, was probably not enough to have altered the nature and trajectory of political scientists' research agenda. There was, however, a palpable, normative distaste for the Bush campaign's tactics. In addition, the 1988 campaign occurred at a time when objective, professional developments were pushing academics to refocus their energies on campaign effects. First, there was the aforementioned identification and elaboration of media effects by political communication scholars. Second, there was renewed interest in the role of issues and political context. This interest had been building slowly since Nie, Verba, and Petrocik's *The Changing American Voter* (1976) and had reached something of a peak with the work of Carmines and Stimson (1989) on "issue evolution" and Rabinowitz and MacDonald (1989) on "directional voting." Political scientists never ruled out the idea that issue opinions could drive significant long-term shifts in either party identification or vote choice, irrespective of exogenous factors. But this possibility had only infrequently been elaborated upon and was even more rarely connected to an assessment of the importance of campaigns.

Other perspectives on the campaign effects debate also emerged in the wake of 1988. There was renewed interest in voter rationality, as evidenced by Samuel Popkin's *The Reasoning Voter* (1991) and Arthur Lupia and Mathew McCubbins's *The Democratic Dilemma* (1998). Both books made the case for collective rationality in the face of the supposed ignorance of individual voters. Relatedly, Michael Alvarez's *Information and Elections* (1997) examined campaign effects on the information levels of voters, finding that campaigns aid citizen knowledge even if they are relatively insignificant with respect to preferences. Each of these studies views campaigns as critical to individual-level information acquisition.

Renewed interest in the campaign effects argument was also spurred by the development of more sophisticated conceptions of information processing. For example, the finding that voters do not remember campaign events or television ads did not disturb proponents of the online processing perspective. After all, the core tenet of this perspective—that people use new information to update prior preferences but do not necessarily retain the particulars of the new information—fits comfortably with the minimal effects findings. In fact, online processing scholars always assumed that using recall measures to assess campaign effects was misguided. Instead, they prefer either experimental manipulations, which capture real-time effects, or dynamic assessments of preference (e.g., Lodge, McGraw, and Stroh 1989; Lodge and Stroh 1993; Lodge, Steenbergen, and Brau 1995).

More surprisingly, recent analyses by those favoring memory-based perspectives—whereby people choose considerations from which to construct opinions by "sampling" from memory bins (e.g., Zaller's reception-acceptance-sample model)—find that persuasive effects are discernible not only for issue opinions but also for candidate preferences. Effects tend to be conditioned, however, by partisanship, awareness, and elite conversation.

On a different front, scholars studying campaign finance in the early 1990s also began to note that the supposed structural equality of presidential campaigning was crumbling. Most obviously, they pointed to discrepancies in presidential campaign resources due to *soft money* (unregulated contributions to the political parties for "party building" activities, outlawed by the 2002 Bipartisan Campaign Reform Act) and independent expenditures (J. Campbell 2003). While the candidates may have been limited to approximately $70 million per campaign, the parties and sympathetic interest groups were not, and these players brought formidable resources to the table (Corrado 2004; Goldstein and Freedman 2002a, 2002b). In addition to money, the supposed equality of expertise between the parties was questioned after 1992 and 1996. The death of GOP strategist Lee Atwater and the semiretirement of James Baker certainly created a vacuum at the top of the Republican hierarchy in those elections, adding weight to the claim that expertise differentials probably exist in any given election, even if they do not sum to a net advantage for one or the other party across elections.

Last, but certainly not least, the interest of political scientists in the campaign effects debate was piqued by the greater availability of data in the 1990s. Since the advent of mass campaigns in the 1830s and 1840s, empirical studies have been hampered by the fact that campaigns (1) do not keep thorough records, (2) jealously guard their secrets for success if they win, (3) disappear from the face of the earth if they lose, and (4) always have an interest in shading their versions of what happened to protect themselves. Although these tendencies still exist, campaigns since 1974 have been forced by federal election law to keep records. Moreover, they have been more willing to systematically transcribe and share resource allocation information since 1988. Scholars, on the other hand, not only have become interested in these data but have been more aggressive in approaching campaigns and securing data-sharing agreements.

On the formal end of the spectrum, there are campaign resource clearinghouses such as the Federal Election Commission (FEC) and the Campaign Media Analysis Group (CMAG), which compile and code expenditure information for all federal (and some state) elections. There are similar entities that compile public opinion and polling information, such as the Roper Center, the Inter-university Consortium for Political and Social Research (ICPSR), and Web sites such as pollingreport.com. Although Roper and ICPSR are by no means new, they have expanded their holdings considerably since the 1980s and have been made available to a wider academic community. There are also the presidential libraries, especially the Eisenhower, Kennedy, Johnson, Nixon, Carter, Reagan, Bush, and Clinton Libraries, which offer internal documents, memos, and even polls from past presidential campaigns.

On the informal end of the spectrum, campaigns and individual scholars have struck agreements that allowed academic use of data after Election Day. That is, in fact, how much of my data on election campaigns have been acquired. Kenneth Goldstein, who has conducted some influential studies of television advertising, has similarly benefited from arrangements with campaign and media consultants. Political pollsters have also used their campaign data to write more formal analyses of broad electoral phenomena (e.g., Stanley Greenberg's *Middle Class Dreams* [1995]).

WHAT HAVE WE LEARNED SINCE 1988?

Even if one accepts my premise that 1988 triggered a renaissance in campaign analyses, it is still reasonable to question whether we actually know any more about presidential campaigns. I think it is clear that we *do* know more. I would point to four areas in which greater understanding has been achieved: (1) estimating the net effects of campaigns, (2) measuring information effects from campaigns, (3) gauging the effects of specific campaign activities, and (4) identifying how candidates and campaigns approach the campaign. The next section considers each of these areas in turn.

ESTIMATIONS OF THE NET EFFECTS OF CAMPAIGNS

Since 1988, there have been several estimates of the total net effect of the presidential campaign. On the whole, these estimates have been fairly conservative. For example, Steven Finkel (1993) uses the Major Panel Survey of 1980 to analyze individual-level movement in presidential preferences. He finds that while many respondents changed their preferences, the net movement is 2 to 3 percentage points at most. At the aggregate level, Gelman and King (1993) demonstrate that there is significant volatility in preelection survey estimations of presidential preferences but that net campaign effects are almost zero because the vote tends to converge on a predictable point on or around Election Day.[6] Erikson and Wlezien (1999) use time series estimation techniques to calculate an aggregate preferences shift of about 5 percentage points in the 1996 presidential campaign. Unlike Gelman and King, however, they attribute the considerable preference volatility over the election cycle to campaign factors. In what is arguably the most comprehensive analysis, James Campbell (2003) analyzes a wide range of American presidential elections and suggests that campaign effects can be broken into two categories, *systematic* and *unsystematic*. He further contends that the average combined effect of these influences on the national vote is about 4 percentage points (J. Campbell 2003, 188).

In addition to studies of preference shifts, some scholars have suggested that general campaign effects can be understood as the residual variance from multivariate models of the presidential vote. These analyses assume that variables such as presidential approval and party identification are exogenous to the campaign and that true campaign effects should be understood as deviations from the estimate derived from an equation of these factors. Larry Bartels (1993) uses this logic to estimate that presidential campaign effects are typically on the order of 2 to 3 percentage points. The forecasting models discussed earlier can be viewed in this light, with their mean error estimates—which generally run between 1 and 4 points—serving as estimates of campaign effects.

CAMPAIGNS AS INFORMATION SOURCES

Despite the natural focus on the presidential campaign's influence on votes, some scholars have argued that this is an overly narrow way to consider campaign effects. In particular, a bevy of analyses examining how campaigns affect voters' political information and knowledge have been produced since 1990. Besides the information-processing models proposed by Zaller (1992), on the one hand, and Lodge and his colleagues, on the other, several other research projects trace the path and impact of campaign information. First, there are the aforementioned studies by Alvarez (1997), Lupia and McCubbins (1998), and Popkin (1991). There is also the work of William Bianco (1998), who finds that voters in Senate elections can fulfill the expectations of both rational choice scholars and political psychologists by using information readily provided in the early stages of political campaigns. Kahn and Kenney (1997) examine the impact of "intensity" in ninety-seven Senate races between 1988 and 1992 and go even farther:[7]

> Intense campaigns encourage individuals to rely more heavily on both sophisticated criteria and simple decision rules when forming impressions of candidates. As campaigns become more hard-fought, people are more likely to consider policy and ideology as well as partisanship and retrospective evaluations of the president and the economy. While the campaign setting clearly affects citizens' decision-making processes, different types of people react differently to the intensity of the campaign. As races become more competitive, novices begin to rely more heavily on issues, sociotropic assessments, party identification, and presidential approval, whereas political experts are less affected by changes in the campaign environment. (Kahn and Kenney 1997, 1173)

Building on these studies of how campaigns affect the information levels of voters, political scientists have recently taken to estimating the "informed preferences" of voters to determine if a fully informed electorate would change election results. In his study of information effects in presidential elections, Bartels (1996) contends that at the individual level, the average deviation of actual vote probabilities from hypothetical "fully informed" vote probabilities is about ten percentage points. In the electorate as a whole, these deviations are significantly diluted by aggregation, but by no means eliminated: incumbent presidents did almost five percentage points better, and Democratic candidates did almost two percentage points better, than they would have if voters had in fact been "fully informed." (Bartels 1996, 194)

Scott Althaus (1998) expands Bartels's analysis by including nonvoters in his study of how full information affects congressional vote preferences. Like Bartels, he finds differences between informed and uninformed voters, although Althaus does not find the same systematic party differences at the congressional level that Bartels finds at the presidential.

In addition to these innovative designs, there have also been a few experimental studies investigating the *kinds* of information that voters want to access about candidates and how this information affects the vote decision. Richard Lau and David Redlawsk (1997) conducted a series of computer-based experiments investigating these questions during the mid-1990s. They found that voters favor biographical information over hard-issue information and that information containing an affective component tends to be more influential than issue-based information. This finding corroborates other recent analyses that demonstrate the considerable role emotion plays in the presidential voting decision (e.g., Marcus and Mackuen 1993).

SPECIFIC CAMPAIGN EFFECTS

While analyses of net movement and information effects help us understand the consequences of presidential campaigns, analyses of specific types of campaign activities sharpen our understanding of *how* campaigns influence voters. This trend toward disaggregating the specific manifestations of presidential campaigning has been matched by a tendency toward more innovative data and research designs. Consider the following aspects of electioneering that have received substantive empirical treatment since the mid-1990s.

Mobilization, Face-to-Face Contacting, Phones, and Direct Mail
As far back as Harold Gosnell's 1927 study of voter turnout, we have evidence that mobilization efforts can increase voting rates. Since then, both experimental and real-life analyses of contacting effects confirm that personal contact can produce votes (Bochel and Denver 1971, 1972; Cain and

McCue 1985; Cutright 1963; Cutright and Rossi 1958; Eldersveld 1956; Eldersveld and Dodge 1954; Katz and Eldersveld 1961; Kramer 1970; Lupfer and Price 1972; Price and Lupfer 1973). But the proliferation of get-out-the-vote (GOTV) efforts beginning in the early 1990s produced a series of innovative studies in political science designed to capture their influences in a more contemporary context. Most notably, we have the "field experiments" conducted by Alan Gerber and Donald Green (2000, 2001). During the 1998 elections in Oregon, Gerber and Green (2000) randomly selected voters from statewide voter lists, assigning them to control and treatment groups. The treatment groups received either (1) direct mail from a candidate but no phone calls, (2) phone calls but no direct mail, or (3) direct mail and phone calls. The control group received no campaign contacts. The authors took pains to insure that their mail and phone calls were as realistic as possible, using genuine campaign consultants to design the materials. Controlling for a host of factors, Gerber and Green found that direct mail increased the candidate's vote share 10 percent beyond what would otherwise be expected but that phone calls actually had a negative impact on aggregate vote share. They also tested the effects of face-to-face contacting, which they found had a highly significant and positive impact on vote share.

More broadly, Rosenstone and Hansen (1993) offer one of the most ambitious arguments of all the recent campaign analyses when they contend that the decline in party mobilization efforts is a significant cause of the decline in aggregate turnout in the United States. This result is corroborated by Verba, Schlozman, and Brady (1995), who argue that party and candidate mobilization efforts can substantially reduce the costs of voting and make it easier for people with limited social capital to overcome the impediments to voting. More recently, Endersby and Petrocik (2001) argue that mobilization is perhaps the critical component to contemporary presidential election campaigns. They use National Election Study (NES) and exit polling data to build a compelling empirical case that while persuasion is minimal in presidential elections, the mobilization efforts of parties and candidates are key to activating partisan predispositions.

Television Advertising
Here is where the renewed interest in campaign effects has been most evident. One of the first of the "modern" works was Darrell West's study of the nature and effects of television advertising in federal elections. While West (1993) upheld the conventional wisdom that TV ads elicit minimal effects, he also observed that campaigns do not expect these ads to persuade a large percentage of voters (see also Kern 1989). Narrow, targeted

effects are what campaigns seek, and, West admits, we have little relevant evidence on their effectiveness. But it was Ansolabehere and Iyengar (1995) who revolutionized the study of campaign and political advertising with their experiments on TV ad effects in California during the 1990 and 1992 elections.[8] They directly confronted the conventional wisdom of minimal effects by demonstrating that campaign ads significantly correlate with changes in candidate appraisals as well as the likelihood of turning out to vote. In particular, they argue that negative advertising mobilizes partisans but depresses turnout among independents.

The Ansolabehere and Iyengar experiments have prompted a slew of challenges. For example, Finkel and Geer (1998) take issue with Ansolabehere and Iyengar on the question of campaign tone and turnout. Using aggregate turnout rates and evaluations of campaign tone, they contend that negative campaigns tend to be coincident with relatively higher turnout. Wattenberg and Brians (1999) also challenge this component of Ansolabehere and Iyengar's argument. They examine individual-level survey data and ultimately side with Geer and Finkel's claim that negative ads *increase* turnout. Interestingly, while there is debate concerning the effects of negativity, all of these studies find that TV ads influence voters.

Candidate Appearances
Several studies have updated the influential work of Stanley Kelley (1961, 1966) on the effects of candidates' visits on local preferences. For example, Bartels (1985) estimated the pattern and impact of Jimmy Carter's travel in the 1976 election. He argues that effects are not substantial but that this finding is understandable because appearances are motivated by multiple factors, some of which are unconcerned with improving the candidate's trial ballot standing. My own research (Shaw 1999a) has examined both the pattern and the effect of presidential candidate appearances from 1988 through 1996. I argue that three extra visits to a state are worth approximately 1 percentage point in the polls. Two current projects in the works, one by Thomas Holbrook and the other by myself (along with Scott Althaus and Peter Nardulli), are re-creating candidate travel from presidential elections going back to 1948. The availability of more reliable data on candidate schedules and public opinion from the libraries of presidential candidates may allow us to calculate even more precise estimates of appearance effects. Looking to the future, there is hope that cooperative campaigns may allow Gerber and Green's field experiment design to be used to gauge the independent impact of candidate visits on earned media, fund-raising, and local voter opinion.

Campaign Events

The work of Holbrook (1994, 1996) on the effects of different kinds of campaign events has been perhaps the most notable advance in this area. Holbrook finds that conventions and presidential debates are the proverbial eight hundred-pound gorillas of campaign events; both clearly influence voters' preferences. This contention is backed by specific studies of campaign events by J. Campbell, Cherry, and Wink (1992), Geer (1988), Lanoue (1991), and Shelley and Huang (1991). Holbrook's estimates of other event effects are much more ambiguous, suggesting that such effects are inconsistent and contextually dependent.

Holbrook's research squares with my own work on the matter (Shaw 1999c), with a few addenda.[9] First, I find that gaffes or mistakes are strongly correlated with changes in candidate preference. Second, I find that scandals are not especially significant for vote change (for a contrary view, see Fackler and Lin 1995). Third, I find that messages (or policy initiatives) tend to be uncorrelated with contemporaneous shifts in candidate preference. Fourth and finally, my own research indicates that not all event effects persist; some effects are durable over a period of ten days while others fade and still others grow. Put another way, the functional form of campaign effects depends on the nature of the event.

Media Effects

Recent studies continue to show that media exposure, while not influencing candidate preferences per se, influences a range of other political attitudes and impressions (Freedman and Goldstein 1999; Hetherington 1996). Collectively, these analyses suggest that (1) vote choice is not the only variable of interest when considering campaign effects, (2) news media coverage matters because it affects impressions of candidates and issues that could in turn influence vote choice (Just et al. 1996; Paletz 1999), and (3) candidate strategy is substantially influenced by the desire to affect news media coverage (Arterton 1984; Patterson 1980).[10]

I should add that while there is no consensus that the news media have an ideological slant, a plethora of recent studies has empirically considered this possibility. Most notably, several studies of the 1992 presidential election show a significant anti-Bush tone to coverage (Kerbel 1995; Lichter and Noyes 1996; Sabato 1993). More specifically, they show that economic coverage was far more negative than the objective condition of the economy and that this was the primary frame used to portray Bush and his administration (Hetherington 1996; Lichter and Noyes 1996). It is also the case that Bush received unfavorable coverage even when he was ahead in the polls (up until late June 1992), so it is difficult to blame "horse race" coverage for the media's overall tone. Clinton, on the other side of the ledger, received positive coverage, but only after he took the lead in the presidential preference polls just before the Democratic convention. No such slant was discernible in 1996, at least not after controlling for Clinton's large and persistent advantage over Dole in the horse race. Internal studies of broadcast and print media conducted by the Bush campaign indicate that coverage of the 2000 race was mixed, essentially following the polls. All of these findings suggest that news media coverage is influenced by professional biases (Robinson and Sheehan 1983; Sigal 1973) that produce favorable coverage for front-runners and unfavorable coverage for underdogs. These biases, however, have not been empirically connected to shifts in support among voters.

CANDIDATE AND CAMPAIGN APPROACHES

In addition to these advances in the study of specific manifestations of the presidential campaign, there have been changes in the way we view both candidates and voters. These new conceptualizations, in turn, have affected our view of what campaigns are about.

Arguably, the most intriguing conceptual advancement in the studies of presidential elections since 1990 is John Petrocik's notion of "issue ownership" (1996). Petrocik posits that candidates use election campaigns to convince voters that their issues are more important than the opposition's issues. Thus, campaigns do not compete for the median voter along some summary Left-Right issue dimension. Instead, they fight to set the agenda, knowing that Democratic and Republican candidates have different credibility on different issues. Democrats, for instance, want to make elections about health care and the environment, while Republicans want to make them about taxes and defense. This strategy comports with common sense, but it is quite different from how political scientists have traditionally conceived of electoral competition and (consequently) campaigns.

Another intriguing area of research focuses on the role of gender and ethnicity in how candidates are perceived. Two studies in this area merit particular attention, the first because of its impact on subsequent research and the second because of its innovative research design. The first study is Kim Kahn's (1994) analysis of gender differences in campaign messages and voters' reactions. Kahn finds that gender does indeed matter to both candidates and voters. Female candidates are more likely than males to emphasize "nurturing" issues such as health care and education. Moreover, voters perceive female candidates as more credible and empathetic on these issues, irrespective of the actual positions or personalities.

The second study focuses on the effects of racial priming in news media coverage of issues such as crime. Nicholas Valentino (1999) conducts experiments in which issues and images are altered slightly to determine whether racial cues are being primed by the local news media's presentation of certain issues. More important for this study, he extends the analysis to claim that such priming can affect candidate evaluations (presumably to the detriment of Democratic candidates) by raising the salience of racially charged subjects. While the evidence linking racial priming and Clinton evaluations in 1996 is weak, the connection posited by Valentino is interesting, particularly in light of the corroborative work by Tali Mendelberg (2001), who contends that racial priming has been a (successful) feature of Republican candidate advertising in recent elections.[11]

THE ROLE OF NEW DATA SETS

I have alluded to innovative campaign research designs and data sets several times in this chapter, but as a capstone to the discussion of post-1988 advances in the study of presidential campaigns, let me now be more specific in calling attention to the most important of them. I will concentrate on nonexperimental studies for present purposes, simply acknowledging the influence of projects led by Ansolabehere and Iyengar, Lau and Redlawsk, and Lodge on the study of electioneering.

Perhaps foremost among the recent wave of campaign projects is the work of Richard Johnston, Kathleen Hall Jamieson, and William Hagen at the behest of the University of Pennsylvania's Annenberg School for Communication in 1996, 2000, and 2004. For the 2000 and 2004 elections, Johnston and his colleagues conducted a rolling cross-sectional survey throughout the election years, interviewing approximately two hundred randomly selected respondents every evening. The resultant data sets allow for the isolation of nightly movement and the analysis of how particular events in the campaigns affected the distribution of opinion. They also facilitate detailed analyses of subgroup reactions to the campaigns as well as how exposure to both paid and free media affected opinions. The sample can even be broken down by media markets to investigate biweekly changes in response to aggregate campaign stimuli. As for the campaign effects debate, Johnston, Jamieson, and Hagen (2004) offer strong evidence that the 2000 election result was significantly affected by a handful of specific campaign events.

The Annenberg project's consideration of campaign effects relies in part on TV ad data gathered under the supervision of Kenneth Goldstein. Goldstein has been instrumental in convincing advertising placement and tracking organizations to partner with academic groups to catalog and make publicly available information on where campaigns, parties, and interest groups are airing their political ads. Groups such as the Brennan Center and CMAG have sponsored and archived these data, which allow academics to analyze media activity in the country's top seventy-five designated market areas (DMAs).[12] In addition, Goldstein has helped the NES retool its media exposure questions so that scholars might get a more accurate representation — in conjunction with the CMAG data — of which ads are seen by which voters.

The limitations of existing frameworks also prompted Simon Jackman, Douglas Rivers, and Sunshine Hillygus to design and implement Knowledge Networks, an enterprise in which a random sample of Americans are given personal computers and high-speed Internet access in exchange for their participation in a series of political, economic, and social surveys. In 2000, thousands participated in the Knowledge Networks project, allowing Hillygus and Jackman (2003; and Hillygus 2005) to track public reaction to events of the presidential campaign. Jackman and Rivers (2001) augmented information from their sample with publicly available state surveys to create highly accurate probability estimates of the likely winner in all fifty states.

Two other studies, both content analyses, also merit inclusion here. First, S. Robert Lichter and Richard Noyes, in conjunction with the Center for Media and Public Affairs (CMPA), have conducted content analyses of news media coverage of presidential elections from 1988 through 2000. The data sets encompass network news and elite-newspaper coverage of politics and elections.[13] CMPA coders identify and quantify coverage of issues and gauge the favorability of coverage toward the candidates. Although the data have not been made publicly available, the CMPA produces newsletters that detail the nature of coverage, including compelling across-time figures.

Second, Roderick Hart has developed his own trademarked software program (DICTION) that "maps" speech and rhetorical discourse, identifying consistencies in language, frames of reference, and the like. Hart has used this program to characterize political speech in general and campaign speech in particular. In *Campaign Talk* (2000), Hart identifies five broad classes of variables that characterize political speech — certainty, optimism, activity, realism, and commonality — and analyzes their frequency and variance in past campaigns compared with the 1996 campaign between Bill Clinton and Robert Dole. The establishment of baseline measures of campaign language allows others to refine the measures and to characterize the rhetoric of subsequent candidates.

WHAT WE DO NOT KNOW

In sum, the empirical attention devoted to presidential campaigns since 1988 has produced consensus with respect to several basic facts. First, most scholars would now agree that campaigns are more about mobilization than they are about persuasion. It is true that many people consider themselves as "undecided," even late in the campaign. But a majority of these voters are strongly predisposed to favor one of the candidates. Furthermore, even if all undecided voters were truly on the fence, garnering anything more than a fifty-fifty split would be difficult, making the investment of resources into persuasive (as opposed to mobilizing) messages a dubious strategy. This is perhaps less true of presidential election campaigns than down ballot races, but it is still the case. Second, net persuasive effects, at least those manifest in vote intentions, tend to be in the single digits. As mentioned earlier, some researchers peg effects at 1 to 2 percentage points, others at 5 to 6, but these are the parameters of the debate. While these effects are consequential, they are not overwhelming. Third, effects of any stripe are conditioned by external circumstances (the state of the economy, presidential approval, previous votes, party identification, etc.). This fact is something that has been assumed since the emergence of the Columbia and Michigan schools and the advent of the forecasting literature, but it has been elaborated in the work of Gelman and King (1993), among others. Fourth, political information and issue and candidate perceptions are influenced by campaign activities, even though votes tend to be less affected. The implication is that subsequent shifts in the vote are made possible by these campaign-driven changes in information and attitudes. Fifth and finally, the so-called "big" events of the campaign both mobilize and persuade voters. Presidential debates and national conventions may not always drive significant shifts in the distribution of candidate preferences, but occasionally they do.

Still, there is much we do not know about presidential campaigns. While the list of potential areas for further inquiry is voluminous, I would draw particular attention to two areas where the need is especially glaring. First, what do presidential general election campaigns try to accomplish with their resources? We hear a great deal about battleground states and swing voters and GOTV plans, but we have surprisingly little idea about the particulars of campaign strategies. For instance, how are electoral strategies developed? Do campaigns adhere to them when allocating resources? Are they dynamic? How much does your opponent's campaigning matter? And do these electoral strategies and their implementation differ between the major parties?

Second, despite estimates of the effects associated with specific campaign activities, we still do not have a consensus regarding the influence of television advertising and candidate appearances. What percentage of voters respond, in any manner, to these activities? And of these "affected" voters, what percentage drift back to their pre-event preference, either due to the activities of the other side or simple memory decay? Moreover, we are even more in the dark with respect to how much these activities mobilize versus how much they persuade voters.

This book takes aim at these questions against the backdrop of the first presidential elections of the twenty-first century. The next three chapters address the broad gaps just identified as well as several smaller, empirical questions. The evidence and arguments presented are only the beginning, of course, and there are a number of caveats that must be acknowledged. But the perfect is the enemy of the good, and the data brought to bear here are good. In fact, despite the occasional qualification, I believe these data facilitate a unique engagement of the presidential campaign effects questions outlined in this chapter and go a long way toward enhancing our more general understanding of what presidential campaigns do.

3

THE TRUTH ABOUT ELECTORAL
COLLEGE STRATEGIES

Perhaps the most unique characteristic of American presidential elections is that the Electoral College decides them. The particulars of this arrangement—winning a sufficient number of statewide contests to amass a majority of available electoral votes—are well known by campaign strategists and political scientists. Furthermore, the normative implications of the Electoral College for democracy in the United States are enormous. Critics point out that the Electoral College is an institution intentionally designed to prevent the direct and popular selection of presidents and as such is vaguely undemocratic (Edwards 2004). They also argue that the Electoral College encourages the subjugation of mass interest to states' interests and that substantial incentives exist within the system to favor policies and groups that can swing competitive states (Schumaker and Loomis 2001).

My concern in this chapter is neither to defend nor to attack the Electoral College as a mechanism for selecting the president. Rather, my goal is to consider more systematically how Electoral College strategies affect presidential campaigning. What did these strategies look like in 2000 and 2004, and which factors drove their development? As a participant in both the 2000 and 2004 campaigns, I thought about those questions even as lists of states were drawn up and considered. From the outset, I was interested in how suppositions derived from political science research would fare in the trenches of real electoral combat. In particular, I went into the Bush elections with four broad expectations about the formation and nature of Electoral College strategies. First, I expected that presidential campaigns would be strategic and that plans would be developed to amass 270 electoral votes (Downs 1957; Enelow and Hinich 1984; Hinich and Munger 1997; Popkin 1991). Second, I expected that these strategies would be constructed through objective, quantifiable analyses but would also be flexible with respect to the relative weight assigned to different factors and to changes in context over time (Campbell 2003). Third, I expected that Electoral College strategies would drive targeting and outreach at the media market level (Shaw 1999b; Shea and Burton 2001). Fourth, I expected that the strategies and actions of the opposition would matter, creating incentives for campaigns to mask their plans especially from the news media (Bartels 1985; Colantoni, Levesque, and Ordeshook 1975).

In this chapter I examine these expectations about the Electoral College and American presidential elections through my experiences in the Bush-Cheney campaigns. In so doing, I draw on the nature and context of those experiences as well as on the political science research that I brought to bear in response to specific campaign questions. The analysis is largely descriptive, but the broader results are suggestive. And be forewarned: I offer a more personal description of circumstances and decisions than is customary, but because I am considering motives and thought processes, this approach seems to me not only appropriate but necessary.[1]

INTO THE FIRE

On a cloudy, cold morning in January 1999, I drove along Highway 360, a scenic, looping, four-lane road that constitutes the western boundary of Austin, Texas. I turned west onto Bee Caves and then south onto Barton Creek Road, which wanders down a valley, rises up the side of a hill, and feeds into the Barton Creek Resort. I had been to the resort once before—I think it was to drop my wife off for a day at the spa. I would return in 2001 and 2002, at the invitation of a colleague and club member, to play golf on both the Canyon and Foothills courses. As I wandered around the hotel lobby on this morning, however, I was unfamiliar with my immediate whereabouts and uncertain about my prospective audience.

Karl Rove and I met at the University of Texas. I joined the faculty in the fall of 1994 as an assistant professor in the Government Department, just as George W. Bush was challenging incumbent Ann Richards for the governorship of the Lone Star State. At the time, Rove was Bush's chief political adviser and the most prominent Republican political consultant in the state. He was also an undergraduate at UT, majoring in government. Fortunately for Rove, he did not have the pleasure of learning the finer points of campaigns under my watchful eye. Truth be told, Robert Luskin, a senior colleague of mine in the department, put me in touch with Rove. Luskin taught Rove in one of his seminars and—knowing that I had worked in a few Republican campaigns as a survey research analyst—thought it a good idea to introduce us. Subsequently, Rove and I had an occasional lunch together. At one point, he gave my parents, who were visiting from San Diego, a ninety-minute tour of the Texas capitol, regaling us with stories of Texas history and contemporary politics. Whatever mutual benefit there might have been to our meetings, I simply enjoyed his conversation and, eventually, his friendship.

As Bush's gubernatorial reelection campaign kicked off in 1998, Rove made a point of introducing me to the governor. Later on, sometime during the late spring of that year, my wife and I attended a quail dinner at Rove's home with Bush and a handful of the state's political cognoscenti. On election night in November, we attended a Bush victory celebration hosted by Rove and his wife at the Shoreline Grill in Austin. We were also invited to Bush's January 1999 inauguration ball. Shortly after the inauguration, the proverbial "other shoe" dropped: I received an invitation from Rove to address a few people on the subject of developing an Electoral College strategy for the 2000 presidential election. The subject matter was unsurprising. During one of our lunches, I had described to Rove an Electoral College model that I had worked on in the 1992 Bush campaign. His interest was palpable and, with the benefit of hindsight, more than academic.

I was not sure exactly what was expected. Rove made clear that the meeting was confidential. I knew that I had about one hour to make my presentation and take questions. I also suspected that I should leave after my session so that presentations on other topics could be heard. I did not know who my audience would be, though, nor did I suspect what would be made of the information I was about to impart.

A more immediate problem was that the meeting was sufficiently secret that I could not figure out which room I was supposed to be in. I guessed that any room festooned with a continental breakfast was likely to house a Republican strategy meeting, and so I followed the aroma of cinnamon buns. This path led me to a circular room straight out of a James Bond movie. Well . . . a James Bond movie in which the villain was from Texas, at any rate. The room was dominated by a large round table framed by eight leather-backed chairs with longhorn armrests. The table itself looked to be made of a black marble, and the center was illuminated by sunlight (the low fog had cleared) pouring down from the sky view. The walls of the room were about twenty feet high and made of dark oak. I half expected Rove to walk in stroking a hairless cat, à la Dr. Evil of the *Austin Powers* movies.

At the table were Robert Teeter and Don Evans. I had known Teeter from my brief stint at Market Opinion Research, his old polling firm, and from my position in the 1992 Bush campaign, for which he had served as campaign manager. Teeter's presence was comforting not only because I knew and liked him but also because he (like Rove) appreciated an academician's point of view. I knew Evans only by reputation—he was a longtime friend of Bush's and had helped put together the financing for Bush's gubernatorial campaigns—so Teeter made a formal introduction as we grabbed orange juice and bagels. Teeter then gave me a bit of insight. There had evidently been a preliminary meeting among the principals, but mine was the first substantive presentation. He led me through a small door at the far end of the "Bond" room and into a smaller, much less intimidating room, where Rove was talking with Joe Allbaugh, Bush's chief of staff. These four men, it turned out, were the audience.

The talk was low-tech. I provided a few handouts and used an overhead projector. I had two major points that I wanted to make to set up the Electoral College model I had previously discussed with Rove. The first point was obvious but needed to be acknowledged—any presidential campaign worth its salt prioritizes among states. Some states are written off at the very beginning as heavily predisposed to go one way or the other. Other states, conversely, are likely to be competitive and therefore worthy of campaign resources. The need for such distinctions is driven by the strategic reality of presidential elections. As noted earlier, the goal in a presidential election is to win a combination of states worth 270 or more electoral votes. A campaign has limited resources with which to accomplish this goal, so a smart campaign should allocate its resources in those states crucial to a minimum winning coalition. The reaction of the principals was perhaps more interesting than this simple jumping-off point. Both Teeter and Rove flipped through the handout and stopped on page two, on which I presented an annotated bibliography along with a litany of "facts" political science has offered on Electoral College strategy. I had not thought these items would be practical enough to incorporate into the talk, but I had underrated my audience.

APPLIED POLITICAL SCIENCE

On page two of the handout, I began by noting that political scientists have long acknowledged that not all states are equal in presidential campaigns. In fact, there have been several cogent journal articles estimating optimal resource allocation strategies within the context of the Electoral College.[2] Applying a game theoretical approach, Brams and Davis (1974) find that local equilibrium strategies—assuming the presidential candidates match each other's campaign activities in each state—dictate allocating resources proportional to a state's relative population raised to the 1.5 (or 3/2s, i.e., "three-halves") power. They go on to point out that this "distortion" in attention could have policy ramifications that students of democratic processes ought to note. Lake (1979) employs a similar model but uses the probability of winning instead of the share of the popular vote as the value that candidates seek to maximize and estimates the exponential power to be 1.72. Bartels (1985) also adopts this basic framework, using television and radio advertising expenditure data from the 1976 presidential campaign of Jimmy Carter to peg the exponential power at 1.70.

But the extant literature also suggests that while the basic contours of Electoral College impact can be gauged, the particulars are more elusive. For example, shortly after the Brams and Davis article, Colantoni, Levesque, and Ordeshook (1975) published a response effectively contending that the so-called 3/2s rule is not plausible. In particular, they argue that two phenomena—"corner solutions" and "sequential learning"—render the Brams and Davis estimates inaccurate. By "corner solutions," Colantoni and his colleagues mean that the estimation techniques used by Brams and Davis overlook the fact that a significant number of states receive *no* presidential campaign attention and thus the functional form of the posited relationship is wrong. By "sequential planning," the authors mean that the underlying strategic imperative guiding the allocation of campaign resources changes from week to week, depending upon (1) what one's opponent is doing, and (2) the receipt and incorporation of new information in the form of polls. Thus, allocation patterns in week one of the campaign may look quite different from those in week ten. More to the point, the 3/2s rule does not account for this dynamic. Instead, Colantoni and his colleagues suggest that presidential candidates typically allocate their resources proportionally to the electoral votes of the states, although there is a great deal of noise in this tendency.

In my handout, I suggested that the critical observation to be gleaned from these studies is that campaigns are rational actors attempting to optimize the probability that their activities will produce an Electoral College victory. Moreover, I pointed out that some studies have begun to document how campaigns grapple with the enormous complexity of allocation factors under the conditions of the Electoral College while expanding on this basic assumption of rationality.[3] In my own analyses, I find that the presidential campaigns of 1988, 1992, and 1996 all categorized states according to their competitiveness and the direction of their aggregate preferences (Shaw 1999b). More specifically, campaigns tended to sort states into one of five categories:

1. Base Republican
2. Lean Republican
3. Battleground
4. Lean Democratic
5. Base Democratic[4]

Tables 3.1 through 3.3 show Democratic and Republican classification schemes from 1988 through 1996. They demonstrate that the overlap between the campaigns' classifications of states in a given year is considerable but far from perfect. Both sides rely on the same historical data and have (in all likelihood) comparable polling information, so this symmetry should come as no surprise. More distantly, the subsequent allocation of resources across these categories is somewhat predictable. States in the battleground category received the most resources, followed by the lean states, and then the base states.

Multivariate analyses of the 1988 through 1996 data demonstrate that the relative importance of a state is affected not only by its competitiveness and population but also by the cost of advertising in its media markets and the amount of recent effort expended there by the opposition. In fact, the interactive effect of competitiveness and cost of advertising is among the most important drivers of campaign resource allocation in these elections. For instance, New Jersey was usually a competitive state from 1988 through 1996, and its fifteen electoral votes presented an attractive target. But advertising in New Jersey means buying television time in the New York City media market to reach the upper third of the state and in the Philadelphia market to reach the lower third. That is, of course, an expensive proposition. But if you are nursing a five-point lead in the statewide polls, and your opponent purchases 1,500 gross rating points statewide (roughly fifteen exposures per person across the state, at a total cost of about $2.26 million), you may feel compelled to respond.

Other scholars have also noted the numerous factors that complicate Electoral College strategy. Bartels, for one, demonstrates that presidential campaigns can, quite rationally, incorporate several nonobvious goals that might affect the allocation of resources (Bartels 1985). He suggests that some resource allocation is geared toward realizing an Electoral College majority, while some is "ornamental" and designed to bolster congressional

TABLE 3.1 A Comparison of Electoral College Strategies, 1988

DUKAKIS'S ELECTORAL COLLEGE STRATEGY	BUSH'S ELECTORAL COLLEGE STRATEGY				
	Base Republican	Lean Republican	Battleground	Lean Democratic	Base Democratic
Base Democratic					District of Columbia* Hawaii* Iowa* Maryland* Massachusetts* Minnesota* Rhode Island* West Virginia*
Lean Democratic					
Battleground			California* Missouri* Ohio* Texas*	Illinois* Michigan* New York* Pennsylvania*	
Lean Republican		Arkansas Colorado Louisiana	New Jersey Oregon* Washington*	Connecticut* Delaware Maine Vermont Wisconsin	
Base Republican		Alabama Alaska Arizona Florida Georgia Idaho Indiana Kansas Kentucky Mississippi Montana Nebraska Nevada New Hampshire New Mexico North Carolina North Dakota Oklahoma South Carolina South Dakota Tennessee Utah Virginia Wyoming			

Source: Data from Shaw 1999b.
Note: Asterisk indicates states that were part of Dukakis's "eighteen-state strategy."

TABLE 3.2   A Comparison of Electoral College Strategies, 1992

CLINTON'S ELECTORAL COLLEGE STRATEGY	BUSH'S ELECTORAL COLLEGE STRATEGY				
	Base Republican	*Lean Republican*	*Battleground*	*Lean Democratic*	*Base Democratic*
Base Democratic					Arkansas California District of Columbia Hawaii Massachusetts Minnesota New York Rhode Island Vermont West Virginia
Lean Democratic			Pennsylvania	Connecticut Delaware Oregon Tennessee Washington	Illinois Iowa Maryland
Battleground		Colorado Montana North Carolina	Georgia Michigan New Jersey Ohio	Kentucky Louisiana Maine Missouri New Mexico Wisconsin	
Lean Republican	Arizona Kansas Nevada New Hampshire	Alabama Florida South Dakota Texas			
Base Republican	Alaska Idaho Indiana Mississippi Nebraska North Dakota South Carolina Utah Virginia Wyoming	Oklahoma			

Source: Data from Shaw 1999b.

candidates of the same party, appease contributors, or achieve some other similar purpose. Along the same lines, West (1983), in his analysis of television advertising in the Reagan-Carter race of 1980, points out that campaign resources are sometimes devoted to "coalition maintenance," even at the expense of reaching out to battleground states and swing groups.

In short, my overview of the discipline's thoughts demonstrated that political science has hardly been silent on the matter of presidential cam-

TABLE 3.3 A Comparison of Electoral College Strategies, 1996

CLINTON'S ELECTORAL COLLEGE STRATEGY	DOLE'S ELECTORAL COLLEGE STRATEGY				
	Base Republican	Lean Republican	Battleground	Lean Democratic	Base Democratic
Base Democratic					Arkansas District of Columbia Delaware Hawaii Iowa Massachusetts Maryland Minnesota New York Oregon Rhode Island Vermont Washington West Virginia
Lean Democratic			California	Illinois Michigan Missouri Pennsylvania	Connecticut Maine Wisconsin
Battleground	North Carolina	Arizona Colorado Florida Georgia Kentucky Tennessee	Louisiana Nevada New Mexico	New Hampshire New Jersey Ohio	
Lean Republican	Indiana Oklahoma South Carolina Texas Virginia	Montana South Dakota			
Base Republican	Alabama Alaska Idaho Kansas Nebraska North Dakota Mississippi Utah Wyoming				

Source: Data from Shaw 1999b.

paign strategy and the Electoral College. But it is one thing to acknowledge that a phenomenon is important and complex, or even to offer expectations about how it works, and quite another to identify and estimate the effects of specific explanatory variables. Political science is interested in the Electoral College because it filters the preferences of voters and thus has implications for democratic functioning in the United States. This interest tends to wax and wane in response to the occurrence of close elections—elections which inevitably raise the question of whether we think it is desirable to retain an arrangement whereby the person who garners the most votes across the nation may not win the presidency. It is therefore curious that there are few studies of Electoral College strategy in the 2000 or 2004 campaigns, despite their competitiveness (but see Burden 2005; Hill 2005). Even more curious is that it never occurred to me on that January morning back in 1999 that our strategic decisions *might* matter to people outside the campaign.

BACK IN THE REAL WORLD

The second point that I wished to make to Rove and his colleagues was that campaigns tend to (wrongly) classify states according to a "weighted view" of recent history. In other words, an Electoral College strategy for 2000 would typically rely on the results from 1996 and 1992, weighting the 1996 results more heavily because they are, after all, more recent. My argument on this matter was that there is no reason, a priori, to assume that 2000 would look more like 1996 than, say, 1988. To be sure, there are some broad temporal trends, such as the movement of the white South away from the Democratic Party, that make 1996 more relevant than 1956 for classifying the partisan presidential predispositions of states. But there are dynamics other than the strict linear progression of time that might drive state-level voting.

Having made this second point, I presented a model that had been developed in 1988 by John Petrocik, while he was working with pollster Fred Steeper. Initially, Petrocik had run a principal-components analysis on state presidential vote results from 1952 to 1984. The principal-components analysis determined commonality in variance and covariance between and among the various state election results and identified dimensions, or *factors,* that appeared to structure these results. The analysis suggested that elections such as 1952, 1956, and (especially) 1960 and 1976 loaded on one factor, while elections such as 1964, 1972, and 1980 loaded on another factor. Petrocik and Steeper agreed that in certain elections the Republican rank order of states was determined by the underlying partisan predispositions of that state, while in other elections it was driven by certain core issue positions (or even the ideological makeup) of the states. More concretely, in 1960 and 1976, the best Republican states were those in which the GOP enjoyed large partisan identification advantages (e.g., New Hampshire, Connecticut, Nebraska, and Utah). In 1964 and

1980, though, the best Republican states were those in which there was a relatively high proportion of conservatives, especially on social and race issues (e.g., Mississippi and Alabama). For 1988, Petrocik used preelection polling data to estimate what kind of election it would be, knowing that the rank order of states would vary according to the answer. While working with Steeper in 1992, I had run a similar model for George H. W. Bush's reelection campaign. Now I was presenting it to Rove.

The meeting lasted well over an hour, with detailed questions from everyone in attendance. I did not offer even a preliminary rank order of states by Republican potential for 2000. I did, however, present five "theoretical" rankings based on differing assumptions about the nature of the 2000 election: (1) a pure party election, (2) a mostly party/some ideology election, (3) an evenly mixed election, (4) a mostly ideology/some party election, and (5) a pure ideology election. When pressed, I said it was unlikely that the election would skew dramatically toward one dimension and that my best guess was that the ultimate rank order would be driven more by ideology than party. This meant that states in the Deep South would be the most reliable Bush fortresses, that border southern states would lean toward Bush more strongly than in party-based elections, and that some of the old bastions of Yankee Republicanism in the New England and Middle Atlantic states would be difficult for Bush to maintain.

WHICH STATES WERE TARGETED (AND WHY)?

Despite whatever nervousness I felt, the presentation was well received: On March 21, 1999, Rove asked me to join the Bush campaign. In fact, one of my primary tasks was to help develop an Electoral College strategy. In looking back on my experiences from the campaign, I believe much of the political science literature and news media punditry was accurate with respect to the strategies and attendant dynamics of the Electoral College.

First, it is true that campaigns do not consider all states equally important. When newspaper reporters write of "battleground" and "nonbattleground" states, they accurately reflect a strategic dichotomy acknowledged by the campaigns. Second, the core insight from political science—that resource priorities are substantially influenced by the electoral votes commanded by the states—is also accurate. Third, the presence of a well-financed, active opposition in the race; the dynamics of the campaign; and a host of goals beyond simply winning a majority in the Electoral College all create an enormous amount of "noise" in determining the optimal allocation of resources in and across the states.

In a broader sense, both political science and the news media also have it right when they assume that presidential campaigns are rational actors seeking to maximize the probability that they will win an Electoral College majority. The utilities of this assumption are that (1) it usually leads to plausible expectations about resource allocation, and (2) it is analytically superior to assuming campaigns allocate resources randomly or that they are stupid. More specifically, it leads one to (correctly) presume that candidates seek to identify those states most at risk *and* most critical to amassing 270 electoral votes when they decide where to campaign.

But while this assumption and its consequent expectations are plausible and useful, they do not go far enough. In fact, the only real failing of political science and the news media is that they have not yet extended their analyses to fully entertain and explore this core assumption of rationality. Put plainly, categories of states are fine, but what happens, for example, when the campaign has to decide where to expend resources *within* the battleground states? Ironically, this was a question I did not think to ask in my first few months with the Bush campaign.

RANK-ORDERING STATES

Over the summer of 1999, many of the main aspects of the Bush campaign's Electoral College strategy were put into place. Indeed, while there was a dizzying array of tasks requiring attention, much of what the Bush campaign's Strategy Department did early on was geared toward identifying the states that ought to be targeted, identifying which groups of voters within those states ought to be targeted, and determining which messages and issue positions ought to be emphasized to persuade and mobilize those groups. This may sound obvious, but anyone who has worked in a campaign knows better; many campaigns lack an identifiable, systematic process to determine where resources are to be allocated.

Two subtle but important decisions guided the formulation and implementation of this process for the Bush team. First, Rove and Matthew Dowd acknowledged that several factors ought to be considered in deciding which states were higher or lower priorities. These factors should (and could) be differentially weighted, but they ought to be listed and, whenever possible, empirically measured. Second, whatever ranking emerged had to be dynamic, in response both to changes in the underlying factors and to the activities of the Gore campaign. This dynamism, however, was most pronounced with respect to those few states on the cusp of battleground status and to market rankings within battleground states (more on this later).

For the 2000 election, we began by assuming that states carried by

Robert Dole in the 1996 presidential election were base states. The question, then, became this: Which states were most likely to be added to the GOP column? The most obvious possibilities came from a handful of southern and Rocky Mountain states, namely, Arizona, Arkansas, Georgia, Louisiana, Missouri, Nevada, and Tennessee. But the relative attractiveness of these states, as well as the potential for moving other states, was unknown.

Rove, of course, had a strong sense of which states were within reach. But he and others on the senior staff wanted a complete ranking of states according to Republican potential. The Electoral College Model that I had presented in January 1999 could generate such a ranking of states, and it was a starting point for the process of classifying states and then rating their relative attractiveness. By July 1999 there were enough publicly available statewide polls with a Bush-Gore matchup question to map the 2000 election against other recent elections in a two-dimensional space. Based on the relative position of the 2000 data point, I calculated a rank order of the states. By early August, with the addition of a few more statewide poll results and some minor adjustments to the rank order, I offered a five-category breakdown of the states.

The categorization followed the format outlined earlier: states were sorted into *base Bush, lean Bush, battleground, lean Gore,* and *base Gore* categories. My suggestion was that we focus on the three middle categories and decide which of four strategies we would pursue. An *offensive strategy* would have meant aggressively campaigning in both the battleground and lean Gore states, largely ignoring the lean Bush states. A *defensive strategy* would have emphasized locking up the lean Bush states, focusing attention on a handful of essential battleground states and largely ignoring the lean Gore states. A *mixed strategy* would have entailed shoring up the most vulnerable lean Bush states, while focusing on the most promising battleground states and perhaps targeting the one or two most susceptible lean Gore states. A *focused, high-risk strategy* would have been to ignore all lean states and focus exclusively on those battleground states most likely to decide the election. These possibilities are outlined in table 3.4.

Although I did not state a preference, I assumed we would employ a mixed strategy. Most recent presidential campaigns appear to have done so, and there were reasons to follow precedent. By early autumn, Bush was leading Gore in the national polls by an average of about 15 percentage points. Even though it was inevitable that this margin would shrink, a defensive strategy seemed completely illogical. Bush's lead in the lean Bush states was approximately 30 points, so what was the purpose of piling on? A high-risk strategy appeared similarly nonsensical. Given Bush's

TABLE 3.4 Theoretical Approaches to Targeting States

| | INCLINATION OF STATE | | | | |
CAMPAIGN STRATEGY	Base Republican	Lean Republican	Battleground	Lean Democrat	Base Democrat
Offensive (example: Bush 2000)	None	None	Much	Much	None
Defensive (example: Dole 1996)	None	Much	Much	None	None
Mixed (example: Reagan 1980)	None	Some	Much	Some	None
Focused, high-risk (example: Gore 2000)	None	None	All	None	None

Note: Cell entries represent the attention given to states falling into that category from the perspective of the example campaign.

early lead, it was very difficult to identify *which* states were most critical to reaching 270 electoral votes. Florida looked to be one, but there were some in the campaign who thought it would eventually be more of a lean Bush state than a true battleground. Michigan and Pennsylvania would almost unquestionably be battlegrounds. But what if Republican Governor John Engler's fights with the unions in Michigan crippled our chances there? Missouri and Ohio seemed likely, too, but local conditions in both of those states were volatile. Of course, I had my rank order, but with every new poll things changed slightly. Moreover, it was certainly possible that the underlying issue or party dynamics of the race would shift in the next fifteen months, and putting all of the campaign's eggs into a small basket did not seem advisable. To me, then, the choice appeared to be between an offensive versus a mixed strategy. As I said, I had no true dog in this hunt, but I leaned toward a mixed strategy simply because it allowed us to hedge our bets—we could always become more aggressive if conditions continued to look propitious.

As it turned out, the campaign's brain trust was less concerned with the nature of the strategy—and the collapsing of categories—than the particular states on the target list. In other words, Rove, Dowd, and others were thinking in more dichotomous terms: states were either in play or not. States that Dole had carried would get minimal resources, while states that had gone Democratic in 1996 but were designated battlegrounds for 2000 would get significant attention. Based on current polling, recent voting trends, and the rank order, we settled on an expansive number of battleground states.

In settling on a broad list of states, the campaign had implicitly decided to be aggressive. In this case, more targets meant including states that had gone Democratic in both the 1992 and 1996 elections. But aggression complicated the particular issue of allocation within the battlegrounds. As mentioned earlier, the question of where—and how heavily—to campaign within these many states would have to be decided based on the systematic consideration of several factors. Battleground states were prioritized according to a weighted algorithm (or "Al Gore-ithm," as I used to say, mostly to courteous but unamused smiles) including:

1. *Past statewide voting history.* States that typically elect Republicans to statewide offices were immediate candidates for battleground status. In addition, any state that George H. W. Bush carried by 5 percentage points or more over Michael Dukakis or that Bill Clinton carried by fewer than 5 points over Robert Dole was a serious candidate. The prime targets using these criteria were Arizona, Arkansas, Florida, Missouri, Nevada, New Hampshire, Ohio, and Tennessee.

2. *Contemporaneous polling numbers.* States in which Bush's lead over presumed Democratic nominee Al Gore was at the national average were considered higher priorities. Assuming the race would tighten across the board, states at or slightly below this average would be the most competitive on Election Day. Following this logic, the campaign identified Arkansas, Florida, Iowa, Missouri, Oregon, Ohio, Pennsylvania, Tennessee, Washington, West Virginia, and Wisconsin as top priorities.

3. *Organizational development and endorsements.* Battleground states in which Bush could count on statewide Republican leaders to organize and campaign for him were much more attractive than states that had either Democratic or unpopular Republican statewide officeholders. Most notably, there was Senator Judd Gregg's presence in New Hampshire, along with Governor Jeb Bush in Florida, Governor John Engler in Michigan, Governor Tom Ridge in Pennsylvania, Governor Robert Taft in Ohio, and Governor Tommy Thompson in Wisconsin. On the other side of the ledger, Illinois had unpopular GOP governor George Ryan, while Arkansas had a divided state party, with one faction supporting Senator Tim Hutchison and the other favoring Governor Michael Huckabee.[5]

4. *The existence of other hot races or solid top-of-the-ticket candidates.* If the campaign could reduce the costs of field staff and television advertising by piggybacking its efforts onto those of a solid Senate or gubernatorial campaign, that would make a state more at-

tractive. Three states appeared to be worth monitoring on these grounds: Nevada, Washington, and Missouri, where GOP Senate candidates John Ensign, Slade Gorton, and John Ashcroft, respectively, had strong campaign organizations.

5. *Issues with cutting potential.* Although the Bush campaign was typically uninterested in tailoring unique campaign appeals for specific jurisdictions, states with favorable issue environments did receive slightly higher prioritization. These states included Washington (where the issue was a Democratic proposal to tear down a number of river dams to protect salmon populations), Michigan (where the issue was Gore's controversial attack on the combustible engine in his book *Earth in the Balance*), and Pennsylvania and West Virginia (where there was a perception that Gore had reneged on a promise to back clean-coal legislation and had thus sold out the miners).

6. *Native-son effects.* While Bush's Texas roots made that state a lock, Arkansas (Bill Clinton's home state) and Tennessee (Al Gore's home state) were considered lean Democratic states because they had ties to the Democratic ticket. Many in the Bush campaign thought this classification was too much of a downgrade and pushed to have them higher on the target list. In addition, vice presidential nominees could bring their states into (or take them out of) play and rearrange the strategic map.

Each of these factors was quantified and weighted, with polling numbers receiving the most consideration. The battleground states were then ranked according to their scores across these factors. States at the top of the list were the highest priority with respect to resource allocation, while states at the bottom were on a "watch" list (no television advertisements or candidate visits, but perhaps some party money and organizational resources). The middle-tier battleground states would receive some campaign resources, but not at the expense of full engagement in the higher-priority states.

It is worth pointing out that, in theory, the 2000 Bush campaign had three Electoral College plans (see table 3.5). The first plan encompassed all of the lean and battleground states, twenty-nine in all, and could be admitted and even disseminated to interested parties. The second plan included twenty-four battleground states—pure battleground states, as well as some lean Bush states that required attention and some lean Gore states that loomed as attainable prizes. This plan could be discussed in more or less specific terms with the news media and some state and local party

TABLE 3.5   The Bush Campaigns' List of Battleground States

	2000			2004	
PUBLIC LIST	THE "REAL" LIST	THE "REAL" REAL LIST	PUBLIC LIST	THE "REAL" LIST	THE "REAL" REAL LIST
Targeted States(29):	*Targeted States(24):*	*Targeted States(15):*	*Targeted States(24):*	*Targeted States(20):*	*Targeted States(15):*
Arizona	Arkansas	Arkansas	Arizona	Arizona	Florida
Arkansas	California	Florida	Arkansas	Arkansas	Iowa
California	Delaware	Iowa	Colorado	Colorado	Maine
Colorado	Florida	Maine	Delaware	Florida	Michigan
Connecticut	Georgia	Michigan	Florida	Iowa	Minnesota
Delaware	Illinois	Minnesota	Illinois	Maine	Missouri
Florida	Iowa	Missouri	Iowa	Michigan	Nevada
Georgia	Kentucky	New Hampshire	Kentucky	Minnesota	New Hampshire
Illinois	Louisiana	New Mexico	Louisiana	Missouri	New Mexico
Iowa	Maine	Oregon	Maine	Nevada	Ohio
Kentucky	Michigan	Pennsylvania	Michigan	New Hampshire	Oregon
Louisiana	Minnesota	Tennessee	Minnesota	New Jersey	Pennsylvania
Maine	Missouri	Washington	Missouri	New Mexico	Washington
Michigan	Nevada	West Virginia	Nevada	North Carolina	West Virginia
Minnesota	New Hampshire	Wisconsin	New Hampshire	Ohio	Wisconsin
Missouri	New Jersey		New Jersey	Oregon	
Montana	New Mexico		New Mexico	Pennsylvania	
Nevada	Ohio		North Carolina	Washington	
New Hampshire	Oregon		Ohio	West Virginia	
New Jersey	Pennsylvania		Oregon	Wisconsin	
New Mexico	Tennessee		Pennsylvania		
North Carolina	Washington		Washington		
Ohio	West Virginia		West Virginia		
Oregon	Wisconsin		Wisconsin		
Pennsylvania					
Tennessee					
Washington					
West Virginia					
Wisconsin					

Source: Author's notes and conversations with Bush campaign staffers.

personnel.[6] The third plan included states that were deemed central to the election effort and therefore worthy of the campaign's resources. This list was known only by those critical to its formulation and implementation (i.e., Strategy Department personnel, the campaign's senior staff, and relevant support personnel). It identified fifteen "true" battleground states.

This list of true battleground states for 2000 requires some elaboration. First, traditionally Democratic states such as West Virginia and Minnesota, as well as Gore's home state of Tennessee, were initially on the watch list. The campaign eventually added them to the list of battlegrounds in late September 2000 when favorable polling data finally convinced the campaign that there were genuine prospects for victory in those states. Second, contrary to popular myth, Illinois and New Jersey were never part of Bush's Electoral College strategy. They were consigned to the lean Gore category early on, and they never left it. In fact, at one point in May 2000, Dowd and I met with Ken Mehlman and Scott Douglas (who were then serving as the political directors of the Midwest and Northeast states, respectively) to discuss the relative merits of Illinois and New Jersey as bottom-rung battleground states. Mehlman offered a discouraging perspective on Illinois, citing Governor Ryan's unpopularity, infighting within the state Republican Party, and several local issues that hampered Republican prospects. He pegged our chances for victory at less than one in five. We all turned to Douglas, who said, "I agree with everything Ken just said, and I still think Illinois is better than New Jersey." Third, the two most persistent strategic debates throughout 2000 were (1) whether we should focus more on Pennsylvania or Michigan in the upper Midwest, and (2) whether we should focus more on Oregon or Washington in the Pacific Northwest.[7] All four states were true battlegrounds, but this categorization was of little help as we were often in the position of choosing between sending the candidate to Flint or Pittsburgh, for example. To the best of my recollection, we never reached a definitive decision on these two matters.

In 2004, the conversation began where the 2000 election left off. Because so many states were decided by a few percentage points, the list of battleground states was almost self-evident. More to the point, it was clear to Rove and Dowd that they had to defend the weakest elements of Bush's 270-vote coalition, a coalition that increased to 279 electoral votes after reapportionment. It obviously included Florida (which Bush had carried by 0.1 points in 2000), New Hampshire (+1.3), Missouri (+3.3), Ohio (+3.5), Nevada (+3.5), and West Virginia (+6.3). To expand the majority to replace potential losses to Kerry, they targeted the weakest links in Gore's coalition: New Mexico (−0.1), Wisconsin (−0.2), Iowa (−0.3), Oregon (−0.4), Minnesota (−2.4), and Maine (−5.1).

Some things had changed since 2000, however. From the Bush campaign's perspective, the rapid growth of minority populations in Phoenix, Denver, and northern Virginia meant that Arizona, Colorado, and perhaps even Virginia required close monitoring. Conversely, the absence of a southern Democrat at the head of the ticket meant that Louisiana, Georgia, Tennessee, and even Arkansas were second-tier battlegrounds at best. Even the emergence of native son John Edwards as Kerry's vice presidential pick never dragged the Carolinas into the fray. In addition, the tragedy of September 11, 2001, and the political implosions of Democratic senator Frank Torricelli and Democratic governor James McGreevey transformed New Jersey back into a state worth watching for Bush.[8]

Other states made the 2004 battleground list by virtue of their size and historical competitiveness, such as Michigan, Pennsylvania, and Washington. Michigan and Washington were viewed skeptically, though, given Bush's failure there in 2000 and his stubbornly low approval ratings in late 2003 and early 2004. And, contrary to some news media accounts, Illinois was never on the Bush campaign's radar screen in 2004. The continuing (and baffling) difficulties of the Illinois GOP rendered that state a nonstarter.

The upshot is that Bush identified at least fifteen states as 2004 battlegrounds before a vote had been cast in the Democratic primaries. Six were states Bush carried in 2000, while nine were Gore states. In addition, one Democratic state (New Jersey) was thought to be worth following, and two heavily contested southern states from 2000—Tennessee and Arkansas—were not considered at risk in 2004. This identification suggested an offensive strategy, with a fallback plan (dropping New Jersey altogether, and perhaps Michigan and Washington, and moving to defend Arizona, Colorado, and maybe even Virginia) that reflected a mixed perspective.

As the fall campaign unfolded, the Bush campaign reclassified Missouri (to lean Bush), and Maine and Washington (lean Kerry). Kerry drove the former decision when he stopped advertising and dropped scheduled campaign stops in those states from his itinerary. Persistent and discouraging private-poll results drove the latter decision. From this it seems reasonable to conclude that offensive strategies are more affected by poll numbers whereas defensive strategies are more affected by the opponent's actions.

MEDIA MARKET PRIORITIES

As suggested earlier, the task of deciding between two important states is an essential one. But identifying (and even ranking) battleground states is not enough. The truth of presidential campaigns is that once a set of battleground states is identified, the focus shifts to media markets. States are, of course, an appropriate unit of analysis—the Electoral College ensures it is so. But political communication is conducted at the level of the media market. Phones, direct mail, and person-to-person contacting can certainly be concentrated in key precincts (or even key blocks within these precincts). Most of the money in contemporary presidential election campaigns, however, is dedicated to television advertising, while most of the candidate's time is wrapped up in visiting cities and towns in an effort to win favorable local media coverage. In planning both of these endeavors, the appropriate unit of analysis is the media market.

Democratic presidential campaigns have been rank-ordering media markets based on an estimated "cost per persuadable voter" since (at least) 1992. James Carville alludes to this practice in his memoir of the 1992 campaign, *All's Fair* (Matalin, Carville, and Knobler 1994), as does Dick Morris (1997) in his tell-all narrative of the 1996 campaign. In 2000, the Bush campaign did the same thing.[9] The mechanics of such an analysis are simple. First, one aggregates county-level voting data from some range of presidential elections over some period of time (usually three or more election cycles) into media markets.[10] Elections in which a home-state candidate is on the ballot (e.g., Texas in 2000 and 2004, Arkansas in 1992 and 1996) are discarded, as they inflate even high-end estimates of the party's underlying support. Second, the number of "swing" (for the Republicans) or "persuadable" (for the Democrats) voters is calculated by taking the difference between the party's high and low percentages.[11] Obviously, it is important to use percentages in these calculations because both population and turnout fluctuations would skew estimates derived from differences in the raw vote. For 2000, I used results from five presidential elections, 1980 through 1996, to estimate swing votes in and across media markets. Usually, the swing was defined by the percentage difference between Reagan's 1984 and Bush's 1992 votes. Third and finally, one multiplies the percentage of swing voters in the market by the estimated number of presidential election voters to determine the average number of available swing voters.[12]

With these estimates in hand, I calculated the relative efficiency of prospective campaign locales by dividing the swing vote by the cost of television advertising in the market. For example, if the cost of reaching every person in a market is twenty-five thousand dollars, and there are one hundred thousand swing voters in the market, the cost is twenty-five cents per swing voter.[13] This cost can be compared with those of all other markets in the battleground states. The most obvious complication for this calculation is that some markets cross state boundaries, and the campaign may need to reach swing voters in only one of these states. Revisiting the New Jersey example here is illustrative. In the 2000 election, the Bush campaign could have decided to advertise in New Jersey (it did not, but let us say it did for the moment). Doing so would have necessitated buying advertising time in the Philadelphia and New York markets. If one takes all swing voters in those markets into account, New York might be more cost-effective than Philadelphia. Unfortunately, residents of New Jersey make up only a small portion of the New York market. The rest of the people in that market live in New York, which was clearly going for Gore. Even if many of these people are swing voters, they cannot be counted in a realistic assessment of cost efficiency. Conversely, people in the Philadelphia market who do not live in New Jersey live in either Pennsylvania or Delaware, both potential battleground states. They would, in all likelihood, be counted in an estimate of the cost per swing voter. The key here is keeping in mind the totality of battleground (and nonbattleground) states when assessing the number of swing voters in multistate markets.[14]

With that in mind, I calculated the relative cost efficiency of advertising for each of the media markets within our list of battleground states. A brief explanation is in order here. Political advertising is measured in *gross rating points* (GRPs), with one hundred GRPs representing the amount of advertising necessary to ensure that on average, every resident within a market sees an ad one time. This concept is used in table 3.6, which presents a quick look at the top twenty markets in 2000, based on cost per swing voter. Such an efficiency listing could then be used in a straightforward manner. Let us say, for instance, that the campaign had two million dollars it wished to spend on TV advertising. We would go down the "cost per swing voter" list of markets, buying one thousand GRPs in the first market, then the second, then the third, and so on until we had exhausted

TABLE 3.6   Top 20 Media Markets by Cost Efficiency of Reaching Swing Voters

MEDIA MARKET	STATE	MEDIA MARKET SIZE	COST PER 100 GROSS RATING POINTS	COST PER SWING VOTER
Flint–Saginaw–Bay City	Michigan	907,455	$4,700	$0.04
Green Bay–Appleton	Wisconsin	—	$3,400	$0.04
Champaign–Springfield Decatur	Illinois	567,244	$3,400	$0.04
Traverse City–Cadillac	Michigan	430,090	$2,800	$0.04
Springfield	Missouri	547,972	$3,300	$0.04
Columbia–Jefferson City	Missouri	281,353	$2,000	$0.05
Little Rock–Pine Bluff	Arkansas	780,160	$5,000	$0.05
Wausau–Rhinelander	Wisconsin	—	$2,000	$0.05
Toledo	Ohio	638,405	$4,900	$0.05
Johnstown-Altoona	Pennsylvania	436,758	$2,800	$0.05
Lansing	Michigan	466,356	$4,100	$0.05
Lafayette	Louisiana	354,366	$2,900	$0.05
Madison	Wisconsin	—	$3,800	$0.05
Wilkes Barre–Scranton	Pennsylvania	818,711	$5,500	$0.06
Grand Rapids–Kalamazoo–Battle Creek	Michigan	1,262,427	$9,900	$0.06
Ft. Smith–Fayetteville–Springdale–Rogers	Arkansas	218,609	$2,400	$0.06
St. Louis	Missouri	1,404,039	$13,700	$0.06
Peoria-Bloomington	Illinois	386,653	$3,000	$0.06
Monroe–El Dorado	Arkansas	264,554	$2,300	$0.06
New Orleans	Louisiana	998,885	$7,300	$0.06

Source: Cost estimates come from Maverick Media (Austin, TX).
Note: Media-market-size figures represent the number of registered voters in the market as of 1998. For Wisconsin I use eligible voter figures, as same-day registration is allowed.

our budget.[15] I say "this is what we did," but the reality is that recommended purchases were sometimes amended by Rove and others, usually to ensure that top-priority states were not "missed" simply because buying within them was relatively inefficient. Again, multiple levels and considerations make developing (or predicting) strategy difficult.

WHAT ABOUT THE DEMOCRATS?

On the other side of the aisle, it is difficult but not impossible to know what the Gore and Kerry campaigns were thinking. Their stratagems have been well guarded by the principals, most notably their targeting guru, Tad Devine. This is, of course, not unusual. As mentioned earlier, one of the difficulties of studying presidential campaigns is that the winners jealously guard their secrets, while the losers disappear, taking with them the records of interest for students of electoral politics. The case of the Gore campaign is even more complex because of two interrelated factors: (1) the closeness of the election, and (2) the divisions within the Democratic Party. The closeness of the election—and, more to the point, Gore's plurality victory in the popular vote—means that members of the campaign could make a credible case that they had the winning strategy. As the guardians of the winning strategy, Gore strategists had an incentive to keep their secrets for success, lest they be called back into battle. The divisions within the Democratic Party also created issues. In particular, Clintonites and members of the Democratic Leadership Council (DLC) took aim at Gore's campaign team as they sought to discredit the more aggressive, populist, class-warfare tack pursued by Gore. This feud, clearly manifest among Democratic consultants looking to line up clients for the 2002 and 2004 elections, led the Gore team members to both aggressively defend their actions and plans in 2000 and to be somewhat circumspect with respect to strategic details.

It is easy, however, to overstate these conflicts. Although my efforts to garner specific information about the static and dynamic particulars of the Gore campaign's Electoral College plan were greeted coolly (given my role in the Bush campaign, who could blame them?), members of Gore's staff were quite collegial and forthcoming in several public forums that I attended. Most notably, high-level members of the Gore team—including senior advisers Bob Shrum and Carter Eskew, media advisor Bill Knapp, and national pollster Stanley Greenberg—were direct and candid during a bipartisan Campaign 2000 conference at the University of Pennsylvania's Annenberg School for Communication.

More specifically, Greenberg offered a list of states in which the Gore campaign was conducting tracking polls. This list almost assuredly bears a strong resemblance to the campaign's list of battleground states. From this list as well as from informal conversations with Shrum and a colleague who worked with Gore's state pollster, Harrison Hickman, it is possible to estimate the rough contours of Gore's Electoral College plan. It seems they targeted twenty-one battleground states: Arizona, Arkansas, Florida, Illinois, Iowa, Kentucky, Louisiana, Maine, Michigan, Minnesota, Missouri, Nevada, New Hampshire, New Mexico, Ohio, Oregon, Pennsylvania, Tennessee, Washington, West Virginia, and Wisconsin. The relative frequency of polling in these states, however, indicates that thirteen— Arkansas, Florida, Iowa, Maine, Michigan, Missouri, New Hampshire, New Mexico, Oregon, Pennsylvania, Tennessee, Washington, and Wisconsin—likely were their true battleground states. Interestingly, members of the Gore campaign indicated that Washington was a top-level battleground state only because the Bush campaign targeted it relentlessly.[16] These operatives said that Gore's internal statewide polling always showed it to be a relatively strong state for the Democratic ticket.

Taken as a whole, the nature of Democratic polling and research attentiveness suggest the Gore campaign, like the Bush campaign, decided that twenty-nine states (plus Washington, D.C.) were uncompetitive. Furthermore, thirteen of the twenty-one competitive states appear to have been especially important targets. While there is no direct evidence that Gore's campaign had a multilevel categorization, it is clear that they developed an empirical method for prioritizing battleground states.

Table 3.7 presents a comparison of the Bush and Gore plans, with the Gore plan being inferred from conversations with Democratic operatives and presentations at the Annenberg conference. The overlap is striking. Assuming that Washington was considered a true battleground state by Gore, only three states were viewed differently by the campaigns: West Virginia, Minnesota, and California. All three were considered strongly Democratic states going into the 2000 presidential election. Ultimately, Gore was able to maintain California and Minnesota, but he did lose West Virginia, which hurt him dearly. There are also those who believe the Gore campaign erred by not targeting Nevada and Ohio—which Bush carried by only 5 and 4 percentage points, respectively—as higher priorities. On the other hand, while Bush's aggressive stabs into West Virginia netted him five electoral votes, the California foray was prohibitively costly and netted little.

Turning to 2004, the Kerry campaign's Electoral College strategy is gleaned from two sources. First, Kerry aides themselves (most notably, Devine and Greenberg) provided insight in their postelection interviews

TABLE 3.7   A Comparison of Electoral College Strategies, 2000

GORE'S ELECTORAL COLLEGE STARTEGY	BUSH'S ELECTORAL COLLEGE STRATEGY				
	Base Republican	*Lean Republican*	*Battleground*	*Lean Democratic*	*Base Democratic*
Base Republican	Alabama Alaska Colorado Georgia Idaho Indiana Kansas Mississippi Montana Nebraska North Carolina North Dakota Oklahoma South Carolina South Dakota Texas Utah Virginia Wyoming				
Lean Republican		Arizona Kentucky Louisiana Nevada Ohio			
Battleground			Arkansas Florida Iowa Maine Michigan Missouri New Hampshire New Mexico Oregon Pennsylvania Tennessee Washington Wisconsin		
Lean Democratic			Minnesota West Virginia	Illinois	
Base Democratic				California	Connecticut Delaware District of Columbia Hawaii Maryland Massachusetts New Jersey New York Rhode Island Vermont

Source: Republican strategic categorizations are drawn from conversations with Karl Rove and Matthew Dowd. Democratic strategic categorizations are drawn from presentations by (and follow-up conversations with) Carter Eskew, Bill Knapp, Stanley Greenberg, and Bob Shrum.

and panels. Second, the particulars of the plan were evident in the innovative and controversial television advertising buy strategy of the Kerry team. Just before Labor Day 2004, Kerry prepurchased advertising in seven states while his strategists openly identified the thirteen others that he would target during the campaign (Sidoti and Fournier 2004). Although he effectively telegraphed his strategy to the Bush campaign, the Kerry team thought the benefits were worth it. As Sidoti and Fournier (2004) point out, "This move allowed Kerry to lock in current advertising rates, which rise sharply in the fall as demand for airtime soars. He can cancel ads later in states he feels he cannot win and redeploy those dollars to others he believes he can win."

Whatever their rationale, the battle map suggested in the TV buy strategy perfectly matches the one described by Kerry aides after the election. Like the Bush team, Kerry's advisers began with the results of the 2000 election. On the offensive side, they simply followed the 2000 vote share to determine that Florida, New Hampshire, Nevada, Ohio, Missouri, Arizona, West Virginia, and Arkansas were the most vulnerable elements of Bush's coalition. Colorado, Louisiana, and North Carolina also emerged as pickup possibilities in the early summer, the last of them due to the presence on the ticket of Tar Heel senator John Edwards. In addition, the Kerry campaign shared the Bush team's curiosity about Virginia. On the defensive side, following the logic of 2000 led Kerry's aides to believe that New Mexico, Iowa, Wisconsin, Pennsylvania, Oregon, Minnesota, Michigan, Maine, and Washington presented the greatest risk. Although Kerry's campaign granted that New Jersey might be closer than they originally expected, they never considered it a battleground state. There were thus thirteen lean states and seven true battlegrounds—Florida, Iowa, New Hampshire, New Mexico, Ohio, Pennsylvania, and Wisconsin.

Table 3.8 shows considerable overlap in the candidates' strategies for 2004. A few states were considered base by one side and lean by the other; Bush's team saw Louisiana and North Carolina as safe while Kerry's campaign deemed them "worth watching." The mirror image existed with respect to New Jersey and Delaware. But eight potential battleground states elicited a difference of opinion—Republicans considered Maine, Michigan, Minnesota, Missouri, Nevada, Oregon, Washington, and West Virginia as battlegrounds whereas Democrats thought of them as leaning toward a particular candidate. Ultimately, both campaigns moved Colorado into the battleground category.

Within their battleground states, there is every reason to assume that Gore and Kerry rank-ordered media markets by cost efficiency to prioritize their media dollars. First, this sort of targeting was (as mentioned

TABLE 3.8   A Comparison of Electoral College Strategies, 2004

KERRY'S ELECTORAL COLLEGE STRATEGY	BUSH'S ELECTORAL COLLEGE STRATEGY				
	Base Republican	*Lean Republican*	*Battleground*	*Lean Democratic*	*Base Democratic*
Base Republican	Alabama Alaska Georgia Idaho Indiana Kansas Kentucky Mississippi Montana Nebraska North Dakota Oklahoma South Carolina South Dakota Tennessee Texas Utah Wyoming				
Lean Republican	Louisiana North Carolina	Arizona Arkansas Colorado Virginia	Missouri Nevada West Virginia		
Battleground			Florida Iowa New Hampshire New Mexico Ohio Pennsylvania Wisconsin		
Lean Democratic			Maine Michigan Minnesota Oregon Washington	Delaware New Jersey	
Base Democratic					California Connecticut District of Columbia Hawaii Illinois Maryland Massachusetts New York Rhode Island Vermont

Source: Republican strategic categorizations are drawn from conversations with Karl Rove, Matthew Dowd, and Ken Mehlman. Democratic strategic categorizations are drawn from public interviews and panel presentations by Bill Knapp and Tad Devine.

earlier) a staple of the Clinton-Gore campaigns in 1992 and 1996. It is difficult to see why the top Democratic staffers would move away from it. They undoubtedly had access to the requisite data and expertise. Moreover, the ultimate success of the Clinton-Gore campaigns leaves little obvious reason for discarding their targeting blueprints. In fact, it is more likely that the Democratic plans included cost-efficiency estimates not only for reaching out to swing voters but also for mobilizing partisans. That is, estimates of cost per swing voter (or "cost per persuadable voter," as the Democrats say) may have been supplemented by analyses of "cost per mobilizable voter", in which Democratic voter turnout variance over some subset of elections would be calculated and divided by media costs for different media markets. Such an analysis would have been in line with the Gore and Kerry campaigns' commitment to increasing turnout among the Democratic base, most obviously manifest in the prominence of Donna Brazille, a mobilization expert who served as Gore's campaign manager, and David Whouley, perhaps the foremost GOTV expert in America, who worked for both Gore and Kerry.

A SELECTIVE OVERVIEW OF LESSONS LEARNED

One Tuesday morning in early October 2000, Dowd and I were updating our state-ranking model. We were entering the latest polling data, changing competitiveness estimates, rethinking organizational ratings, and making several other small adjustments. At one point, he turned to me and said, "If we do this just right, we'll get what we would have gotten by ranking these states off the top of our heads." I have thought about that comment a dozen times since then. The nugget of truth—that campaigns desperately want to have logical, systematic, and empirical backing for their intuitions and prejudices—is priceless. But it also suggests the single most important lesson to be drawn from this delineation of Republican and Democratic Electoral College plans: presidential campaigns *are* rational and strategic. They are rational in that they act to maximize the chances they will achieve their ultimate goal of winning the election. The existence of plans with targeting distinctions evidences this rationality. In 2000 and 2004, the campaigns were also strategic in the sense that these plans were concocted to guide the allocation of resources, although I will save my comments on the extent to which activity patterns matched the plans for chapter 4.

But the evidence for rational and strategic behavior does not mean that one can easily predict what a given presidential campaign might do. As suggested earlier, this unpredictability is precisely because strategic considerations are numerous and dynamic. Furthermore, the election is made up of multiple contests across many states, and the activities and organizations of Senate, House, and gubernatorial candidates can matter, as can internal party factors.

Three other lessons from 2000 and 2004 stand out. First, the dynamic and granular character of targeting decisions suggests measuring campaigns and their effects at multiple times during the campaign and at multiple levels. Both Republicans and Democrats ultimately targeted small subsets of voters and locales within high-priority states, and their efforts may have waxed and waned over the fall. This reality ought to inform how we measure impact.

Second, the overlap between the Republican and Democratic plans is considerable but not perfect. In particular, it is likely that the Democrats' targeting was even leaner than the Republicans' due to the horse race (the Democrats trailed throughout much of 2000 and 2004) and finances (the Democrats had considerably less television ad money than the Republicans did, at least in 2000).

Third, the campaigns had a number of reasons to be secretive about their plans. Most obviously, if there is an advantage to be gained by outgunning your opponent in a given state or media market, you do not want to announce your activities on the off chance that the opposing campaign may be unaware of your efforts. Moreover, state and local candidates and party officials who are left out of a targeting plan can be very touchy. Presidential candidate visits and advertising dollars are considered a big boost to their election prospects, and they do not like being left out. A snub may not damage the candidate's chances of winning the election, but it could affect the degree of enthusiasm and cooperativeness of these officials in subsequent electoral and legislative battles. Consequently, even among the faithful, presidential campaigns are reluctant to give out their true electoral map.

Another reason for secrecy is that the media clamor for the details of presidential campaign plans but (for some reason) cannot seem to keep a secret and rarely feel compelled to provide the context that goes into the construction of plans. Campaigns are therefore in the position of wanting to satisfy the media's craving for horse race information without giving away the truly significant distinctions that animate planning decisions. In 2000, it meant that the Bush campaign would talk freely about the broad list of important states but not about the narrower list. Indeed, the media could be used to publicize a feint; both Clinton (in 1992 and 1996) and Bush (in 2000) visited or bought television time in states that were not true battleground states in an effort to achieve favorable publicity about the aggressiveness of the campaign and to draw the opposition into committing resources that were better spent elsewhere.

Besides these lessons, the tea leaves of 2000 and 2004 clearly show a trend toward tighter, leaner targeting. For all of the recriminations aimed at the Gore and Kerry campaigns, both had extraordinarily focused targeting plans. Not only were they more focused than Bush's, they were undoubtedly more focused than either of Clinton's. Again, in part this focus was due to their position; both trailed in the polls for much of the campaign and neither had as much money as Bush and the Republican National Committee nor the attendant luxury of adding media markets and states to their lists.

This trend toward leaner targeting may be troubling, as it could reduce the number of markets and states receiving presidential campaign resources. Such an outcome is not a certainty, however. The closeness of the national vote distribution could increase incentives to compete in more states and markets such that there is little net change in the proportion of the population receiving presidential election campaign visits and TV ad dollars.[17]

But perhaps a more basic question about this trend merits attention: Who cares if the campaigns target their efforts, and, more particularly, who cares if these targeting schemes are becoming narrower? The simple answer is that everyone in states left off the targeting list might care. If one believes that candidates offer policy inducements to persuade and mobilize voters and that they follow through on these promises when elected, then voters in nonbattleground states ought to be concerned. If a state—or even a media market within a state—is ignored, its voters' more particularized interests are receiving less attention and commitment than the particularized concerns of voters in battleground states.

Again, I hasten to reiterate that all this speculation is based on an assumption for which there is currently little supportive evidence. Neither I nor anyone else has provided empirical support for the notion that campaigns *follow through* on these stratagems. There is some reason to believe that campaigns, in fact, are imprecise and nonstrategic when allocating the television dollars and candidate visits that dominate our conception of presidential electioneering. In other words, I have not yet established that electoral plans, however they look, are actualized. It is toward this subject that I turn in chapter 4.

4

ALLOCATING CAMPAIGN RESOURCES
ACROSS STATES AND MEDIA MARKETS

It is clear that the Republicans and Democrats had plans to win Electoral College majorities in 2000 and 2004. If these presidential campaigns did not follow their strategic plans, however, knowledge of these plans does not necessarily add much to our understanding of electoral politics. Of course, the mismatch between strategy and behavior would tell us *some* things—it would tell us that factors not related to winning the election drive what the candidates say and to whom they say it. It would also tell us that political consultants are not calling the shots.[1] Perhaps, then, it is more appropriate and accurate to state that deviations from Electoral College plans yield information on how the context of American presidential campaigns affects candidate decisions and behavior. The influence of context, in turn, could have profound implications for what voters see and how elected officials ultimately understand their mandates. But nonstrategic behavior would be surprising given the pull of the presidency and the attendant incentive not to waste a single minute or dollar. Therefore the most useful working hypothesis is that presidential campaigns strictly adhere to their Electoral College plans when it comes to devising their schedules and buying television advertising time.

Unfortunately, few previous studies have empirically engaged this hypothesis. This gap is curious given the fundamental questions that cannot be answered absent these data. Are reliably Republican or Democratic states totally ignored? How much variation is there in the amount of campaign activity lavished on the battleground states? To what extent are campaigns influenced by the activities of the opposition? Is there any discernible dynamic that affects the absolute or relative amount of campaigning from late August through Election Day? This chapter engages these questions by estimating the allocation of certain resources across battleground states and media markets in the 2000 and 2004 presidential election campaigns. The implicit assumption is that describing the distribution of resources is critical to assessing campaign strategies and, ultimately, shifts in voters' preferences.

Based on the words of strategists both during and after the elections, it is evident not only that they had plans but that they believe the campaigns adhered closely to those plans. In an interview with the *Milwaukee Journal Sentinel*, Gore strategist Tad Devine posited that they had concentrated their television ads and candidate appearances more precisely than any presidential campaign in history.[2] Gore's pollster Stanley Greenberg and media consultant Bill Knapp both repeatedly expressed this same belief at the bipartisan Campaign 2000 conference at the University of Pennsylvania's Annenberg School for Communication. Despite having a large portion of their anti-Bush resources in the hands of independent 527 organizations, the Kerry team members conveyed comparable confidence in their precision in 2004.

On the Bush side, Karl Rove, Matthew Dowd, and media consultant Mark McKinnon appear to have been only slightly less maniacal in their focus. In 2000, GOP party officials and office holders in nonbattleground states called and e-mailed Rove on a daily basis, begging for resources to boost state and local candidates. Rove employed a variety of approaches to assuage their concerns and accommodate their requests. He did not, however, impart advertising dollars or, even more preciously, a visit from the candidate unless it fit into the campaign's broader strategic plan. This restraint caused enormous strains between the Bush campaign and the rather far-flung and disparate components of the GOP. Furthermore, the strains often were manifest in sniping about the controlling nature of the Austin-run campaign.[3] The strains were less evident in 2004, but that there were strains is undeniable.

This purported adherence to strategy fits with the pattern discerned from other recent presidential elections. As mentioned in chapter 3, my research on the presidential campaigns of 1988 through 1996 suggests that in these years the campaigns' resource allocation patterns tended to match their strategies (Shaw 1999b). More specifically, the data show that three factors had strong effects on the distribution of television advertising and candidate visits. First, whether a state was considered *base, lean,* or *battle-*

ground had a statistically and substantively significant influence on the amount of resources it received during the campaign. Base states typically received a modest allocation of resources, lean states received a considerable amount of attention, and battleground states were inundated with both TV ads and visits from the candidates. Candidates departed from this general pattern according to their position in the polls; underdogs spent money and time shoring up their lean and occasionally even their base states, whereas favorites ignored their base and lean states and spent disproportionately on battleground and the other side's lean states. There is little evidence that these tendencies varied by party. There is some indication, however, that targeting became increasingly narrow over time.

A second factor driving resource allocation was the competitiveness of the state, coupled with the cost of advertising. In other words, states where the race was close and where TV advertising was relatively inexpensive tended to get more commercials and more visits. Competitive states dominated by one or two affordable media markets, such as New Mexico and Maine (five and four electoral votes, respectively), consistently received resources from the campaigns even though they are relatively tiny. This scenario is a more complicated version of reality than has been advanced in the literature and contradicts the commonly held belief that the largest electoral prizes (such as California, New York, Florida, Illinois, and Pennsylvania) get a disproportionate share of the campaigns' attention (see Bartels 1985; Colantoni et al. 1975).

Third and finally, the resource allocations of one presidential campaign were strongly correlated with those of the other. Presidential and vice presidential candidate appearances, in particular, varied much more directly with the movements of the opposition than the campaign's own Electoral College plan. This interrelationship is one of the main arguments that Colantoni, Levesque, and Ordeshook (1975) make in their criticism of Brams and Davis's "3/2s rule" for presidential campaigning (see chapter 3).[4]

QUESTIONS AND HYPOTHESES ABOUT RESOURCE ALLOCATION IN 2000 AND 2004

Although we have some sense of how the 2000 and 2004 campaigns behaved, it is instructive to begin by establishing a formal baseline of knowledge. How much campaigning occurred in the 2000 and 2004 elections? How much money was spent? How many TV ads were aired? How many appearances did the candidates make? The critical task in answering these questions is to first present aggregate, state-by-state information on the allocation of time and money and then to break these data down by (1) date, and (2) media market. Because campaign communication is typically changed every week across dozens of media markets, understanding this communication requires measuring it within this context. In short, I propose investigating where the campaign occurred by paying attention to appropriate spatial and temporal variation in the allocation of key resources.

These baselines allow me to comment on several broader issues:

1. How closely did the campaigns adhere to the plans identified in chapter 3? Can we understand whatever deviation there was?
2. Did the candidates alter the fundamentals of their resource allocation patterns between Labor Day and Election Day?
3. Was there any variance between the Republican and Democratic campaigns with respect to where they campaigned and how closely they adhered to their plans?

Given these questions, it is pedagogically useful to have clearly stated research hypotheses about what we will find in the 2000 and 2004 data. These hypotheses are based largely on a more formal rendering of conventional wisdoms and the assumed rationality of campaigns manifest in much of the minimal effects literature. My first hypothesis is that the volume of campaigning in 2000 and 2004 was quite high—extensive television advertising and many personal appearances. What exactly is "high"? It strikes me as reasonable to expect that a voter in a typical state was exposed to twenty or so presidential advertisements and two or three candidate visits from each side.[5] These numbers would constitute a nominal increase from the 1988 through 1996 election campaigns.

The second hypothesis posits that the campaigns adhered to their plans, with almost no resources being allocated to nonbattleground states. This hypothesis is understandable given the closeness of the races and the increased ability of the campaigns to target pockets of persuadable or nonmobilized voters. But while understandable, the result is that only a subset of the American electorate gets to experience the presidential campaign firsthand in either 2000 or 2004. On the other side of the ledger, the overall number of states receiving resources ought to have been substantial—possibly greater than in previous elections—because of the number of battleground states in 2000 and 2004.[6] Based on the campaigns' Electoral College strategies, I would estimate that as many as twenty states received nontrivial resources from at least one side in 2000 and 2004.

The third hypothesis is that there were no allocation differences between the Republican and Democratic campaigns in 2000 or 2004. This hypothesis is consistent with the assumption that presidential campaigns are equally strategic, motivated, and well-heeled. My instincts tell me that this hypothesis—though appropriately framed and plausible—will be falsified. In particular, it seems to me that the partisan overlap in television and appearance allocations will be considerable but not complete. Furthermore, I expect that discrepancies exist even in important battleground states and that the Democrats—Gore and Kerry—were more focused and consistent in their resource allocations. Once again, this is not a prediction about the campaigns' relative expertise. Instead, the Democrats were in a slightly more defensive position (even though Gore led the race for at least three weeks in September) and thus had greater incentive not to be adventurous. To the extent that Gore and Kerry deviated from their plans, it would almost surely have been a reaction to Bush's expenditures of time and money.

The fourth hypothesis is that campaign resource allocation ramps up after the conventions and the debates and in the days immediately before the election. This hypothesis assumes candidates think voters pay more attention to the campaign when relevant information is available and in the closing days, right before they have to make a decision. More specifically, TV advertisements and candidate appearances are both front-loaded (during the Labor Day weekend) and back-loaded (just before Election Day) to coincide with voter interest and news media coverage of the fall campaign. Call this the *timely events* hypothesis. This hypothesis stands in contrast to other reasonable possibilities, such as a "pure" front-loaded strategy (to set the agenda and frame issues), a "pure" back-loaded strategy (to insure maximum exposure when the most people are paying attention), or a proportional strategy (to insure a presence no matter when voters want to hear from the candidates). I would guess that the timely events hypothesis will hold, though perhaps less for relatively underfunded campaigns (such as Gore's in 2000), for whom the incentive to marshal resources for the end game is greatest.

DATA AND DESIGN

As stated in chapter 1, the focus here is on television advertisements and candidate appearances. I do not consider direct mail, phone banks, canvassing, get-out-the-vote drives, and other forms of campaign contacting. Based on my own observations, it is clear that these other activities are extensive and finely targeted. Because the bulk of campaign dollars go to television advertisements and the planning and execution of the candidates' appearances at local venues, however, I focus on these activities in gauging whether campaigns follow through on their Electoral College plans.

For both 2000 and 2004, I have television spending figures for the presidential campaigns, the parties, and interest groups. The raw data consist of estimates of dollars allocated by the candidates and parties over a given week in the fall campaign for each of the nation's 210 media markets.[7] These estimates are from the Bush-Cheney campaigns, which used both the Republican National Committee (RNC) and a professional tracking service (National Media Inc.) to estimate the television advertising purchases of all relevant players. It is, of course, theoretically possible that estimates of the Democratic buys are inaccurate due either to the intentional inflation of the GOP advantage by both the Republicans and their tracking service or to undetected (presumably last-minute) buys by the Democrats. The first possibility makes little sense, however. Why would a campaign prefer to be misled about the activities of its opponent? The second possibility is also highly unlikely, given the technology used to track ad placements[8] and the public nature of broadcast transmission records in the United States. In addition, these data are consistent with the aggregate, statewide Democratic spending figures presented by Bill Knapp, who helped devise and implement the TV ad strategies of both Gore and Kerry.

Although the estimates are of dollars spent, for analytic purposes I convert these dollar figures into *gross rating points* (also known as *GRPs* or *points*).[9] GRPs provide an estimate of audience reach, with one hundred GRPs representing a TV ad buy that would be seen, on average, one time by every person in the market. The analytic utility of this measure is that it tells us how often voters in a market were exposed to TV ads and thus equalizes advertising cost discrepancies that exist between and across markets. It allows us, for example, to see that even though a campaign might have spent more money on ads in San Francisco than in Des Moines, voters in the Des Moines market saw many more ads than did their Bay Area counterparts.[10]

For state analyses, GRP estimates are calculated by taking the total GRPs purchased for each market in a state, weighting them by each media market's contribution to the state's electorate, and summing across all markets.[11] Similar data from previous elections have been used in recent studies (Freedman and Goldstein 1999; Goldstein and Freedman 2002a, 2002b; Shaw 1999a), but the estimates used here are still quite unusual. Furthermore, these particular data improve upon those used in some of the earlier studies. For example, these data encompass all media markets and not simply Nielsen's top seventy-five or one hundred, a limitation in the analyses of Goldstein and Freedman. In addition, the data encompass both soft money and the candidates' hard-dollar expenditures, unlike my own previous research (Shaw 1999a). Finally, the data also include cable television buys, an increasingly important component in the total paid advertising story.[12]

For candidate appearances, I estimate the number of both presidential and vice presidential visits, relying on information provided by the Republican and Democratic campaigns. This information is cross-checked against accounts published in the *Hotline* and the *New York Times*.[13] The specific measure is of the number of public appearances a candidate made in a state or media market. For instance, a candidate could have made three separate appearances in Florida on October 12, which would be coded as "3." This approach is a slight departure from my previous work, in which I used days in the state as my measure of candidate appearances. The logic here is that one wants to measure the "earned" (or "free") news media coverage an appearance generates, thus additional events on a given day warrant additional weight. Neither fund-raisers nor vacation days are tallied for this analysis, reducing the possibility that the results will be dominated by nonpublic events.

My time frame is dictated by data considerations. Although the campaigns were on the air and the candidates in the field throughout 2000 and 2004, I do not have sufficient polling data to measure the impact of these activities, which is regrettable but not fatal. For example, analyses of the influence of preconvention campaigning in 2000 tend to be skeptical of effects. On the one hand, Kenneth Goldstein and Kathleen Hall Jamieson (in press releases for the Brennan Center) have indicated that data from the Annenberg School's rolling cross-sectional survey show the Democrats' summertime TV ads moved voters in battleground media markets. On the other hand, statewide numbers were stable, and strategists from both campaigns expressed doubt that a sufficient number of voters were paying enough attention to move either state or market numbers (see Jamieson and Waldman 2001).

Similarly, in 2004 the national trial heat numbers for Bush and Kerry shifted no more than 5 percentage points one way or the other between March 13—when Kerry clinched the nomination—and Labor Day. This broad pattern of stability was also manifest in battleground states such as Ohio, Florida, Pennsylvania, and Wisconsin. Certainly the campaigns' activities framed the race in ways that facilitated later developments; in particular, the Bush camp's attempt to paint Kerry as a "flip-flopper" and the late summer attacks on Kerry by the independent 527 group Swift Boat Veterans for Truth. But much of the 2004 race's volatility, however circumscribed, did not materialize until the fall.

I therefore concentrate on the nature of presidential campaigning from August 24 through November 6, 2000, and from September 3 through November 1, 2004. This is a conservative examination of the total scope of electioneering, in that primary election and preconvention campaigning is discounted, as are the conventions themselves. Still, volume and patterns revealed during the fall give us substantial leverage on the research hypotheses posed earlier.

RESULTS

WHERE DID THEY CAMPAIGN AND HOW MUCH DID THEY DO?

Table 4.1 shows state-by-state television advertising dollar outlays for the 2000 and 2004 general election campaigns. The cumulative figures, counting candidate, party, and interest group spending, are about $206 million in 2000 and $248 million in 2004. Of these totals, slightly more than 50 percent came from the candidates' campaigns. For example, in 2000, the Bush campaign spent more than $61 million, and the Republican National Committee (RNC) spent more than $53 million, while the Gore campaign spent more than $47 million, and the Democratic National Committee (DNC) spent more than $31 million. In 2004, the first election after the passage of the Bipartisan Campaign Reform Act of 2002, party and candidate expenditures declined for both Republicans and Democrats during the general election campaigns (by 25 percent and 30 percent, respectively), while independent expenditures by interest groups skyrocketed. Republican-leaning interest groups spent $33.8 million in 2004, compared to $2.4 million in 2000. For Democratic-leaning groups, the increase was also dramatic: $72.4 million in 2004, compared to $10.9 million in 2000.

Furthermore, the data show that the "air war" was concentrated in a select sampling of states. A typical state received approximately $4 million in television ad money in the 2000 and 2004 fall campaigns, but twenty-four battleground states received an average of $8.6 million in 2000 and $12.9 million in 2004. Conversely, nonbattleground states received no appreciable television advertising dollars.

Within the battleground states, the pattern of resource allocation was also uneven. At the high end, Florida received $27.2 million in 2000 and an astounding $57.5 million in 2004 from the campaigns and their

TABLE 4.1 TV Advertising Money in 2000 and 2004

	2000					2004				
	BUSH / RNC	GORE / DNC	REP. SPECIAL INT.	DEM. SPECIAL INT.	CUM. DIFF.	BUSH / RNC	KERRY / DNC	REP. SPECIAL INT.	DEM. SPECIAL INT.	CUM. DIFF.
Alabama	$0	$0	$0	$0	$0	$0	$0	$0	$0	$0
Alaska	$0	$0	$0	$0	$0	$0	$0	$0	$0	$0
Arizona	$0	$0	$0	$0	$0	$397,465	$0	$0	$0	$397,465
Arkansas	$2,297,467	$2,045,748	$35,887	$4,949	$282,657	$206,995	$0	$238,530	$441,831	$3,694
California	$5,914,444	$0	$11,193	$93,867	$5,831,770	$0	$2,486,702	$725,550	$2,137,486	-$202,939
Colorado	$0	$0	$0	$0	$0	$0	$0	$0	$0	$0
Connecticut	$0	$0	$0	$0	$0	$0	$0	$0	$0	$0
Delaware	$371,142	$350,308	$0	$0	$20,834	$0	$0	$0	$30,000	-$30,000
District of Columbia	$0	$0	$0	$0	$0	$0	$0	$0	$0	$0
Florida	$16,670,690	$8,218,090	$299,217	$2,054,778	$6,697,039	$21,259,859	$14,722,660	$5,158,200	$16,327,892	-$4,632,493
Georgia	$555,940	$0	$0	$0	$555,940	$0	$0	$0	$0	$0
Hawaii	$0	$0	$0	$0	$0	$0	$0	$0	$0	$0
Idaho	$0	$0	$0	$0	$0	$0	$0	$0	$0	$0
Illinois	$2,756,425	$1,487,526	$7,782	$81,531	$1,195,150	$0	$0	$0	$0	$0
Indiana	$0	$0	$0	$0	$0	$0	$0	$0	$0	$0
Iowa	$3,986,936	$3,423,245	$38,505	$44,941	$557,255	$3,848,030	$2,803,561	$3,389,614	$4,291,197	$142,886
Kansas	$0	$0	$62,015	$461,844	-$399,829	$0	$0	$0	$0	$0
Kentucky	$1,143,915	$125,220	$0	$0	$1,018,695	$0	$0	$0	$0	$0
Louisiana	$3,791,298	$3,040,407	$0	$0	$750,891	$0	$0	$0	$0	$0
Maine	$1,764,159	$1,074,085	$36,886	$53	$726,907	$1,431,717	$889,626	$0	$1,279,130	-$737,039
Maryland	$0	$0	$0	$0	$0	$0	$0	$0	$0	$0
Massachusetts	$0	$0	$0	$0	$0	$0	$0	$0	$0	$0
Michigan	$12,230,378	$10,694,475	$305,053	$1,708,903	$132,053	$7,033,595	$3,367,012	$682,475	$4,596,125	-$247,067
Minnesota	$1,574,590	$809,090	$195,963	$471,992	$489,471	$4,340,619	$2,268,705	$1,611,761	$3,087,215	$596,460
Missouri	$8,974,615	$7,314,171	$105,603	$1,064,936	$701,111	$850,195	$0	$1,679,935	$894,830	$1,635,300
Montana	$0	$0	$0	$0	$0	$0	$0	$0	$0	$0
Nebraska	$0	$0	$0	$0	$0	$0	$0	$0	$0	$0

continued

TABLE 4.1 *continued*

	2000					2004				
	BUSH/RNC	GORE/DNC	REP. SPECIAL INT.	DEM. SPECIAL INT.	CUM. DIFF.	BUSH/RNC	KERRY/DNC	REP. SPECIAL INT.	DEM. SPECIAL INT.	CUM. DIFF.
Nevada	$2,188,216	$939,458	$145,772	$439,812	$954,718	$2,870,390	$1,563,421	$1,588,865	$4,167,666	-$1,271,832
New Hampshire	$1,313,175	$279,605	$0	$0	$1,033,570	$2,274,889	$1,128,270	$0	$978,779	$167,840
New Jersey	$0	$0	$0	$0	$0	$0	$0	$0	$0	$0
New Mexico	$2,084,867	$1,711,035	$31,232	$185,756	$219,308	$1,497,572	$1,818,834	$1,428,705	$1,529,980	-$422,537
New York	$0	$0	$0	$0	$0	$0	$0	$0	$0	$0
North Carolina	$542,665	$0	$104	$2,155	$540,614	$0	$0	$125,655	$0	$125,655
North Dakota	$0	$0	$0	$0	$0	$0	$0	$0	$0	$0
Ohio	$9,045,793	$7,828,493	$0	$0	$1,217,300	$11,057,010	$7,652,379	$6,689,005	$11,611,853	-$1,518,217
Oklahoma	$0	$0	$0	$0	$0	$0	$0	$0	$0	$0
Oregon	$5,103,980	$4,174,748	$152,818	$558,099	$523,951	$2,499,023	$1,655,685	$0	$814,265	$29,073
Pennsylvania	$13,375,593	$11,389,653	$818,182	$2,518,762	$285,360	$13,228,568	$8,353,996	$6,086,420	$10,164,845	$796,147
Rhode Island	$0	$0	$0	$0	$0	$0	$0	$0	$0	$0
South Carolina	$0	$0	$0	$0	$0	$0	$0	$0	$0	$0
South Dakota	$0	$0	$0	$0	$0	$0	$0	$0	$0	$0
Tennessee	$2,176,429	$1,822,485	$0	$0	$353,944	$0	$0	$0	$0	$0
Texas	$0	$0	$234	$1,280	-$1,046	$0	$0	$0	$0	$0
Utah	$0	$0	$0	$0	$0	$0	$0	$0	$0	$0
Vermont	$0	$0	$0	$0	$0	$0	$0	$0	$0	$0
Virginia	$0	$0	$0	$0	$0	$0	$0	$0	$0	$0
Washington	$8,346,330	$5,797,215	$45,728	$603,894	$1,990,949	$698,075	$1,155,900	$0	$1,588,141	-$2,045,966
West Virginia	$1,820,835	$811,705	$2,277	$18,799	$992,608	$3,711,292	$1,530,470	$464,434	$2,727,320	-$82,064
Wisconsin	$5,999,452	$5,335,261	$117,657	$610,634	$171,214	$4,982,040	$3,928,666	$3,976,201	$5,750,724	-$721,149
Wyoming	$0	$0	$0	$0	$0	$0	$0	$0	$0	$0
National	$114,029,334	$78,672,023	$2,412,108	$10,926,985	$26,842,434	$85,883,033	$55,325,887	$33,845,350	$72,419,279	-$8,016,783
National Avg.	$2,235,869	$1,542,589	$47,296	$214,255	$526,322	$1,683,981	$1,084,821	$663,634	$1,419,986	-$157,192
Battleground Avg.	$4,751,222	$3,278,001	$100,505	$455,291	$1,118,435	$4,771,280	$3,688,392	$1,410,223	$3,017,470	-$524,360

Source: Television advertising figures are provided by the Bush–Cheney campaign and are validated by data from the nonpartisan organization National Media Inc. They reflect purchases between August 20 and November 6, 2000, and between September 3 and November 1, 2004.

advocates. The Republicans had a $6.7 million spending advantage there in 2000, but were $4.6 million behind the Democrats in 2004. Pennsylvania received only slightly less attention, with campaign expenditures totaling $28.1 million in 2000 and $37.8 million in 2004. Here, the parties were at virtual parity in both elections. More generally, eight states (Florida, Michigan, Missouri, Ohio, Oregon, Pennsylvania, Washington, and Wisconsin) received at least $10 million in combined television ad money from the presidential election candidates, the national parties, and interest groups in 2000. In 2004, the campaigns reached the $10 million mark in another eight states (Florida, Iowa, Michigan, Minnesota, Nevada, Ohio, Pennsylvania, and Wisconsin). A few states (Kansas, North Carolina, and Texas) received token TV ad dollars in 2000, but such minor spending was nearly nonexistent in 2004.

The balanced partisan spending distributions in 2004 raise a fundamental question: how did the Republicans outspend the Democrats so substantially in 2000? Two explanations exist. First, the Republicans put a greater emphasis on television advertising than the Democrats did. Many scholars have observed that after the 1996 elections, labor unions began to shift their focus away from providing money for television ads and toward investing in personal contacting (J. Campbell 2003; Corrado et al. 2003; Herrnson 2002; Magleby 2003). This shift appeared to be a smart move after 1998 and 2000, when the unions' Election Day mobilization efforts helped fuel Democratic successes. During that time, the DNC and Democratic candidates supplemented union investments by contributing their own money to contacting activities. Thus, while TV ads still commanded the lion's share of the Democrats' budgets, this dominance was not total. Beginning in 2000 and accelerating rapidly in 2002 and 2004, the Republicans also began to invest substantial resources into individual-level voter contacting. These efforts attracted considerable media attention and were credited with helping the Republicans regain control of the Senate in 2002 and retain the White House in 2004.[14] But the GOP's commitment to grassroots outreach did not come at the expense of television advertising expenditures, at least not in 2000.

Second, the Republican Party simply had more money than the Democratic Party. The GOP advantage in 2000, which was about $12 million heading into the summer of that year, grew to about $22 million when the DNC spent $10 million on an August advertising blitz leading up to the Democratic National Convention, a move that can be described as "controversial." At the time, Democratic operatives argued that the initiative was necessary to shore up Gore's sagging poll numbers and make him competitive before his convention. They also cited internal polls indicating that this goal was, in fact, accomplished. The Republicans, meanwhile, matched the spending for about a week and then let up when their internal polls showed that no one was paying attention. After the election, Gore campaign officials suggested that these expenditures were driven by advice from Democratic Party lawyers, who argued that soft money raised in the primaries had to be spent prior to the convention (see Jamieson and Waldman 2001). This is an interesting interpretation of federal laws—one that was not held by either Republican Party lawyers or Democratic Party lawyers outside the DNC. Whatever the cause, the expenditures exacerbated the Democrats' financial disadvantage heading into the fall campaign.

This resource allocation picture changes slightly when one considers the reach of television advertising. Table 4.2 shows how many gross rating points (GRPs) were purchased in each state in 2000 and 2004. Recall that 100 GRPs corresponds to each voter seeing an ad, on average, one time. Thus, on average, a voter in a given state saw 111 presidential campaign advertisements (61 Republican, 50 Democratic) between August 24 and November 6, 2000. Assuming consistent expenditures over the course of the campaign (a dubious assumption, as I discuss later), this equates to almost nine ads per week. In battleground states, the average voter was exposed to 142 Republican and 115 Democratic ads over the eleven weeks of the 2000 fall campaign. In 2004, the average voter saw 75 presidential campaign ads (38 Republican and 37 Democratic). This equates to 8.3 TV ads per week over the nine-week general election campaign. The average voter in a battleground state viewed 103 Republican and 106 Democratic TV ads over this period.

Interestingly, if one goes by GRPs, the top states for 2000 were Michigan (49,253 GRPs or 493 ads per voter), Wisconsin (46,452), Washington (44,010), and Oregon (42,829). Six other states received at least 30,000 GRPs over the fall (Arkansas, Iowa, Maine, Missouri, New Mexico, and Pennsylvania), while another five states received at least 20,000 GRPs (Florida, Louisiana, Nevada, Ohio, and West Virginia).

In 2004, seven states received at least 30,000 GRPs: New Mexico (37,137), Wisconsin (35,395), Ohio (34,257), Nevada (34,265), Pennsylvania (32,155), Florida (31,075), and Iowa (30,980). Minnesota, Colorado, and Maine received at least 20,000 GRPs, while Michigan, and West Virginia received just under 20,000 GRPs.

Irrespective of the ranking, the exposure suggested here is truly extraordinary. Over the seventy-seven days of the 2000 campaign, for instance, Michiganders saw an average of 6.4 presidential campaign ads a

TABLE 4.2 GRPs in 2000 and 2004

	2000							2004						
	BUSH/ RNC	GORE/ DNC	REP. SPECIAL INT.	DEM. SPECIAL INT.	CUM. REP.	CUM. DEM.	CUM. GRP DIFF.	BUSH/ RNC	KERRY/ DNC	REP. SPECIAL INT.	DEM. SPECIAL INT.	CUM. REP.	CUM. DEM.	CUM. GRP DIFF.
Alabama	0	0	0	0	0	0	0	0	0	0	0	0	0	0
Alaska	0	0	0	0	0	0	0	0	0	0	0	0	0	0
Arizona	0	0	0	0	0	0	0	1,320	0	0	0	1,320	0	1,320
Arkansas	18,106	16,582	279	39	18,385	16,621	1,764	582	0	509	887	1,091	887	204
California	2,715	0	5	42	2,720	42	2,678	10,089	6,375	1,304	2,948	11,393	9,323	2,070
Colorado	0	0	0	0	0	0	0	0	0	0	0	0	0	0
Connecticut	0	0	0	0	0	0	0	0	0	0	0	0	0	0
Delaware	2,614	2,465	0	0	2,614	2,465	149	0	0	0	0	0	0	0
District of Columbia	0	0	0	0	0	0	0	0	0	0	0	0	0	0
Florida	16,096	8,249	286	1,966	16,382	10,215	6,167	12,646	9,045	2,229	7,155	14,875	16,200	-1,325
Georgia	0	0	0	0	0	0	0	0	0	0	0	0	0	0
Hawaii	0	0	0	0	0	0	0	0	0	0	0	0	0	0
Idaho	0	0	0	0	0	0	0	0	0	0	0	0	0	0
Illinois	3,770	2,065	11	111	3,781	2,176	1,605	0	0	0	0	0	0	0
Indiana	0	0	0	0	0	0	0	0	0	0	0	0	0	0
Iowa	20,163	18,636	189	220	20,352	18,856	1,496	9,725	7,765	6,941	6,549	16,666	14,314	2,352
Kansas	0	0	304	2,264	304	2,264	-1,960	0	0	0	0	0	0	0
Kentucky	5,244	468	0	0	5,244	468	4,776	0	0	0	0	0	0	0
Louisiana	14,384	11,600	0	0	14,384	11,600	2,784	0	0	0	0	0	0	0
Maine	19,111	11,969	397	1	19,508	11,970	7,538	9,138	5,573	0	5,365	9,138	10,938	-1,800
Maryland	0	0	0	0	0	0	0	0	0	0	0	0	0	0
Massachusetts	0	0	0	0	0	0	0	0	0	0	0	0	0	0
Michigan	23,931	21,402	586	3,280	24,517	24,682	-165	9,693	4,727	636	4,188	10,329	8,915	1,414
Minnesota	5,490	2,834	680	1,639	6,170	4,473	1,697	10,139	5,722	2,424	5,570	12,563	11,292	1,271
Missouri	20,198	16,680	237	2,388	20,435	19,068	1,367	1,552	0	2,383	1,141	3,935	1,141	2,794
Mississippi	0	0	0	0	0	0	0	0	0	0	0	0	0	0
Montana	0	0	0	0	0	0	0	0	0	0	0	0	0	0
Nebraska	0	0	0	0	0	0	0	0	0	0	0	0	0	0
Nevada	13,368	5,856	900	2,715	14,268	8,571	5,697	12,279	7,213	4,574	10,199	16,853	17,412	-559

continued

TABLE 4.2 *continued*

	2000							2004						
	BUSH/ RNC	GORE/ DNC	REP. SPECIAL INT.	DEM. SPECIAL INT.	CUM. REP.	CUM. DEM.	CUM. GRP DIFF.	BUSH/ RNC	KERRY/ DNC	REP. SPECIAL INT.	DEM. SPECIAL INT.	CUM. REP.	CUM. DEM.	CUM. GRP DIFF.
New Hampshire	2,617	558	0	0	2,617	558	2,059	7,020	3,956	0	3,282	7,020	7,238	-218
New Jersey	0	0	0	0	0	0	0	0	0	0	0	0	0	0
New Mexico	17,284	14,346	260	1,548	17,544	15,894	1,650	11,054	12,065	7,573	6,445	18,627	18,510	117
New York	0	0	0	0	0	0	0	0	0	0	0	0	0	0
North Carolina	0	0	0	0	0	0	0	0	0	200	0	200	0	200
North Dakota	0	0	0	0	0	0	0	0	0	0	0	0	0	0
Ohio	12,624	11,132	0	0	12,624	11,132	1,492	12,493	8,354	5,018	8,392	17,511	16,746	765
Oklahoma	0	0	0	0	0	0	0	0	0	0	0	0	0	0
Oregon	21,959	17,832	653	2,385	22,612	20,217	2,395	7,318	5,332	0	1,694	7,318	7,026	292
Pennsylvania	17,518	15,310	1,067	3,284	18,585	18,594	-9	12,127	8,267	4,570	7,191	16,697	15,458	1,239
Rhode Island	0	0	0	0	0	0	0	0	0	0	0	0	0	0
South Carolina	0	0	0	0	0	0	0	0	0	0	0	0	0	0
South Dakota	0	0	0	0	0	0	0	0	0	0	0	0	0	0
Tennessee	6,456	5,536	0	0	6,456	5,536	920	0	0	0	0	0	0	0
Texas	0	0	5	24	0	24	-19	0	0	0	0	0	0	0
Utah	0	0	0	0	0	0	0	0	0	0	0	0	0	0
Vermont	0	0	0	0	0	0	0	0	0	0	0	0	0	0
Virginia	0	0	0	0	0	0	0	0	0	0	0	0	0	0
Washington	24,880	17,155	139	1,836	25,019	18,991	6,028	1,554	2,157	0	2,457	1,554	4,614	-3,060
West Virginia	14,362	6,445	18	150	14,380	6,595	7,785	8,514	3,878	948	4,860	9,462	8,738	724
Wisconsin	22,963	20,730	446	2,313	23,409	23,043	366	11,000	8,765	6,492	9,138	17,492	17,903	-411
Wyoming	0	0	0	0	0	0	0	0	0	0	0	0	0	0
National	305,853	227,850	6,462	26,205	312,315	254,055	58,260	148,243	99,194	45,801	87,461	194,044	186,655	7,389
National Avg.	5,977	4,468	127	514	6,124	4,981	1,142	2,907	1,945	898	1,715	3,805	3,660	145
Battleground Avg.	13,902	10,357	294	1,191	14,196	11,548	2,648	8,236	6,613	2,082	3,976	10,318	10,588	-271

Source: Television advertising figures in gross rating points (GRPs) are provided by the Bush-Cheney campaign and are validated by data from the nonpartisan organization Campaign Media Monitor. They reflect purchases between August 20 and November 6, 2000, and between September 3 and November 1, 2004.

day! Over the sixty days of the 2004 campaign, they saw another 3.2 ads per day.

Not surprisingly, the GRP estimates also show a Republican advantage across the states in 2000. In the twenty-three states that witnessed appreciable campaigning, the Democrats had an exposure advantage in three states (Kansas, Michigan, and Pennsylvania) and in one of those states (Pennsylvania) the advantage amounted to nine GRPs. In contrast, the average GOP advantage in the battleground states was 2,648 GRPs, which equates to 26.5 additional TV ad exposures. It is worth observing that voters in these states certainly saw their share of Democratic ads; a typical battleground state voter was exposed to 11,548 GRPs or 115.5 Democratic ads. Still, the GOP advantage is noteworthy. The Republican edge was particularly significant in West Virginia (+7,785 GRPs), Maine (+7,538), Florida (+6,167), Washington (+6,028), and Nevada (+5,697).

In 2004, the GOP edge evaporated. Bush and the Republicans maintained an appreciable cumulative GRP advantage in Colorado (+2,070 GRPs), Iowa (+2,352), Michigan (+1,414), Minnesota (+1,271), Missouri (+2,794), and Pennsylvania (+1,239). But Kerry and the Democrats managed advantages (in table 4.2 indicated with negative numbers because they are disadvantages to the Republicans) in Florida (−1,325), Maine (−1,800), and Washington (−3,060), and more or less fought to a draw in Arkansas, Nevada, New Hampshire, New Mexico, North Carolina, Ohio, Oregon, West Virginia, and Wisconsin.

Moving on to candidate appearances, we again see an impressive volume of campaign activity in 2000 and 2004. Table 4.3 presents the number of appearances made by both the presidential and vice presidential candidates between August 24 and November 6, 2000, and between September 3 and November 1, 2004. In 2000, Bush made a total of 133 campaign appearances, compared to 100 for Gore. This averages to about twelve appearances a week for Bush and nine for Gore. Dick Cheney and Joe Lieberman made 112 and 94 appearances, respectively. Combined, the presidential and vice presidential candidates made 439 campaign appearances over the fall 2000 campaign. In 2004, Bush made 123 appearances, compared to 102 for Kerry. Bush thus averaged more than thirteen appearances a week, while Kerry checked in at eleven. Cheney made 114 appearances, compared to 123 for John Edwards. Combined, the presidential and vice presidential candidates made 462 campaign appearances over the fall 2004 campaign.

As with TV advertising, appearances were concentrated in strategically important states. In 2000, twenty-four states received no appearances and another two states received only a single appearance. In 2004, twenty-one

TABLE 4.3 Candidate Appearances in 2000 and 2004

	2000							2004						
	BUSH	GORE	CHENEY	LIEBERMAN	CUM. REP.	CUM. DEM.	CUM. DIFF.	BUSH	KERRY	CHENEY	EDWARDS	CUM. REP.	CUM. DEM.	CUM. DIFF.
Alabama	0	0	0	0	0	0	0	0	0	0	0	0	0	0
Alaska	0	0	0	0	0	0	0	0	0	0	0	0	0	0
Arizona	1	0	0	0	1	0	1	2	3	0	1	2	4	-2
Arkansas	3	1	3	4	6	5	1	0	0	0	0	0	0	0
California	17	3	7	7	24	10	14	0	0	0	2	0	2	-2
Colorado	0	0	1	0	1	0	1	4	3	3	2	7	5	2
Connecticut	0	0	0	0	0	0	0	0	0	0	0	0	0	0
Delaware	0	0	1	1	1	1	0	0	0	0	0	0	0	0
District of Columbia	0	0	0	0	0	0	0	6	3	5	8	11	11	0
Florida	11	12	10	14	21	26	-5	22	21	16	25	38	46	-8
Georgia	0	2	1	0	1	2	-1	0	0	9	0	9	0	9
Hawaii	0	0	0	0	0	0	0	0	0	1	0	1	0	1
Idaho	0	0	0	0	0	0	0	0	0	0	0	0	0	0
Illinois	11	6	6	6	17	12	5	0	0	1	1	1	1	0
Indiana	0	0	0	0	0	0	0	0	0	0	0	0	0	0
Iowa	6	11	4	3	10	14	-4	8	9	10	11	18	20	-2
Kansas	0	0	0	0	0	0	0	0	0	0	0	0	0	0
Kentucky	2	1	3	4	5	5	0	0	0	0	1	0	1	-1
Louisiana	2	3	3	0	5	3	2	0	1	1	0	1	1	0
Maine	2	1	2	4	4	5	-1	1	0	0	2	1	2	-1
Maryland	0	0	0	0	0	0	0	0	0	0	0	0	0	0
Massachusetts	0	0	0	0	0	0	0	0	0	0	0	0	0	0
Michigan	18	8	9	4	27	12	15	7	3	9	6	16	9	7
Minnesota	1	0	1	3	2	3	-1	7	3	6	5	13	8	5
Missouri	8	10	7	5	15	15	0	4	2	2	1	6	3	3
Mississippi	0	0	0	0	0	0	0	0	0	0	0	0	0	0
Montana	0	0	0	0	0	0	0	0	0	0	0	0	0	0
Nebraska	0	0	0	0	0	0	0	0	0	0	0	0	0	0

State														
Nevada	0	1	4	1	4	2	2	3	3	3	1	6	4	2
New Hampshire	2	1	2	2	4	3	1	4	4	1	3	5	7	-2
New Jersey	0	2	0	4	0	6	-6	1	0	1	3	2	3	-1
New Mexico	3	3	4	2	7	5	2	3	6	3	1	6	7	-1
New York	0	0	0	0	0	0	0	3	2	0	5	3	7	-4
North Carolina	2	1	1	0	3	1	2	1	1	0	3	1	4	-3
North Dakota	0	0	0	0	0	0	0	0	0	0	0	0	0	0
Ohio	7	5	10	5	17	10	7	17	17	13	16	30	33	-3
Oklahoma	0	0	0	0	0	0	0	0	0	1	0	1	0	1
Oregon	3	4	7	2	10	6	4	1	0	2	4	3	4	-1
Pennsylvania	12	8	12	4	24	12	12	13	6	8	9	21	15	6
Rhode Island	0	0	0	0	0	0	0	0	0	0	1	0	1	-1
South Carolina	0	0	0	0	0	0	0	0	0	0	0	0	0	0
South Dakota	0	0	0	0	0	0	0	0	0	0	0	0	0	0
Tennessee	6	5	3	4	9	9	0	7	0	0	1	7	1	6
Texas	0	0	0	0	0	0	0	0	0	0	0	0	0	0
Utah	0	0	0	0	0	0	0	0	0	0	0	0	0	0
Vermont	0	0	0	0	0	0	0	0	0	0	0	0	0	0
Virginia	0	0	0	0	0	0	0	0	0	0	0	0	0	0
Washington	5	4	5	4	10	8	2	0	0	0	0	0	0	0
West Virginia	2	1	2	0	4	1	3	1	0	3	6	4	6	-2
Wisconsin	9	7	4	11	13	18	-5	9	15	11	5	20	20	0
Wyoming	0	0	0	0	0	0	0	0	0	5	0	5	0	5
National	133	100	112	94	245	194	51	123	102	114	123	238	225	13
National Avg.	2.6	2.0	2.2	1.8	4.8	3.8	1.0	2.4	2.0	2.2	2.4	4.7	4.4	0.3
Battleground Avg.	6.0	4.5	5.1	4.3	11.1	8.8	2.3	7.2	6.0	6.7	7.2	14.0	13.2	0.8

Source: Appearance figures are provided by the Bush-Cheney campaign and validated by data from the *New York Times* and the *Hotline*. They reflect travel between August 20 and November 7, 2000, and between September 3 and November 1, 2004.

states were shut out and four others merited only one appearance. Of course, the usual suspects got the most play. Florida saw 47 total candidate appearances in 2000 and 84 in 2004, Pennsylvania 36 and 36, Michigan 39 and 25, Missouri 30 and 9, Wisconsin 31 and 40, Iowa 24 and 38, Ohio 27 and 63. This means that a voter in Florida or Pennsylvania could expect a candidate visit about every 2.1 days during the 2000 fall campaign and every 1.5 days in 2004.

The candidate differential—Bush making more appearances than his Democratic opponents—is surprising given the popular perception that Bush did not work hard on the campaign trail while Gore and Kerry were attempting to overcome their personality deficiencies with Stakhanovite work ethics. But in fact, Bush had an appearance advantage in several key battleground states in both elections. In 2000, for example, Bush had the edge in Maine (2 to 1), Michigan (18 to 8), Ohio (7 to 5), Pennsylvania (12 to 8), Tennessee (6 to 5), Washington (5 to 4), and Wisconsin (9 to 7). Gore did have the advantage in Florida (12 to 11), Iowa (11 to 6), Missouri (10 to 8), and Oregon (4 to 3), but Bush's average statewide advantage was about half a point (0.6 appearances) and his average battleground advantage was over a point (1.5 appearances). Cheney also enjoyed a slight advantage over Lieberman—0.4 more average statewide appearances and 0.8 more battleground state appearances—although this edge was only marginally significant by standard statistical measures.

In 2004, the spread is roughly even across battleground states. Bush made more appearances than Kerry in Florida (22 to 21), Pennsylvania (13 to 6), Michigan (7 to 3), Minnesota (7 to 3), Missouri (4 to 2), West Virginia (1 to 0), and Colorado (4 to 3), while Kerry held the upper hand in Wisconsin (15 to 9), Iowa (9 to 8), and New Mexico (6 to 3). Ohio was even (17 apiece). Bush's overall battleground advantage was 1.2 appearances. Edwards reversed the slight edge Cheney held over Lieberman in 2000, even though Cheney increased his visibility on the trail.

There are reasons, however, to view the candidate differences reported here with caution. Most important, the Republican and Democratic tickets appear to have had different conceptions about how to get the most out of an appearance. The Republicans favored shorter appearances, while the Democrats tended to "camp out" both at singular appearances and within a particular media market. For 2000, it is also important to remember that Gore was still encumbered by his responsibilities as vice president, and Lieberman was still a member of the U.S. Senate (with a reelection campaign to run), while Bush and Cheney were free to campaign as they wished.[15] In addition, the 2000 Democratic convention was held after the

Republican convention, allowing the Republicans to get a head start on the campaign trail.

These preliminary data allow us to directly consider the first three of the four research hypotheses. First, as expected, the sheer volume of campaign outreach is impressive for both elections, but especially for 2004. In hotly contested states, voters were targeted with between two and five TV ads a day, and a candidate appearance every 2.5 days. The data are also consistent with the second hypothesis—that resource allocation is concentrated in battleground states. The data here are unequivocal, although there does appear to be differentiation between top-level and middle-level battleground states, as suggested in chapter 3. The third hypothesis does not receive as much support, however, as resource allocation patterns do vary by party, especially in 2000.

PARTY VERSUS CANDIDATE PATTERNS

Before examining these data across media markets and over time, I pause now to briefly consider a particular feature of the 2000 television ad expenditure data: the differences between national party and candidate spending. That such differences exist is to be expected. The party is more interested than the presidential campaign in the success of Senate and congressional candidates and in cultivating good feelings with states that have significant donor bases. Thus, it is more likely that the party will be on the air in states that are not critical to the presidential candidate's minimum winning coalition.

This possibility is borne out on a couple of occasions in table 4.1.[16] One of these cases is California, where the RNC's $4.3 million allocation in 2000 can be seen as an attempt by the party not only to bolster Bush's chances in the Golden State, but also to establish a top-of-the-ticket message and presence for Republican candidates across the board.[17] Another case is New Hampshire, where the Gore campaign spent $273,480 on TV ads, while the DNC spent only $6,125. Evidently, the campaign believed that Gore had a shot at winning the state, whereas the party was less optimistic. (Gore ultimately lost New Hampshire by about seven thousand votes.) Of course, it could be argued that both the party and the campaign thought the state was winnable but decided the campaign should shoulder the financial burden. A similar situation occurs for the Republicans in Illinois—the campaign laid out a substantial amount of money for TV ads in 2000 while the party did little or nothing.

But these examples are exceptional. Party spending patterns tend to mimic those of the presidential candidates. As suggested earlier, there are two obvious explanations for occasional asymmetries. First, the party has no important, competitive candidates outside of the presidential race and might decide to let the campaign do all of the heavy lifting in a particular state while it engages elsewhere. Second, the party and campaign might disagree on the competitive status of a state, with the party refusing to invest its resources in what it feels to be an unwinnable contest.

A less obvious third explanation also looms: the party might sponsor a substantively different type of TV ad than the campaign, and there could be a decision that one of them is more appropriate than the other for a specific state. In particular, most political professionals believe that party ads tend to be more negative than candidate ads. Therefore, one would expect the party to be shouldering a disproportionate share of the load in states and markets where the opposition is to be attacked. Conversely, the candidate will be sponsoring a relatively higher proportion of the ads in states and markets where the emphasis is on advocacy.

For 2000, the logic behind this hypothetical possibility is somewhat supported by previous empirical work. Jamieson and her colleagues at the Annenberg School conducted content analyses of TV ads aired by the candidates and parties in 2000 and demonstrated that while the RNC's ads were indeed significantly more likely to be classified as "contrast" or "attack" than those of the Bush campaign, there was no difference between the ads of the DNC and the Gore campaign.[18] In other words, the sponsoring agent mattered for the content of Republican ads in 2000 but not for Democratic ads. This division of labor on the GOP side was of little practical consequence, however, because the Bush campaign and the RNC were typically on the air in the same places at about the same volume—Bush averaged $2.54 million on TV ad expenditures in battleground states compared to $2.21 million for the RNC, with little significant variation in this ratio across the states (except for California and Illinois).

THE VIEW FROM THE MEDIA MARKETS

Statewide measures of candidate activity can, of course, mask variation in the distribution of campaign resources across a state's media markets. But from appendix 1 (television advertising by media market) and appendix 2 (candidate appearances by media market) at the back of this volume, we see there is little consistent, significant variation across media markets within a given state. This is not to say that campaigns distribute resources evenly. In Florida, for example, the Mobile-Pensacola market saw 39,060 total GRPs from the two candidates and their parties in 2000, compared to 18,322 GRPs for Jacksonville-Brunswick. This is a difference of 20,738 GRPs (or 207 additional TV ad exposures) between the markets. It is important to bear in mind, however, that this difference is unusually large. Furthermore, voters in the Jacksonville-Brunswick market still saw, on average, 181 presidential TV ads.

In absolute terms, targeting differences between the campaigns were also unusual. For the most part, the Republicans and Democrats aired their TV ads in the same markets. Unlike the states, however, market differences did exist with respect to volume, especially in 2000. Most notably, as seen in appendix 1, the Democrats did nothing in California markets in 2000, while the RNC targeted Los Angeles (4,631 GRPs) and the Bush campaign made late plays in Sacramento-Stockton-Modesto (1,049 GRPs), Los Angeles (889; bringing the Bush/RNC total for the market to 5,520), San Diego (773), and San Francisco (606).

For both 2000 and 2004, the most striking difference in the figures is the resource allocation chasm between markets in battleground versus nonbattleground states. For the first time since the advent of commercial television, no national spots were aired and many markets received no presidential campaign ads. Interestingly, markets received *less* play if even a portion of their population fell outside a battleground state. For instance, the Omaha market covers Nebraska and part of Iowa, yet it received only about 3,700 GRPs across the 2000 campaign. Similarly, the El Paso market covers much of eastern New Mexico but received virtually zero attention in 2000 or 2004.[19] This lack of attention is clearly linked to the costs of advertising and the inefficiency of paying to reach voters who do not matter for the Electoral College.

As was evident from the statewide data, the absolute exposure achieved in given markets was extraordinary. The Iowa markets are particularly striking, with voters in two markets—Davenport–Rock Island–Moline and Des Moines–Ames—receiving over 60,000 and 50,000 GRPs, respectively, in 2000. (This averages out to voters being exposed to about seven presidential ads a day for eleven weeks.)

Despite both sides gaining significant exposure, the partisan advantage across the markets was consistent (obviously) with general statewide patterns that favored the Republicans. In both elections, the Republicans appear to have cast broader nets, allocating significant TV dollars in less-populous markets. This finding fits with the conventional wisdom that the GOP attempted to mobilize rural Republican-leaning voters in 2000 and (especially) 2004. Differences across the Florida markets effectively demonstrate this point. In 2004, for instance, the Republicans purchased

7,236 more GRPs than the Democrats did in the conservative Panhandle market of Mobile-Pensacola. Similarly, the GOP advantages in Panama City and Gainesville were 4,076 and 4,533 GRPs, respectively. Note that Kerry and the Democrats actually held the edge in the large left-leaning markets of Miami, Orlando, and Tampa–St. Petersburg.

This slight pro-GOP tendency is more pronounced in 2000: Bush and the Republicans held massive advantages in Fort Myers–Naples, Jacksonville-Brunswick, Mobile-Pensacola, and Panama City. Gore and the Democrats, however, managed to hold the Republican advantage down in the larger media markets; the Republicans were "only" up 4,339 GRPs in Tampa–St. Petersburg–Sarasota, 7,507 in Orlando, and 7,939 in Miami–Fort Lauderdale. These data suggest that the Democrats attempted to minimize the GOP's financial superiority in 2000 by concentrating their spending in the major metropolitan media markets, allowing the Republicans to rack up relatively large advantages in the more sparsely populated markets.

These findings are essentially repeated with respect to candidate appearances. Appendix 2 shows that twelve markets received ten or more collective appearances from the presidential and vice presidential candidates in 2000. They rank as follows: Chicago (16), Detroit (15), Los Angeles (14), St. Louis (14), Pittsburgh (14), Tampa–St. Petersburg–Sarasota (12), Miami–Fort Lauderdale (12), Portland, Oregon (12), Milwaukee (12), Grand Rapids–Kalamazoo–Battle Creek (11), Seattle-Tacoma (11), and Cedar Rapids–Waterloo–Dubuque (10).

The Republican ticket's greatest advantages in 2000 were in Grand Rapids–Kalamazoo–Battle Creek (+7 appearances), Detroit (+5), Los Angeles (+4), Chicago (+4), Philadelphia (+3), Wilkes-Barre–Scranton (+3), Yakima-Pasco-Richland-Kennewick (+3), and Green Bay–Appleton (+3). The GOP had an edge in 59 of 103 media markets (58 percent) that received an appearance in 2000. The Democrats had more appearances in 25 markets (24 percent). Their greatest advantages (set as negative figures in appendix 2 because they are disadvantages to the Republicans) were in Miami–Fort Lauderdale and Orlando–Daytona Beach (–4), Davenport–Rock Island–Moline (–3), New York (–3), Philadelphia (–3), and La Crosse–Eau Claire (–3).

In 2004, ten markets received ten or more appearances: Miami–Fort Lauderdale (17), Orlando–Daytona Beach–Melbourne (17), Columbus (16), Tampa–St. Petersburg–Sarasota (16), Milwaukee (16), Philadelphia (13), West Palm Beach–Fort Pierce (11), Cleveland (11), and Minneapolis–St. Paul (10). The Bush-Cheney campaign had its greatest advantages in Grand Rapids–Kalamazoo–Battle Creek (+5) and Harrisburg-Lancaster-Lebanon-York (+4). The GOP held an edge in 41 percent of media markets that received at least one visit. The Kerry-Edwards ticket dominated in Miami–Fort Lauderdale (–7), Orlando–Daytona Beach–Melbourne (–5), West Palm Beach–Fort Pierce (–3), and Detroit (–3). The Democrats held advantages in 39 percent of markets that received a visit.

Although the Republicans managed an overall advantage in the raw number of appearances in both states and media markets, it is important to reiterate the earlier observation that Republican stops tended to be briefer. In addition, it also appears that the Democrats did not think it necessary to send the candidates around to Democratic strongholds to mobilize their base. Instead, their candidates made a handful of appearances in the major urban markets of battleground states — such as Detroit, Philadelphia, and Cleveland — and then opted not to match the GOP tickets' visits. Rather, they concentrated their appearances across the competitive and (especially) Democratic-leaning lesser markets, such as Wilkes-Barre, Madison, and Flint. They also spent an enormous amount of time in Florida, especially their vice presidential candidates.

The presence of Los Angeles and Chicago at the top of the appearance list in 2000 is surprising, given that neither California nor Illinois was considered a top-tier battleground state. It may indicate a strategic miscalculation on the part of the campaigns, especially on the GOP side, or it may indicate that the need to drive news media coverage in influential markets is such that these markets warrant attention even if their states are only marginally competitive. Of course, it does not explain why New York did not receive a commensurate number of appearances. Another possibility is that the central location of Chicago (en route from Austin or Nashville to Wisconsin, Iowa, or Minnesota and within easy striking distance of Michigan and Missouri) and the unusual competitiveness of states near Los Angeles (Oregon, Washington, New Mexico, and Nevada) made these media markets attractive in spite of the pro-Gore leanings of Illinois and California acknowledged by both parties.

Turning back to the research hypotheses, campaign resource allocations across media market patterns mimic those found across the states. First, by any measure, television ads and candidate appearances were liberally sprinkled over a wide range of markets. Second, and as expected, markets within battleground states attracted far more activity than non-battleground markets. Once again, however, the third hypothesis receives sketchy support at best — there are partisan campaign differentials across media markets. Let us now turn our attention to the fourth hypothesis, which predicts allocation levels will follow the occurrence of major events in the campaign calendar.

PATTERNS OVER THE FALL CAMPAIGN

Figures 4.1a and 4.1b present the combined outlays of the Republican and Democratic campaigns in a typical battleground state over the 2000 and 2004 fall campaigns. A cursory glance offers encouragement for the timely events hypothesis. Figure 4.1a shows that although both sides were on the air in the aftermath of the Democratic National Convention in 2000, the average exposure level in a battleground state was only about 1,500 GRPs (791 Republican and 726 Democratic GRPs). Granted, fifteen TV ad exposures during the first week of the fall campaign is not inconsequential, but it hardly qualifies as a blitz. Looking more generally at TV ad exposure throughout September, two patterns emerge. First, the Republicans were on the air more heavily than the Democrats. This advantage peaks with an accelerated schedule of GOP buys in the first two weeks of September (1,308 and 1,202 GRPs, respectively). Second, despite this brief uptick on the part of Republican TV ad buys, the general absolute level of ads is relatively low and consistent. The Democrats' efforts are especially restrained; they average about 800 GRPs per week in battleground states for the first six weeks of the race, with a high of 855 and a low of 629 GRPs. After their minor splurge of 1,202 GRPs in battleground states for the week of September 10–16, the Republicans average 982, 925, and 964 GRPs for the next three weeks.

The second week of October brought the first of the debates and a significant change in television advertising outlays. The Democrats dipped down to 557 GRPs (from 850) in battleground states for the week of October 8–14, while the Republicans went up to 1,179 (from 984). These trends apparently represent different takes on voter responsiveness to paid advertising during the debates, and the contrast is striking. It is also the point at which Bush regains the lead from Gore, although it is impossible to ascertain causation from these data alone. From October 15 until Election Day, both sides increase their TV ad outlays on a weekly basis. The Republicans go from 1,179 GRPs for the week of October 8–14 to 2,901 GRPs for the final week of the campaign. The Democrats go from 557 GRPs to 1,928 GRPs over this same interval. This means that a typical voter in a battleground state saw forty-eight presidential election ads during the final week of the campaign. Put another way, battleground voters saw seven presidential ads a day in the last days of the race! The average weekly increase over this four-week period is approximately 600 GRPs. The average GOP advantage is approximately 650 GRPs, or almost one ad every day.

In 2004, the broad patterns shown in figure 4.1b fit the 2000 template,

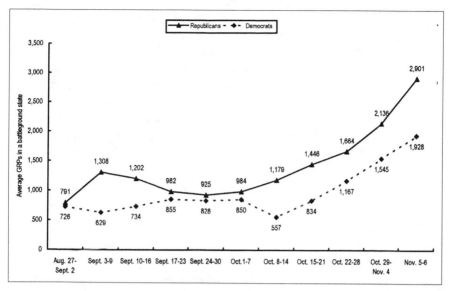

FIGURE 4.1A   Total TV ad outlays over the 2000 campaign

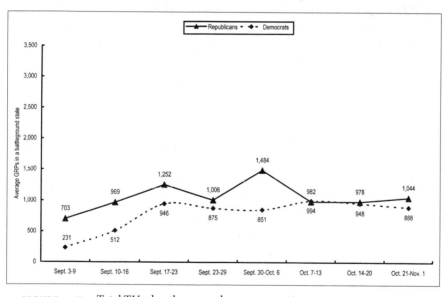

FIGURE 4.1B   Total TV ad outlays over the 2004 campaign

but with some important differences. The week after the Republican National Convention saw modest TV ad outlays, followed by a significant increase, especially by the Republicans, between mid-September and early October. In battleground states, the Republicans go from an average of 703 GRPs for the week of September 3–9 to 1,484 GRPs for the week of

September 30–October 6. Meanwhile, the Democrats move up from an average of 231 GRPs for the week of September 3–9 to 946 GRPs for the week of September 17–23 and essentially stay at about that level through the debates. Although the time series data do not include special interest expenditures, it seems reasonable to conclude that the Democrats figured a baseline of approximately 850 GRPs would be sufficient to hold or increase Kerry's support across battlegrounds, particularly with Democratic 527 groups providing supplemental, anti-Bush advertising. The divergent strategies with respect to the debates are again evident here; GOP spending spikes in early October as the Bush-Cheney campaign seeks to reinforce earned media messages while Democratic spending flatlines or goes down as the Kerry-Edwards campaign seeks to marshal resources as debate coverage dominates. The absence of a late increase in TV spending in 2004 is an artifact of the time frames; spending did, in fact, increase on both sides over the final weekend. Unfortunately, I was only able to estimate spending over the last ten days of the campaign, necessitating the consolidation of the final two weeks of the race (weeks 8 and 9, respectively). Still, the records indicate an average of about 1,500 GRPs in battleground states over the final four days of the campaign—a decline from the average of 2,500 GRPs registered in 2000. This difference reflects the effects of campaign finance reform (and the attendant rise in 527 group spending at the expense of national party expenditures), as well as a modest retreat from the implementation of the timely events strategy.[20] The dominance of the timely events perspective over other explanations of TV ad strategy should not be minimized, however.

Of course, the basic TV spending patterns are not absolute. Figures 4.2a through 4.2e demonstrate that the aggregate pattern revealed by figure 4.1 masks variation across the battleground states. Television advertising outlays across the fall for five states—Florida, Tennessee, and West Virginia in 2000 and Ohio and Pennsylvania in 2004—are presented in these figures. In figure 4.2a for Florida 2000, we see the aggregate battleground state pattern repeated almost perfectly. Relatively low outlays are followed by a brief Republican uptick, which is followed by consistent increases by both sides through the last week of the campaign.

Tennessee (figure 4.2b) and West Virginia (figure 4.2c) show something else entirely. For Tennessee in 2000, we see one piece of conventional wisdom confirmed and another repudiated. On the confirmation side, the Bush campaign did, in fact, launch a TV ad initiative during the week of October 8–14 that went unanswered for seven days. This may not seem like much, but given that polls showed Tennessee to be an even state at that point, it could have been critical in allowing Bush to assume command of

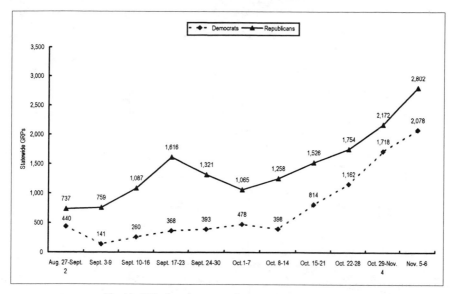

FIGURE 4.2A   Florida TV ad outlays over the 2000 campaign

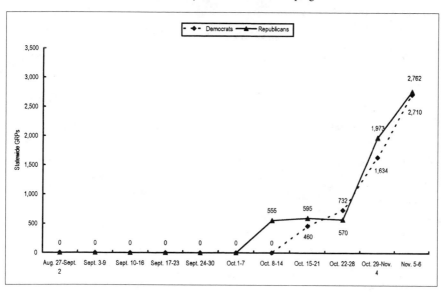

FIGURE 4.2B   Tennessee TV ad outlays over the 2000 campaign

the race in that state. On the repudiation side, it is not true that Gore and the Democrats took the state completely for granted. After the Republican initiative, the Democrats matched GOP TV ad outlays over the next four weeks. This finding is especially important given that the Democrats rarely matched the Republicans' TV ad outlays in battleground states. It is

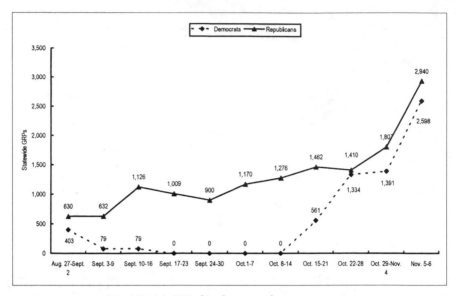

FIGURE 4.2C   West Virginia TV ad outlays over the 2000 campaign

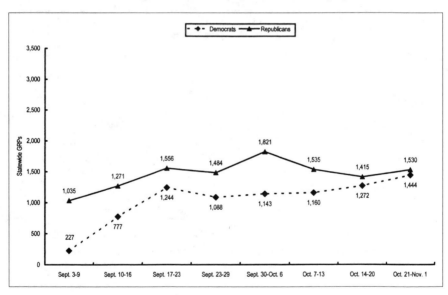

FIGURE 4.2D   Ohio TV ad outlays over the 2004 campaign

clear from these data that Gore knew the importance of holding Tennessee, even if he waited too long in responding to Bush.

The conventional wisdom about Tennessee—a belated and halfhearted Democratic response to Republican spending—is actually more appropriate for West Virginia in 2000. The data show that after roughly match-

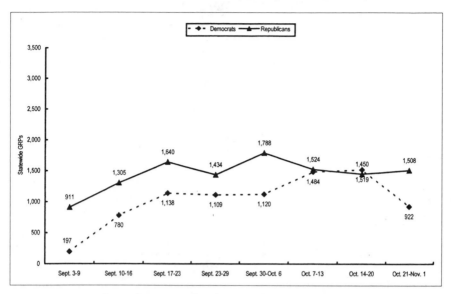

FIGURE 4.2E   Pennsylvania TV ad outlays over the 2004 campaign

ing the Republicans during the week of the Democratic convention, the Democrats allowed the Republicans to run unopposed on the airwaves for six weeks. Even when they went back up for the week of October 15–21, the Democrats were outmatched, 1,462 GRPs to 561. Over the last three weeks of the campaign the Democrats matched the Republicans (and this includes a 2,598 GRP Democratic buy for the last week), but they lost West Virginia's five electoral votes for the first time since 1984 and only the second time since 1960.

In 2004, state-by-state analyses reveal much less significant variation from the general battleground pattern. In Ohio (figure 4.2d), for example, the data look almost identical to the aggregate figures. In Pennsylvania (figure 4.2e), though, we see another example of the high-stakes gambles the Democrats seemed willing to take. After increasing their TV ad outlays in mid-October, Kerry-Edwards and the DNC scaled back for the last week in response to polls showing a Democratic lead of 2 to 5 percentage points. This move might have cost them the state had the polls been off by even a point or two, but it allowed them to allocate greater campaign resources to states that looked even more precarious, such as Ohio, Iowa, and Wisconsin.

Taken together, the figures from 2000 and 2004 indicate that the Democrats matched the Republicans during the first week of the general election campaign but then concentrated competitive buying patterns in a handful of states while allowing the Republicans to dominate elsewhere. They assumed a particularly low profile in early October, possibly believ-

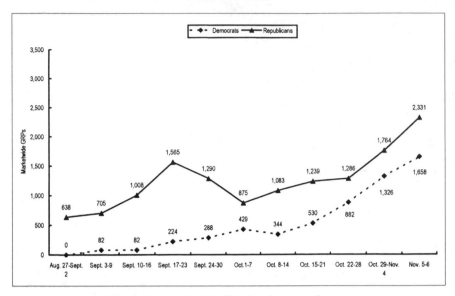

FIGURE 4.3A   Miami–Fort Lauderdale TV ad outlays over the 2000 campaign

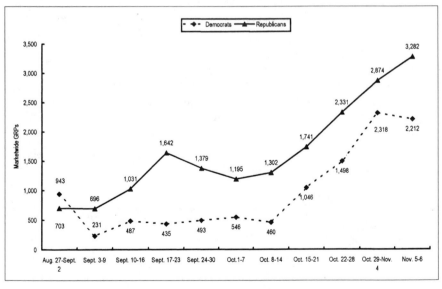

FIGURE 4.3B   Orlando–Daytona Beach TV ad outlays over the 2000 campaign

ing that paid advertisements would be less effective during the debates. The Democrats then largely matched Republican TV ad buys from mid-October to Election Day.

But do the strategic dynamics that existed with respect to state buy patterns also exist at the media market level? Figures 4.3a through 4.3d

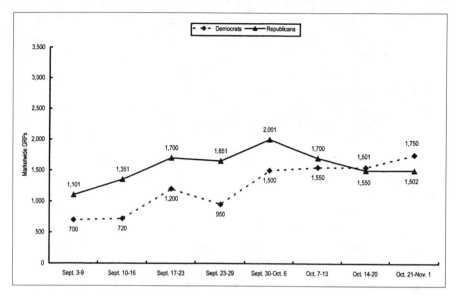

FIGURE 4.3C   West Palm Beach–Fort Pierce TV ad outlays over the 2004 campaign

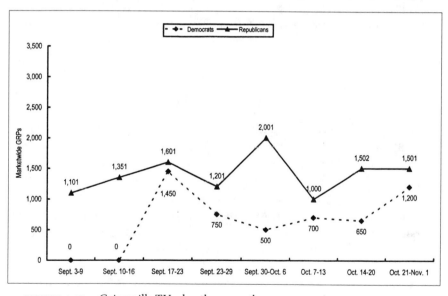

FIGURE 4.3D   Gainesville TV ad outlays over the 2004 campaign

examine four Florida markets—Miami–Fort Lauderdale and Orlando–
Daytona Beach in 2000 and West Palm Beach–Fort Pierce and Gainesville
in 2004—to answer this question. Although there is some variation in
both the absolute magnitude and the over-time pattern of TV ad outlays,
the overall picture suggests that market dynamics mirrored those at the

state-level. In particular, figures 4.3a and 4.3b show that the Republicans opened 2000 with substantial buys and then increased their buys slightly, while the Democrats tended to open more conservatively and then escalate their buys along with the GOP (with the Republicans maintaining a slight edge) through Election Day. In 2004, the data from West Palm Beach (fig. 4.3c) show a relatively even distribution, both between parties and over time. This pattern matches the general pattern observed in the states for that election. Conversely, the Gainesville data (fig. 4.3d) show significantly greater GOP attention to a conservative market, at least until the final ten days. This pattern fits with the contention, alluded to earlier, that the Republican ticket made a special effort to mobilize supporters in heavily GOP areas.

The Gainesville example notwithstanding, the consistency of the data stands out. So does (once again) the absolute level of TV advertising. Over the last three weeks of the 2000 campaign, voters in Miami saw an average of 4.3 ads per day. In the last week, the average climbed to 5.7 ads per day. In Orlando, the parties bought a combined total of over 5,500 GRPs during the last week of the 2000 race. In West Palm Beach, the total for the last week of 2004 was 3,200 GRPs. These are not numbers that would overwhelm executives at Coca-Cola or General Motors, but for political advertising they represent extraordinary outreach.

DO RESOURCES FOLLOW CAMPAIGN PLANS?

Although I have presented a considerable amount of data attesting to the volume and dynamic patterns of television advertisements and candidate appearances in the 2000 and 2004 campaigns, I have not up to this point directly engaged the question of whether these resource allocations adhered to the campaigns' Electoral College strategies. I have only offered evidence that resources tend to be disproportionately allocated to certain states, which I refer to as *battlegrounds*. But it is now time to return to the plans concocted by the campaigns themselves and to conduct a more precise test of the second hypothesis.

Table 4.4 addresses this charge by charting how the campaigns allocated GRPs and candidate appearances across the categories of their Electoral College plans. As expected, none of the four campaigns under scrutiny invested time or money in the Republican or Democratic base states. Gore and Kerry in fact purchased an average of 4 and 0 GRPs, respectively, in the Democratic base states. It should also be unsurprising—given the ebb and flow of the candidates' fortunes across the 2000 and 2004 campaigns—that the campaigns invested some resources in the

TABLE 4.4 Campaigning by Electoral College Strategies in 2000 and 2004

CATEGORIES OF STATES	2000				2004			
	BUSH PLAN & CUM. REP. TV BUYS	GORE PLAN & CUM. DEM. TV BUYS	BUSH PLAN & CUM. REP. CANDIDATE APPEARANCES	GORE PLAN & CUM. DEM. CANDIDATE APPEARANCES	BUSH PLAN & CUM. REP. TV BUYS	KERRY PLAN & CUM. DEM. TV BUYS	BUSH PLAN & CUM. REP. CANDIDATE APPEARANCES	KERRY PLAN & CUM. DEM. CANDIDATE APPEARANCES
Base Republican	1,152	1,256	1.00	0.76	0	0	0.74	0.21
Lean Republican	7,753	2,961	4.67	2.86	653	222	0.75	2.00
Battleground	16,412	14,513	8.43	7.42	12,659	12,077	12.93	12.60
Lean Democratic	4,188	7,554	6.33	5.40	770	2,307	1.00	1.50
Base Democratic	272	4	1.50	1.30	0	0	1.55	2.56
Total	6,124	4,981	3.88	3.18	3,805	3,660	4.51	4.55

Note: Cell entries represent average GRPs or appearances in the particular category of states.

lean states. I say this is unsurprising, but that characterization is somewhat revisionist—I believed the Gore and Kerry campaigns would have been even more reticent to invest outside the pure battleground states. Instead, they allocated an average of 4,900 GRPs in states that they believed leaned Democratic. The investment in states that leaned toward the Republicans was also substantial, though considerably less than for the Democratic leaners (the overall average was approximately 1,550 GRPs, and Kerry averaged only 222). Bush and the RNC allocated significant TV ad resources in Democratic lean states (averaging 4,188 GRPs in 2000 and 770 GRPs in 2004), though perhaps not as much as one might have expected given the common perception of Republican aggressiveness. These investments in lean states, however, are dwarfed by the campaigns' efforts in the battleground states. Across these states, Bush and the RNC allocated 16,412 and 12,659 GRPs in 2000 and 2004, respectively, compared with 14,513 and 12,077 GRPs for the Democrats. That equates to a typical voter seeing 145 Republican and 133 Democratic ads over the fall.

The story is slightly more complicated when one examines candidate appearances in the right-hand columns of table 4.4. The campaigns most assuredly concentrated the lion's share of their time in the battleground states, but the lean states (especially the Democratic lean states) received almost as much attention. In 2000, Bush and Cheney averaged 8.43 appearances in their battleground states, with Gore and Lieberman averaging 7.42. But Bush and Cheney also averaged 6.33 appearances in Democratic lean states, compared to 5.40 for the Democrats. The campaigns' travel itineraries thus more closely match the hypothesis that the Republicans were more aggressive. One statistic worth noting is the standard error for the GOP tickets' appearances in lean Democratic states—it is quite substantial and leads one to believe that although Bush and Cheney campaigned hard in some Democratic states, they did not hit all of these states with the same fervor. Indeed, they appeared to cherry-pick the choicest Democratic targets, such as Minnesota and California, while ignoring states such as New Jersey. In 2004, Bush-Cheney averaged 12.93 appearances in battleground states, with Kerry-Edwards averaging 12.60. This time, however, there are few interparty differences in the lean states.

A more rigorous examination of the relative effect of the campaigns' Electoral College plans on resource allocation is offered in table 4.5. Television advertisements and candidate appearances are modeled as a function of (1) the campaign's plan, (2) the opposing campaign's plan, and (3) the state's electoral votes. The rationale for these explanatory variables is straightforward. I am, of course, fundamentally interested in the degree to which a campaign's plan drives its allocation of resources. The opposing campaign plan is also included in the model because a campaign is likely to allocate resources in a state that the other side has targeted.[21] Finally, electoral votes are included to account for the possibility that campaigns are more likely to spend money and time in states with a relatively large number of electoral votes. As mentioned earlier, several studies in political science (Bartels 1985; Brams and Davis 1974; Colantoni, Levesque, and Ordeshook 1975) have explored the relationship between electoral votes and campaign "volume." There is a strong consensus that electoral votes drive campaign resource allocation, but there is no consensus regarding the functional form of this relationship. Having estimated the model using a variety of assumptions about the functional form of this relationship, I settle on a proportional relationship for the sake of parsimony.

The ordinary least squares (OLS) regression coefficients presented in table 4.5 suggest several compelling story lines. Initially, television advertising allocations are strongly correlated with the campaign's Electoral College plan, less strongly correlated with the opposition's plan, and uncorrelated with the state's electoral vote total. In both 2000 and 2004, the Republicans were as likely as the Democrats to allocate GRPs in accordance with their Electoral College plan—contrary to my tentative expectations. Both sides followed their plans, and the differences are not statistically significant. The Democrats seem to have been more attentive to the strategic plans of the Republicans than the Republicans were to the Democrats' plans. In fact, in 2000 Bush's plan is more correlated with Democratic GRPs than is Gore's plan.

The dynamic shifts when one examines the distribution of candidate appearances. Here, campaign strategies are less predictive of resource allocation. At the same time, the states' electoral votes are highly predictive. Another specific finding from 2000 is also worth mentioning: Bush's strategy was significantly correlated with both Bush's appearances and *Lieberman's appearances*. This finding is not totally unexpected, though. Lieberman was often dispatched in 2000 to markets that needed attention in the wake of Republican outreach. Most notably, Lieberman went to Minnesota twice and California once after Bush and the RNC opened advertising blitzes in those states. Interestingly, while Lieberman was deployed in lean Democratic states, Cheney was disproportionately deployed in lean Republican states such as Nevada, Kentucky, and Georgia. This finding suggests that vice presidential candidate appearances were used to shore up the candidates' bases.

As a general matter, however, the statistical and substantive significance of the states' electoral votes on the frequency of candidate appearances is striking. Moreover, the contrast with the paltry effect of electoral

TABLE 4.5   Predicting Resource Allocation by Electoral College Strategy in 2000 and 2004

	2000								2004					
	BUSH GRPS	GORE GRPS	RNC GRPS	DNC GRPS	BUSH VISITS	GORE VISITS	CHENEY VISITS	LIEBERMAN VISITS	BUSH/RNC GRPS	KERRY/DNC GRPS	BUSH VISITS	KERRY VISITS	CHENEY VISITS	EDWARDS VISITS
Intercept	-4,264 (-1118)	-4,086 (1,025)	3,504 (896)	-2,211 (781)	-3.29 (0.83)	-2.26 (0.74)	-2.11 (0.58)	-2.14 (0.63)	-570 (453)	-380 (387)	-1.41 (0.77)	-0.92 (0.81)	-0.49 (0.66)	-1.09 (0.85)
Rep. EC plan[a]	2,897* (-1190)	1,516 (1,090)	2,665** (953)	1,609 (831)	1.77* (0.88)	0.83 (0.79)	1.10 (0.62)	1.23* (0.67)	2,127** (879)	714 (752)	0.08 (1.50)	-1.03 (1.57)	-0.22 (1.27)	1.10 (1.65)
Dem. EC plan[a]	1,464 (1,250)	2,494* (1,146)	791 (1,001)	588 (873)	0.28 (0.93)	0.92 (0.83)	0.61 (0.65)	0.27 (0.71)	2,853** (939)	2,720*** (803)	3.34 (1.60)	4.28* (1.67)	3.19* (1.36)	1.85 (1.77)
Electoral votes	4.40 (46.49)	-2.00 (42.61)	26.10 (37.23)	13.00 (32.48)	0.18*** (0.04)	0.09** (0.03)	0.09*** (0.02)	0.10*** (0.03)	12.23 (28.53)	5.70 (24.41)	0.15*** (0.05)	0.09 (0.05)	0.06 (0.04)	0.15** (0.05)
Standard error	3,123.80	2,862.70	2,501.20	2,181.90	2.32	2.07	1.63	1.77	1,929.01	1,650.87	3.28	3.43	2.79	3.63
Adjusted R^2	0.57	0.59	0.57	0.40	0.52	0.38	0.49	0.43	0.83	0.75	0.49	0.40	0.45	0.37

Note: Cell entries represent the results of least squares regression equations (standard errors in parentheses). $N = 51$ states for all models.

[a] Electoral College strategy categories were collapsed: Battleground = 2, Lean Rep./Dem. = 1, Base Rep./Dem. = 0.

$*p < .05$ $**p < .01$ $***p < .001$

votes on the allocation of TV ads is puzzling. I believe the difference has to do with the costs of candidate travel versus those of television advertising. It is no more difficult to book TV airtime in a small state than in a large one. And while competitive states with a substantial number of electoral votes are attractive, their relative attractiveness diminishes once one takes into account the costs of running TV ads to reach the greater number of voters residing within them. In other words, you get as much bang for your buck in a competitive small state, such as New Mexico, as you do in a competitive large state, such as Florida. This equalization of costs does not occur with candidate travel. It costs almost as much to send a candidate to Albuquerque as it does to send him to Miami. Granted, the dominant media markets in smaller states tend to reach a larger portion of the statewide electorate, but the purchase on electoral votes is still not as great as it is for markets in larger states. For example, Albuquerque contains 86 percent of the population of New Mexico, which means it is worth 4.3 electoral votes (0.86 multiplied by 5 electoral votes for the state). Tampa–St. Petersburg, in contrast, contains 29 percent of the population of Florida, which means it is worth 7.3 electoral votes (0.29 multiplied by 25 electoral votes for the state in 2000). Applying this logic, Miami's market in 2000 is worth 5.3 electoral votes, while Orlando's is worth 4.5. What you get, therefore, is an incentive to send the candidates to markets within the larger states. And, so long as a candidate has made the trip, there is also an incentive to have him visit one of the "lesser" markets while he is there.

Ironically, the peculiar circumstances of the 2000 campaign may have ameliorated the magnitude of the relationship between electoral votes and candidate appearances. Most presidential campaigns are based out of Washington, D.C., or northern Virginia (e.g., Dole and Clinton in 1996, Bush in 1992, Bush in 1988, Reagan and Mondale in 1984, Carter and Reagan in 1980), which makes travel to the more sparsely populated states of the West more difficult and costly. In 2000, the campaigns were based in Austin and Nashville, making travel to smaller battleground states—Oregon, Nevada, New Mexico—more cost-effective than is typically the case.

WHAT WE HAVE LEARNED

The data suggest several generalizations that can be made about presidential campaigning in 2000 and 2004. First, the volume of campaigning was impressive, with both the Democratic and Republican campaigns (and their friends) flooding the airwaves with television ads and stumping aggressively across a range of local markets.

Second, the candidates and parties did allocate a large proportion of their resources to battleground states, which were identified well before the fall campaign. Resource allocations were not as targeted as one might expect, though, and candidate appearances were especially likely to be dispersed in lean or even base states.

Third, the GOP ticket enjoyed a considerable television advantage in 2000, thanks to its larger war chest and the DNC's decision to put ads on TV during the summer. Democratic-leaning groups helped eradicate part of this disadvantage, and Gore was able to achieve parity in some critical states (most notably, Pennsylvania and Michigan). But it is reasonable to ask whether this edge helped Bush carry states such as Tennessee and West Virginia. More surprisingly, the Republicans also averaged slightly more appearances than the Democrats in 2000, probably because of the GOP tendency to make "quick" appearances and hit multiple markets in a day. The Republican campaign advantage disappears in 2004. The reasons are not obvious, although campaign finance reform, the mobilization of Democratic donors against Bush's policies in Iraq, and having candidates who were not tied down by White House responsibilities loom as plausible explanations.

Fourth, the campaigns did not allocate resources evenly over the course of fall 2000 and 2004. In 2000, the campaigns sponsored an initial flurry of activity in the first week or so of September, then trailed off until the end of September, after which they increased allocations on a weekly basis through the final week of the campaign. In 2004, the allocation pattern was similar to that of 2000, except that resources were distributed more consistently on a weekly basis from mid-October through Election Day. The parties' strategies varied in two important ways: (1) the Democrats curtailed activities more significantly than the Republicans for the "dead" weeks of September, and (2) the Democrats were relatively quiet during the debates. This pattern was more evident in 2000 and was undoubtedly affected by the Democrats' financial disadvantage in that race. But it also indicates that Democratic strategists believed events (and the attendant news media coverage) would dominate the campaign during that time, allowing them to throttle down.

Finally, the data from 2000 demonstrate that the national parties' activities paralleled those of the campaigns. Minor differences occur, but RNC and DNC spending on TV ads clearly complemented that of the campaigns.

In sum, we have compelling evidence from 2000 and 2004 that campaigns make plans and that these plans drive some appreciable portion of TV ad buys but a much smaller portion of candidate appearances. Spending patterns fluctuate with the occurrence of campaign events, and discrepancies do occasionally exist between the major parties and their campaigns. There are, to be sure, many twists and turns to these simple points, but the points themselves are undeniable. What we do not know is the extent to which these campaign activities influence the perceptions and behavior of voters. The question of campaign effects is dealt with squarely in the next chapter.

5

MEASURING THE CAMPAIGN'S IMPACT

YOU GOTTA HAVE POLLS

Campaigns are obsessed with polls. Some acknowledge and even embrace this obsession. Others, like the Bush campaigns, wrestle with it. Bush often and openly expressed disdain for polling during the 2000 campaign. This disdain was genuine and meant that it was pointless to even suggest policy priorities based on public opinion data. By extension, Bush was skeptical of spending money on polls. The polling budget for 2000 could be generously characterized as "spartan." All told, the Bush campaign conducted three surveys of battleground states—in March, June, and July—and did tracking polls in the most competitive states throughout the fall. That was it. The campaign never conducted a national poll of any kind.

Still, polls are the ultimate campaign scoreboard. It is relatively easy to dismiss them in May, but as the clock winds down, the inclination to check the polls becomes irresistible—even in the Bush campaigns. Moreover, polls are critical for diagnosing what is working (or failing) and where it is doing so. This is, ironically, one point on which practitioners and political scientists agree. Fortunately, the 2000 and 2004 Bush campaigns ultimately did enough polling to provide an unprecedented opportunity to estimate the effects of presidential electioneering. This chapter aims to capitalize on this opportunity.

The mechanics of tracking polls are straightforward. By mid-September in both 2000 and 2004, the Bush camp was tracking opinion in all of its battleground states. Every night, Monday through Thursday, 150 to 200 likely voters per state were asked a brief set of questions about the upcoming election: "Are you following the campaign?" "How do you feel about the candidates?" and (most important), "For whom do you intend to vote?" Not every battleground state was tracked every week. In fact, many were polled every other week. As long as the campaign was tracking, though, the emotional well-being of everyone on the team hinged on the results of those nightly surveys.

During the 2000 race, the compilation, absorption, and incorporation of the tracking poll estimates of public reaction to the campaign's activities drove the daily routine. On weekdays, I would get into the campaign headquarters at 301 Congress Avenue at about eight o'clock in the morning. My first stop was the Lincoln Lounge, a lengthy cubicle on the south side of the second floor of the building. Once there, I would go to the large stack of output stashed in a filing box. Two interns in the Strategy Department, Michael Shannon and J. D. Estes, would have stayed very late the night before, waiting to receive and process the nightly polling data from all states where we were tracking. On some nights, they would receive the data from the last midwestern states at about midnight, format the results, and finish around two o'clock in the morning. Other nights, when we were tracking in Oregon and Washington, they would not even receive the West Coast data until two o'clock and would not finish formatting until four. The polling data would go to a very small set of top-level advisers, including Rove and Dowd. Shannon and Estes would usually return to the office—if they had bothered to leave—by eight-thirty. In the meantime, I would peruse the overnight tracking results. My day was made, one way or the other, by what I saw in those numbers. Given what we know about the errors and random fluctuations in surveys such as these, pegging my feelings on them was somewhat nonsensical. It is impossible, however, to keep entirely rational in the middle of a presidential campaign.

Sometime in mid-September of 2000—my notes are a little hazy on the exact date—I began to use these tracking poll data to gauge the effects of the campaign's two major outreach endeavors, television advertising and candidate appearances. For starters, I took the relative volume of Republican and Democratic advertising and the number of candidate appearances in a state, controlled for the historical Republican presidential vote, and used these figures to predict candidate vote share. To get a more sharply defined picture, I took the weekly changes in the aggregate amounts of these activities and used them to predict attendant shifts in candidate preferences. Through early October 2000, the results were eye-catching: television advertising was only nominally associated with candidate preferences, and neither Bush nor Gore appearances seemed to be helping their respective cases. As for the vice presidential candidates, Joe Lieberman's appearances produced positive changes in the vote, while Dick Cheney's produced *negative* shifts.

I updated this analysis for the campaign every few days, and the basic relationships evolved during the race. The Lieberman effect dissipated considerably as October progressed, possibly due to the Gore campaign's decision to deploy Lieberman in one or two Florida media markets for several days at a time. In contrast, Cheney appeared to rally, especially after the vice presidential debate. He never drove the numbers the way the Republican ticket might have wished, but the negative effect evident in September faded as the last leaves began to fall. The influence of television advertising, at least in terms of volume differentials, continued to be marginal.

These on-the-fly analyses were somewhat lost in the aftermath of the election and the subsequent controversy in Florida. But I had several conversations with members of the Bush campaign—as well as with academics who collected and analyzed data from the campaign—about the broad dynamic I have outlined here. These conversations corroborated much of the initial analysis and produced some interesting extensions and corollaries. A few months after the election, Dowd commented that he believed that both Bush and Cheney—but particularly Cheney—had trouble moving the numbers with their appearances. Dowd's explanation was that local media coverage was not especially favorable when the candidates came calling, reducing (and perhaps even reversing) the expected bump. If this assessment is correct, the implication is that local news media have adopted a posture akin to that of the national news media as described by Thomas Patterson (1993): negative and cynical, and driven by the horse race and narrative considerations. With respect to paid advertising, both Dowd and I were skeptical of the influence of television advertising on voters' preferences in 2000. Yet we also believed that Bush's ultimate victory, especially in the state of Florida, might not have happened without a sizable television advantage over the Democrats.

Sam Popkin, author of *The Reasoning Voter* (1991) and consultant to several Democratic presidential campaigns, told me that Gore's surveys also showed the candidates' appearances had minimal effects. In fact, the Democratic numbers may have been even less favorable for Cheney than the Republican numbers were. On the matter of television advertising,

Popkin said that Gore's polling showed small effects, with one major exception: the barrage of Social Security advertising that ran in the last ten days of the campaign helped the Democrats gain 2 to 3 percentage points. This finding is consistent with data presented by the Democrats' national pollster Stanley Greenberg and media adviser Bill Knapp at the bipartisan Campaign 2000 conference at the University of Pennsylvania's Annenberg School for Communication.

Two academic studies shed additional light on the question of presidential campaign effects in 2000. First, using available public polls and records of candidate travel from the *New York Times*, Charles Franklin analyzed the effects of candidate visits to various states in 2000. While he found modest movement in conjunction with presidential candidate appearances, Franklin also showed that Cheney's appearances had a negative impact, corroborating both Popkin's claim and my preliminary analyses (Franklin 2001). Franklin did not test for the reversal of the effect after the vice presidential debate that I note earlier, but outside verification of this anomalous finding cannot help but further pique one's interest.

Second, Johnston, Jamieson, and Hagen (2004) validate Popkin's recall of the effectiveness of Gore's Social Security advertisements. According to their rolling cross-sectional survey, Gore's standing began to trend up around the time of the third debate, as both the Gore campaign and the DNC significantly increased the proportion of Social Security ads in their overall advertising mix. Johnston, Jamieson, and Hagen also suggest that Democratic contrast ads—in which Gore hammers Bush for "promising the same money to two different groups"—were particularly effective.[1]

These preliminary investigations, however, can be augmented and sharpened. More specifically, in this chapter I rely on weekly data from the states and media markets on voters' perceptions of the candidates, their vote intentions, and their likely exposure to television advertising and candidate appearances for both 2000 and 2004. These data allow me to more effectively test the argument that presidential campaigning influences voters. From chapters 3 and 4, we know that the campaigns had electoral plans and that they mostly adhered to these plans when allocating resources. We also know that the campaigns deployed sufficient resources to expose voters to their messages many times over, that the volume of outreach coincided with important events in the campaign, and that the Republicans occasionally had a television advertising advantage over the Democrats. What we do not know yet is the effect of strategy or the allocation of resources. Furthermore, we do not know *how much* voters are affected by campaigns, nor do we know *how* different factors condition campaign effects.

EXPECTATIONS OF CONDITIONAL EFFECTS

Following in the footsteps of Thomas Holbrook (1996) and others, I contend that campaigns can produce small but significant effects on presidential elections. The conceptual and analytical difficulty is that both the opposing campaign and the news media work to minimize the cumulative advantage that one side can affect. Put another way, the opposing campaign is likely to target its activities in roughly the same places as you, with roughly the same volume. Meanwhile, the news media often focus on aspects of the election that conflict with your agenda (such as the horse race) and aggressively scrutinize your policy positions and general claims. These tendencies undoubtedly reduce aggregate movement in candidate support. Still, the fundamental research hypothesis in this chapter is that campaign activity positively correlates with voters' preferences and produces small improvements in the prospects for victory.

To guide the analysis, I propose several more particular hypotheses. Initially, the expectation of minimal aggregate change is partly a product of using vote choice as the sole measure of influence. That is, changing the vote distribution is a tough standard for gauging campaign effects, but few studies focus on other measures of influence. This choice of focus is, of course, defensible given that votes ultimately decide election outcomes.[2] Numerous studies, however, suggest that candidate appraisals are the proximate attitudinal correlate of the vote (e.g., Fiorina 1981). In light of this finding, I treat candidate favorability scores as an alternative, complementary dependent variable. Let me be clear: vote choice and candidate favorability ratings are conceptually distinct yet inextricably related. I presume that campaign activities are likely to affect candidate favorabilities. I further presume that candidate favorabilities, in turn, affect vote choice. In fact, I hypothesize that changes in feelings toward a candidate often precede similar (if lesser) changes in the vote. If correct, my measures of candidate favorability ("would you say that your impressions of Al Gore are strongly favorable, somewhat favorable, somewhat unfavorable, or strongly unfavorable") have the additional virtue of being more flexible than binary measures of the vote and may therefore be more sensitive in detecting campaign influence.

Another of my research hypotheses concerns the level of analysis. States are, as I have mentioned, entirely appropriate units of analysis because presidential elections are ultimately decided by the aggregation of state results in the Electoral College. Media markets, however, provide an intriguing alternative for estimating effects, since this is the level at which campaign activities are conveyed to voters. My estimates of electioneering at this level are thus more precise. Consistent with the chapter 4 examination of resource allocation, I employ media-market-level estimates to complement state-level estimates at several points in this chapter. I hypothesize that campaign effects are more likely to exist at the media market level given the absence of aggregation errors in the allocation and exposure measures.

My final research hypothesis draws on a broader theme of this study: campaign effects are more likely to be discerned through time series analyses. Campaign resource outlays vary by the day, in response to the activities of the opposition, to the occurrence of events, and to new information about voters. Consequently, campaigning differentials over a few days may affect preferences but may also be subsequently offset by compensatory activities from the other side. In addition, there may be long stretches of the campaign in which activities do not affect changes in voters' opinions and preferences but a single week or two in which the influence of the campaign is substantial. These possibilities argue against reliance on cross-sectional data. And while I do offer cross-sectional analyses of campaign influences, I also break the campaign into weeks (eleven in 2000 and nine in 2004) to estimate dynamic effects. One would prefer day-to-day information (or even hour-to-hour), but such detail is possible only if one is content to rely on national data (see Erikson and Wlezien 1999; Holbrook 1996).

Do I expect to find that the campaigns were decisive in 2000 or 2004? The closeness of the elections, especially 2000, renders that question much less interesting than it might have been for, say, 1988. Everything was decisive in 2000: ballot design, overseas absentee votes, get-out-the-vote drives, voter roll purges, and so on. In fact, the 2000 race is perhaps the best evidence for Holbrook's simple but important claim that the underlying distribution of preferences is critical for understanding the significance of the campaign on the election outcome. More intriguing are the issues of whether voters moved in response to campaign activities and whether a net advantage accrued to particular candidates.

My expectations for both elections are that campaigning mattered but that the net advantages were relatively small. We already know that Republicans and Democrats focused on roughly the same set of states and that both camps inundated these states with massive amounts of television advertising and numerous candidate appearances. There were differences in the amount of campaigning, as well as in its timing, though, and these factors should lead to some net advantages. Such is particularly the case in 2000, when campaigning discrepancies existed in the handful of states that turned the race: Florida, Missouri, New Hampshire, Ohio, Tennessee, and West Virginia.

The remainder of the chapter proceeds in a straightforward manner. In the Data and Design section, I briefly explain the candidate support and favorability variables and discuss model specification and estimation issues. In the Changes in Candidate Standing section, I describe the opinion dynamics of the 2000 and 2004 campaigns, while in the Campaigning Effects section I present the multivariate models of campaign influence. In the Further Discussion section, I expand on the empirical findings of the campaign effects analysis. Finally, in the concluding section, I discuss the findings and what they mean for 2000 and 2004 and the broader debate on campaign effects.

DATA AND DESIGN

This analysis focuses on three critical pieces of information: (1) polling data, to measure candidate standing, (2) television ad buy data, to measure voter exposure to campaign ads, and (3) candidate appearance data, to measure voter exposure to the local news media coverage that accompanies these visits. The TV ad and candidate appearance measures were delineated in chapter 4 and need not be rehashed here, except to reiterate that they have been gathered at both the state and media market level for every week of the 2000 and 2004 fall campaigns.

The data used to measure vote intention and candidate favorability are from statewide tracking surveys conducted by Voter/Consumer Research and Market Strategies Inc. for the Bush-Cheney campaigns.[3] As described earlier, during a given week, between 150 and 200 likely voters from each of several battleground states were interviewed every evening. Surveying was generally confined to Monday through Thursday evenings, and only high-priority states were tracked every week (other battleground states were tracked every other week). The Bush polling data are especially useful for two reasons. First, they yield continuous estimates of voters' opinions over the entirety of the general election campaigns. Second, large numbers of respondents from each of the battleground states allow me to estimate support within media markets. On the few occasions for which I require data but do not have campaign polls—such as when I calculate baseline estimates of candidate support in nonbattleground states—I rely on publicly available statewide surveys.

As discussed in chapter 4, my time frame is dictated by data considerations. Although the campaigns were on the air and the candidates in the field well before Labor Day in both 2000 and 2004, polling data that would allow me to gauge early effects are hard to come by. I therefore concentrate on campaigning and movement across eleven weeks of the 2000 campaign (August 24 through November 7) and nine weeks of the 2004 campaign (September 3 through November 1). This focus leads to a conservative estimation of effects, in that the impact of primary elections and preconvention campaigns are discounted, as are the conventions themselves.

Besides offering basic descriptive information on changes in candidate preferences and favorabilities over the course of the fall campaign, I propose two rigorous empirical analyses. First, I estimate pooled time series models for 2000 and 2004, employing campaign differentials to explain week-to-week changes in Bush's share of the two-party vote in battleground states and media markets.[4] Second, I estimate similar pooled time series models for 2000 and 2004 to explain week-to-week changes in the candidate favorability differential—(Republican favorability – unfavorability) – (Democratic favorability – unfavorability)—for the same battleground states and media markets. For 2000, I have appropriate data from twenty-four states and fifty media markets. For 2004, the data are from seventeen states and fifty-nine media markets.

The pooled time series models also include three control variables that minimize the possibility that campaign effects are overstated. The first is a measure of the extent to which the Republican poll share deviates from the average Republican presidential vote in that state or media market. This measure controls for the possibility that movement in candidate support is a simple reversion of aggregate preferences to the historical mean (such a reversion can be interpreted as mobilization).[5] The second control variable is the percentage of undecided voters in the state or market. This measure controls for the possibility that candidate support is more likely to shift when a relatively high proportion of voters have not made up their minds (such a shift can be interpreted as persuasion).

These first two control variables can also be combined with the TV advertising and candidate appearance variables to explore, in a preliminary manner, mobilization and persuasion effects that are directly tied to campaign differentials. Presumably, mobilization is more likely to occur when a candidate is "underachieving" compared with his party's expected vote share but manages to outcampaign his opponent. Interaction terms between deviation from the historical average and the measures of TV advertising and candidate appearances estimate this effect. By the same token, persuasion is more likely to occur when there is a high proportion of undecided voters and a candidate manages to outcampaign his opponent. Interaction terms between the percent of undecided voters in the polls and the measures of TV advertising and candidate appearances estimate this effect. Although measurement and specification errors make estimating interactive campaign effects difficult, data from 1988 through 1996 show that these measures can drive statistically significant changes in the vote (Shaw 1999a). I therefore include them in the initial specifications of the models, though I am open to dropping them in favor of more parsimonious and robust specifications.

The third control variable is early September support for Ralph Nader. The assumption here is that some Naderites were likely to defect to the Democrats—the more liberal-progressive major party—as Election Day neared. Such an assumption was certainly the belief of Gore and, to a lesser extent, Kerry strategists, who courted, cajoled, and even insulted Nader supporters.

CHANGES IN CANDIDATE STANDING

A preliminary inspection of the data reveals a complex series of dynamics in both 2000 and 2004. In 2000, for example, Bush gained on Gore over the course of the fall. The fact that Bush improved his standing between late August and early November could be somewhat surprising to the casual fan of politics, given that Bush seemed to have been the front-runner throughout the race. The reality, though, is that while Bush led during the spring and summer of 2000, Gore was in front by the end of the Democratic National Convention in Los Angeles. Indeed, as shown in figure 5.1a's daily aggregation of national polls on candidate preference, Gore surged to the lead around Labor Day, stretching this advantage to approximately 5 percentage points by mid- to late September.[6]

From there, Bush closed to within 2 percentage points by early October. Johnston, Jamieson, and Hagen (2004) argue that Bush's rally was caused by news media scrutiny of Gore's September 22 call to release thirty million barrels of oil from the six hundred million barrel Strategic Petroleum Reserve. (The Energy Department did, in fact, approve the release of oil from the reserve on September 22.) The attendant coverage was largely negative, focusing on whether this call was a cynical move by the vice president to curry favor among swing voters in the Northeast and Midwest (Johnston, Jamieson, and Hagen 2004).

The Annenberg team also claims that this media hit was exacerbated by three ongoing stories that gained momentum in late September and early October. First, on September 19, reporters questioned Gore's claim—made in one of his standard stump speeches—that his mother-in-law paid more

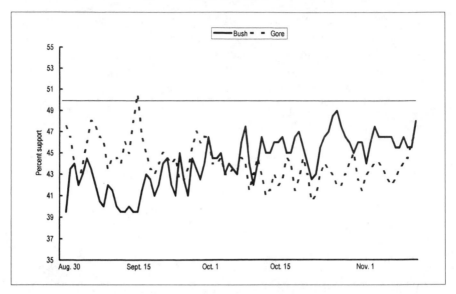

FIGURE 5.1A   Movement in national candidate preferences during the 2000 fall campaign. Lines are moving averages based on all available national surveys. Surveys of likely voter populations are used whenever they are available.

for arthritis medicine than it cost to treat his dog with the same drug.[7] Second, on September 21, reporters challenged Gore's claim that his mother had sung the tune "Look for the Union Label" to him as a childhood lullaby.[8] Third, reporters scrutinized another Gore stump speech claim—repeated during the first presidential debate—that children in a Sarasota, Florida, high school classroom had been forced to stand for days due to classroom overcrowding.[9] According to the Annenberg group's research, the net effect of these stories, and subsequent media coverage suggesting Gore had problems telling the truth, was a 2-to-3-point reduction in Gore's vote and a dead heat in the polls.

By mid-October, after the first two presidential debates, Bush had reclaimed a 2-point lead. But Gore fought back during the last three weeks of the race and pulled slightly ahead by the last weekend. As mentioned earlier, Johnston, Jamieson, and Hagen (2004) point to the campaign, citing both candidates' late emphasis on Social Security as critical to Gore's last-minute surge. This interpretation matches the argument advanced by Gore strategists, who contend that the late barrage of television ads alleging that Bush had promised Social Security money to two different groups—young people and retired people—drove the movement toward Gore. Neither the Annenberg team nor the Democrats, however, offer more than correlational or suggestive evidence for their interpretations.

A comparable series of ebbs and flows also characterized the 2004 campaign. The difference, however, is that there were fewer lead changes. In 2004, Bush's postconvention advantage remained reasonably solid through September but disappeared around the time of the first presidential debate (see fig. 5.1b). In truth, Bush's early October support was not all that different from September; rather, it was an increase in vote intention for Kerry that drove the margin to zero. A moment-by-moment unpacking of movement indicates Kerry's performance in the first debate was the proximate event associated with his rise. Kerry's support appears to have had an upper boundary of 46 percentage points throughout September, whereas Bush frequently broke 50. After the Miami debate, Kerry's lowest share of the vote was 44 percent, and he averaged 47 percent. But while Kerry expanded his electorate, Bush managed to recover enough of the ground he lost to reassume a 3-point lead throughout the remainder of the debate season.

Two late episodes also merit attention. First, Kerry benefited from the conclusion of the debate season and the initiation of the final stretch. This benefit was slight—only a single point—but it put him within 2 percentage points of Bush during the final week of the campaign. Second, the release of the Osama bin Laden videotape on the Friday before the election (October 29) aided Bush. Kerry's support dipped 4 points in two

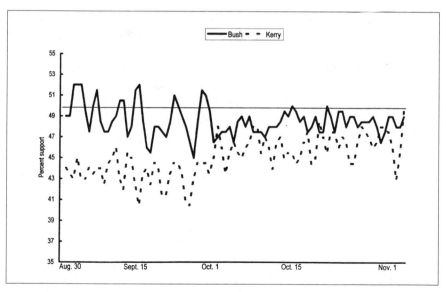

FIGURE 5.1B   Movement in national candidate preferences during the 2004 fall campaign. Lines are moving averages based on all available national surveys. Surveys of likely voter populations are used whenever they are available.

days, although he recovered all of this loss by the eve of the election. These episodic movements should not obscure the main change over the course of fall 2004—Kerry's expansion of his base vote.

Table 5.1 summarizes the complex movements of 2000 and 2004 in a variety of ways. The first columns focus on the presidential candidates' standing in the national polls, while the second two columns focus on their standings in the states and media markets. The national numbers tell the most conservative story. In 2000, Bush picked up 2.7 points on Gore over the course of the campaign. The average movement toward Bush was 4.9 points across battleground states and 3.3 points across media markets.[10] Third-party support, particularly support for Green Party candidate Ralph Nader, declined from September to November, although not as much as one might have expected. Nader's share of the national vote decreased by 0.8 points, while his average support in media markets and battleground states each dropped by 0.6 points.

In 2004, Kerry picked up 3.1 points on Bush over the campaign. As suggested earlier, much of this gain was driven by an increase in absolute support for Kerry—he rose from 43.4 percent in early September to 48.3 percent on Election Day. Unlike 2000, the underdog candidate's gains were relatively smaller in battleground states and media markets. Kerry picked up 1.1 percentage points in the most critical states over the campaign and a paltry 0.1 points in the most important media markets. The relatively smaller movement in numbers at the media market level is inconsistent with my hypothesis that campaign effects ought to have been more powerful there, but I would emphasize that cross-sectional estimates can mask significant weekly or daily shifts in voter preferences. Ironically, Kerry was checked despite the complete collapse in support for Ralph Nader: the Green Party candidate went from 5 percent of the September vote to 0 percent of the Election Day vote in battleground states. He also dropped from 2.5 percent to 0.2 percent in battleground media markets.

Looking for even more variance, table 5.2 examines shifts in candidate favorability differentials over the 2000 and 2004 fall campaigns. The 2000 numbers go a long way toward explaining what happened in that election: Al Gore's favorability ratings dropped 12 percentage points from September to November. Bush's ratings, in contrast, remained constant. Gore's plunge was less dramatic in battleground states and markets, but Bush's favorability ratings actually improved, leaving the vice president 3.7 and 6.8 points worse off, respectively, in those categories after eleven weeks of campaigning. It is worth noting that these findings are consistent with the hypothesis that candidate favorability ratings ought to be more variable (or sensitive) than vote choice.

TABLE 5.1 Movement in Candidate Preferences over the Fall Campaign

	2000			2004		
	NATIONAL AVERAGE	BATTLEGROUND STATE AVERAGE	BATTLEGROUND DMA AVERAGE	NATIONAL AVERAGE	BATTLEGROUND STATE AVERAGE	BATTLEGROUND DMA AVERAGE
Vote Share						
Bush	47.9	48.1	51.6	50.7	50.4	52.5
Gore/Kerry	48.4	48.1	45.3	48.3	49.6	47.3
Nader	2.7	2.8	2.2	0.4	0.0	0.2
Margin (Bush-Dem.)	−0.5	0.0	6.3	2.4	0.9	5.2
Bush share of two-party vote	49.7	50.0	53.3	51.2	50.4	52.6
September Poll Standing						
Bush	42	40	44.4	48.9	44.7	49.5
Gore/Kerry	45.2	44.9	41.4	43.4	44.9	44.2
Nader	3.5	3.4	2.8	2.1	5.0	2.5
Undecided	7.8	11.4	9.8	5.3	7.6	3.8
Margin (Bush-Dem.)	−3.2	−4.9	3.0	5.5	−0.2	5.3
Bush share of two-party vote	48.2	47.1	51.7	53.0	49.9	52.8
Campaign Movement						
Change in the margin	+2.7	+4.9	+3.3	−3.1	+1.1	−0.1
Change in Bush's vote share	+1.6	+2.9	+1.5	−1.8	+0.6	−0.2

Source: The September national numbers are based on an average of all publicly available national polls conducted between September 3 and September 20. For the 21 battleground states, the averages encompass the same time frame and are based on tracking polls conducted for the Bush–Cheney campaign by Voter Consumer Research and Market Strategies Inc. Positive movement numbers reflect increases in Bush's relative share of support.

TABLE 5.2   Movement in Candidate Favorability over the Fall Campaign

	2000			2004		
	NATIONAL AVERAGE	BATTLEGROUND STATE AVG.	BATTLEGROUND DMA AVG.	NATIONAL AVERAGE	BATTLEGROUND STATE AVG.	BATTLEGROUND DMA AVG.
November Favorability						
Bush						
Favorability	56.0	58.4	58.7	52.0	50.6	52.1
Unfavorability	36.0	39.4	38.7	45.0	46.6	44.9
Net favorability/unfavorability	20.0	19.0	20	7.0	4.0	7.2
Gore/Kerry						
Favorability	54.0	53.4	54	46.0	51.3	49.8
Unfavorability	39.0	41.1	42.3	44.0	45.4	47.1
Net favorability/unfavorability	15.0	12.3	11.7	2.0	5.9	2.7
Favorability margin						
(Bush fav./unfav. − Dem. fav./unfav.)	5.0	6.7	8.2	5.0	−1.9	4.5
September Favorability						
Bush						
Favorability	56.0	58	57.9	55.0	51.6	53.3
Unfavorability	36.0	41.3	42	44.0	45.5	43.7
Net favorability/unfavorability	20.0	16.7	15.9	11.0	6.1	9.6
Gore/Kerry						
Favorability	60.0	58.1	56.9	52.0	49.5	48.2
Unfavorability	33.0	44.4	42.5	44.0	46.2	47.3
Net favorability/unfavorability	27.0	13.7	14.4	8.0	3.3	0.9
Favorability margin						
(Bush fav./unfav. − Dem. fav./unfav.)	−7.0	3.0	1.5	3.0	2.8	8.7
Campaign Movement						
Bush favorability	+0.0	+2.3	+4.1	−4.0	−2.1	−2.4
(Nov. net fav./unfav.) − (Sept. fav./unfav.)						
Gore/Kerry favorability	−12.0	−1.4	−2.7	−6.0	+2.6	+1.8
(Nov. net fav./unfav.) − (Sept. fav./unfav.)						
Bush fav. movement − Dem. fav. movement	+12.0	+3.7	+6.8	+2.0	−4.7	−4.2

Source: The September national numbers are based on an average of publicly available national polls conducted between September 3 and September 20. For November, the favorability estimates come from an average of U.S. national polls conducted between October 28 and Election Day. For the 21 battleground states, the averages are based on tracking polls conducted for the Bush-Cheney campaign by Voter Consumer Research and Market Strategies Inc. Positive movement numbers reflect increases in Bush's relative share of support.

In 2004, Bush's favorability numbers declined over the campaign, but not as much as Kerry's. In fact, Bush emerged 2 points to the better. This slight improvement did not hold across the battleground states and markets, however. Kerry increased his favorability compared to Bush by 4.7 points in battleground states and 4.2 points in battleground markets.

A comparison of the vote choice and candidate favorability dynamics from 2004 presents an apparent anomaly. Bush's favorability differentials declined less than his vote share across the nation but significantly more than his vote share in battleground states and markets. Recall that my first research hypothesis predicts a smaller drop in Bush's national vote share and a larger drop in his battleground vote share given the observed shifts in his favorability numbers. The solution to this puzzle lies in the apparent lack of early mobilization of Republican voters in battleground states (and especially in smaller battleground media markets) in 2004. Even as voters felt slightly less favorable to Bush, his Republican base returned to his side as the campaign moved toward Election Day.

It is also intriguing that Bush's relative favorability ratings improved more nationally than in the battleground states in both elections. In 2000, Bush does 8.3 points better nationally than in battleground states (12.0 – 3.7), while in 2004 he does 6.7 points better (2.0 – -4.7). The tendency could be idiosyncratic, though. In 2000, Gore collapsed outside the battlegrounds; and in 2004, Kerry improved inside the battlegrounds.

Both the trial ballot and favorability data provide some evidence that challengers (Bush in 2000 and Kerry in 2004) are better positioned to increase their support over the campaign. First, challengers usually become better known during the fall, and their vote share may improve as voters get more comfortable with them. Second, challengers can benefit as in-party candidates are forced to defend their records and past statements. This tendency appears to be slight, however, and these two elections may not be particularly representative.

Of course, presidential elections are not won by amassing popular votes or even by scoring an impressive average vote across many states—they are won in the Electoral College. Table 5.3 documents the cross-sectional movement in the Electoral College between early September and Election Day for both 2000 and 2004. The data suggest a significant Bush comeback in 2000 and no net advantage in 2004. From the top rows of the table, we see that Gore led Bush at the outset of fall 2000 in 27 states worth 337 electoral votes.[11] This placed him 67 votes above the 270 needed to become president. Bush was carrying 23 states worth 197 electoral votes, with one state (worth 4 electoral votes) tied. By Election Day, Bush picked up the "tied" state (New Hampshire) and six of Gore's states (Florida, Ken-

TABLE 5.3 Movement in Electoral College Votes over the Fall Campaign

	SEPTEMBER		ELECTION DAY		MOVEMENT	
	Electoral Votes	States	Electoral Votes	States	Electoral Votes	States
2000						
Bush	197	23	270	30	+73	+7
Gore	337	27	268	21	−69	−6
Tied	4	1	0	0	−4	−1
2004						
Bush	279	29	286	31	+7	+2
Kerry	249	20	252[a]	20	+3	0
Tied	10	2	0	0	−10	−2

Source: The September numbers are based on an average of all publicly available statewide polls conducted between September 3 and September 20. Positive movement numbers reflect increases in Bush's
relative share of support.
[a]For analytic purposes, I report Kerry's electoral vote as 252 despite the fact that one Kerry elector failed
to vote for him in the Electoral College ballot.

tucky, Louisiana, Missouri, Tennessee, and West Virginia), worth 73 electoral votes, to give him exactly 270. Gore, needless to say, lost 69 electoral
votes, leaving him 2 votes shy of a majority.

In 2004, Bush led Kerry by 30 electoral votes following the GOP convention—279 to 249, with New Mexico and West Virginia (10 electoral
votes) tied. Bush picked up 17 electoral votes from 3 states (Iowa, New
Mexico, and West Virginia) but also lost 10 votes from 1 state (Wisconsin).
Kerry picked up 10 electoral votes from 1 state (Wisconsin) but lost 7 votes
from 1 state (Iowa). The net gain for Bush over Kerry was 2 states and 4
electoral votes.

Figures 5.2a and 5.2b present a more dynamic picture, using the Bush
campaign's internal tracking poll numbers to chart the Electoral College
story on a week-to-week basis over the 2000 and 2004 fall campaigns.[12]
In 2000, as shown in figure 5.2a, Gore's support level peaked during the
week of September 22 (recall his Strategic Petroleum Reserve gambit) at
310 projected electoral votes. This zenith is later than suggested in the
cross-sectional analysis offered in table 5.3 and with considerably fewer
electoral votes (310 versus 337). In addition, these data show that Bush did
not assume the electoral vote lead until October 21 and *never* had a clear
majority.[13] This lag between the national trial ballot results from 2000
(see figure 5.1a) and the state results makes it easy to see why the GOP
"doomsday" scenario most often advanced in October had Bush winning
the popular vote and Gore carrying the Electoral College.

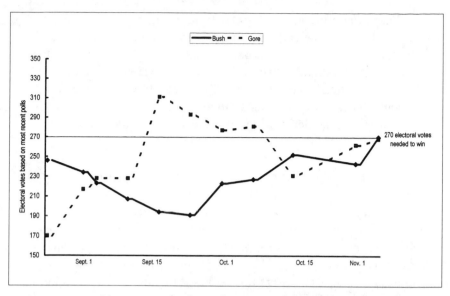

FIGURE 5.2A Movement in the electoral vote count during the 2000 fall campaign. Weekly estimates are based on all available statewide polls conducted between September 3 and Election Day.

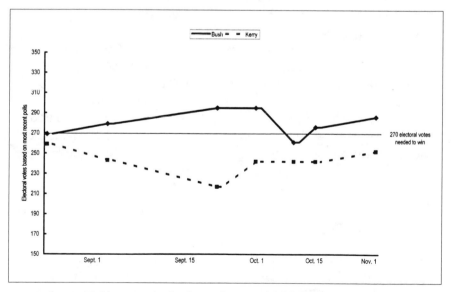

FIGURE 5.2B Movement in the electoral vote count during the 2004 fall campaign. Weekly estimates are based on all available statewide polls conducted between September 3 and Election Day.

Perhaps the most interesting result occurs in the last seventy-two hours of the 2000 race. As Gore's surge was consolidated, it left him at the threshold of 270 electoral votes on November 5. But in the last two days, Bush rebounded slightly, throwing several Gore states (including Iowa, New Mexico, Oregon, and Wisconsin) back into the even category. If the election had been held on Monday, there is every reason to believe Gore would have won the electoral as well as the popular vote.

In 2004, as shown in figure 5.2b, the time frame prevents us from seeing Bush's ascension in the aftermath of his convention. Furthermore, we do not see a dramatic reversal in the last few days such as we saw in 2000. Instead, Bush consolidated his convention edge throughout September, peaking at about 306 electoral votes during the week of September 26. The Electoral College outlook then slowly shifted during the debate season, with Kerry dropping Bush below a 270 electoral vote majority during the week of October 7. But this deadlock was short-lived, and Bush moved over the 270 threshold during the week of October 14 and pushed to 286 by Election Day. Interestingly, there was more back-and-forth movement in 2004 than in 2000, with Ohio, Pennsylvania, Florida, Wisconsin, Iowa, and New Mexico flipping from Bush to Kerry, or vice versa. The net effect of this movement was never especially great, however, as the candidates tended to split these prizes. Moreover, Bush always held the upper hand because of his large base in the southern and Rocky Mountain states.

More generally, these figures support the hypothesis that time series analyses will pick up shifts in candidate support that are not evident in cross-sectional data. They may even help us detect small net advantages that accrued to specific candidates. Granted, we do not see enormous week-by-week changes in the aggregate distribution of popular support or projected electoral votes. There is a clear ebb and flow to both campaigns, however, which is masked by simple August-to-November comparisons of support. And, perhaps more important, the result is not a reversion to the Labor Day equilibrium.

CAMPAIGNING EFFECTS

The most important question for this chapter is whether Republican and Democratic activities and expenditures influenced any of the movement described earlier. Although there is some indication that campaigning coincided with fluctuations in candidate support, there is certainly no a priori reason to *assume* marginal differences in the quantity or quality of campaigning caused these shifts.

SIMPLE RELATIONSHIPS BETWEEN
CAMPAIGNING AND VOTE SHARE

Table 5.4 offers a first glimpse at the link between campaigning and candidate support by examining resource allocation in states where the Republicans gained support over the campaign versus states where the

TABLE 5.4   Breakdown of Support Changes by Campaigning

	2000			2004		
	BUSH GAINS	GORE GAINS	OVERALL	BUSH GAINS	KERRY GAINS	OVERALL
States (Sept. to Nov.)						
Television advertising differential (R – D)	1,138	1,152	1,143	201	43	145
Bush appearances	2.08	2.33	2.16	2.12	3.00	2.43
Gore/Kerry appearances	1.61	1.80	1.67	2.09	2.11	2.10
Cheney appearances	1.44	2.40	1.73	1.91	2.39	2.08
Lieberman/Edwards appearances	1.44	1.67	1.51	2.58	2.22	2.45
Total	36	15	51	33	18	51
Media Markets (Sept. to Nov.)						
Television advertising differential (R – D)	3,404	4,194	3,778	578	1,213	901
Bush appearances	1.04	1.23	1.13	1.86	1.55	1.70
Gore/Kerry appearances	0.73	1.06	0.89	1.50	1.59	1.54
Cheney appearances	0.90	0.98	0.94	1.07	1.52	1.30
Lieberman/Edwards appearances	0.67	0.81	0.73	1.61	1.48	1.54
Total	69	40	109	28	29	57
States (weekly)						
Television advertising differential (R – D)	2,010	2,147	2,069	389	253	308
Bush appearances	0.33	0.55	0.44	1.06	0.60	0.79
Gore/Kerry appearances	0.20	0.53	0.36	0.81	0.63	0.71
Cheney appearances	0.32	0.33	0.33	0.79	0.59	0.68
Lieberman/Edwards appearances	0.30	0.35	0.32	1.02	0.63	0.79
Total	117	109	226	48	68	116
Media Markets (weekly)						
Television advertising differential (R – D)	433	398	415	395	340	367
Bush appearances	0.18	0.2	0.19	0.22	0.21	0.22
Gore/Kerry appearances	0.13	0.2	0.17	0.22	0.18	0.2
Cheney appearances	0.07	0.19	0.13	0.21	0.12	0.17
Lieberman/Edwards appearances	0.14	0.17	0.15	0.22	0.2	0.21
Total	127	136	263	198	201	399

Source: Cell entries are the average allocations (or differences) across the states within the given category. The cross-sectional state analysis is based on an average of all available statewide public polls conducted between September 3 and September 20. Other analyses are based on tracking polls conducted for the Bush-Cheney campaign by Voter Consumer Research and Market Strategies Inc. across 21 battleground states. The weekly analysis uses a one-week lag to gauge TV effects.

Democrats gained. The analysis is separated out by election; as we know, the GOP had a significant campaigning edge in 2000 but not in 2004. In addition, I move from broader to more specific views of the relationship between campaigning and vote shift as one proceeds down the table. For example, focusing on the time period from Labor Day to Election Day, the top block simply shows the mean level of campaign activity in states where the Republican candidate gained in the polls versus states where the Democratic candidate gained. More specifically, the top left cell shows the average TV ad differential (1,138 GRPs for Bush) in states where Bush picked up ground over the campaign. The cell adjacent and to the right shows the pro-GOP TV ad differential was even greater (1,152 GRPs for Bush) in states where Gore gained. The cells below show the average appearances by specific candidates in states where the Republican or Democratic candidate gained over the campaign.

The second block down similarly focuses on campaign differences by vote improvement, only at the level of the media market. Thus, the top left cell in this block tells us that Bush has an average TV advertising advantage of 3,404 GRPs in markets where he gained over the period from September to November. The third and fourth blocks consider *weekly* resource allocation averages in states or markets broken down by whether the Republican or Democratic candidate picked up ground during the week.

I expect, of course, that Republican campaign advantages are larger in states or markets in which the Republicans gained on the Democrats. The relationship between net positive movement in the polls and mean campaigning advantages is uneven at best, however, in the cross-sectional numbers displayed in the top two blocks. Only once (at the state level in 2004) is Bush's average TV advertising advantage greater in areas in which he gained. In the same vein, only once (at the media market level in 2004) is Bush's average appearance advantage greater in areas in which he gained. Furthermore, only once (at the media market level in 2000) is Cheney's average appearance advantage greater in areas in which GOP standing in the polls improved.[14]

The estimates of weekly movement in the polls show an entirely different story, one much more consistent with my research hypotheses. In the bottom two blocks, we see that in three out of four cases, the average Bush TV advertising advantages are greater in states in which Bush gained support over the campaign (the exception is at the state-level in 2000). For presidential and vice presidential candidate appearances, we see much the same story; only once (for presidential appearances at the media market level in 2004) is the hypothesized positive relationship between average resource allocation differences and net poll movement not observed.

The reality is that these estimated relationships must be read with a certain degree of skepticism. This dichotomous rendering of candidate support movement (e.g., "Bush gains" versus "Gore gains") could mask subtler but equally legitimate effects. For example, positive movement in response to one candidate's campaigning could be offset by a more substantial response to increased campaigning by the other side. The weekly time frame mitigates but does not eliminate this possibility. More important, comparing means by category fails to control for other independent variables that can affect candidate favorability and standing. I therefore turn now to multivariate models of campaign effects.

MULTIVARIATE RELATIONSHIPS

Table 5.5 presents weekly shifts in candidate standing within battleground states and media markets. As mentioned earlier, the data constitute a pooled time series, with twenty-four cross sections (states) and eleven time points (weeks) in 2000 and seventeen cross sections and eight time points in 2004. I do not have candidate support numbers for every week, but I do have appropriate data for a sufficient number of time points to generate large overall sample sizes (64 state and 276 media market cases for 2000; 65 state and 226 media market cases for 2004).[15]

The specification of the models requires some explanation. Bivariate scatterplots indicate that TV advertising differences had a nonlinear effect on changes in Bush's share of the two-party vote, leading me to use the difference of logged TV advertising for the Republicans and Democrats.[16] In addition to the difference of logged TV advertising, I include appearance variables for the presidential and vice presidential candidates, controls for the percentage undecided and deviation from the average historical vote, and a full slate of interaction terms combining campaigning variables with these two control variables.[17] I also include a control for Nader's share of the vote and dummy variables for each cross section and week (the baseline states are Florida in 2000 and Ohio in 2004, and the baseline week is week 1 for both elections). The cross-sectional and timing dummies isolate effects associated with specific states or weeks of the campaign. The latter is critical given the possibility that shifts in voters' preferences may be disproportionately driven by the debates. All told, the specifications and estimators chosen for the models are extremely conservative and ought to significantly tax the campaign effects argument.

The pooled time series models (see table 5.5) offer several striking results. Let us first consider the independent effects of campaign activities. As expected, the logged TV advertising differentials are correlated with

TABLE 5.5 Estimations of Relationship between Candidate Preference Change and Campaign Activities (Weekly)

DEP. VAR. = BUSH SHARE OF THIS WEEK'S VOTE – BUSH SHARE OF LAST WEEK'S VOTE	2000		2004	
	STATES	DMAS	STATES	DMAS
Television Advertising				
Television advertising differentials	0.393**	0.128	0.371	0.440
log(Rep. TV lagged one week) – log(Dem. TV lagged one week)	(0.167)	(0.398)	(0.200)	(0.400)
Candidate Appearances				
Bush	0.046	0.255	0.023	0.955
	(0.207)	(1.231)	(0.200)	(1.000)
Gore/Kerry	−0.494**	−1.549	0.170	−0.627
	(0.202)	(1.287)	(0.300)	(1.000)
Cheney	0.129	0.621	−0.188	1.277
	(0.266)	(1.575)	(0.300)	(1.100)
Lieberman/Edwards	−0.186	−1.901	0.025	−0.142
	(0.217)	(1.222)	(0.200)	(0.900)
Control Variables				
% undecided in Sept. polls (lagged one week)	0.154**	0.157	−0.307*	0.216
	(0.050)	(0.172)	(0.200)	(0.200)
Deviation from hist. avg. in Sept. polls (lagged one week)	0.498***	1.540***	0.839***	0.216***
	(0.073)	(0.096)	(0.148)	(0.043)
Intercept	−4.533***	−0.776***	−1.456	−0.976
	(1.074)	(0.053)	(0.900)	(0.900)
N	64	276	65	226
Standard error	2.121	10.455	1.971	5.977
Adjusted R^2	0.190	0.502	0.343	0.091

Note: Cell entries represent the results of least squares regression equations (standard errors in parentheses). The models are of pooled time series data, with states or DMAs serving as cross sections and weeks serving as units of time. Dummy variables for the states/DMAs and the weeks were included in the estimations but are omitted from the table for presentational clarity. Regression coefficients are calculated using a least squares estimator. Standard errors are actually panel-corrected standard errors (see Beck and Katz 1995). Most of the complications associated with time series analysis (e.g., serial autocorrelation, random walks, etc.) are ameliorated by the use of a differenced dependent variable. Television advertising is measured in hundreds of gross rating points (GRPs).
$*p < .05$ $**p < .01$ $***p < .001$

positive shifts in candidate support. The influences at the state level are particularly noteworthy: they are statistically significant at the 0.01 level in 2000 and at the 0.09 level in 2004. The substantive effects are even more intriguing. Holding all other factors constant, a 1,000-GRP increase in Bush's statewide TV advertising advantage for a given week produces a 0.1-point increase in the Republican share of the 2000 presidential vote. If Bush had managed five such weeks in battleground states, he would have carried Iowa, New Mexico, Oregon, and Wisconsin. Conversely, a Gore edge of this magnitude would have tipped Florida and New Hampshire (and the election). In 2004, the same TV advertising increase is also worth

0.1 points. This difference over five weeks would have shifted Wisconsin to Bush or Iowa and New Mexico to Kerry.

At the media market level, the effects are more variable: in neither 2000 nor 2004 do they meet conventional levels of statistical significance. Still, the coefficients are sufficiently close to statistical significance to warrant using them to estimate effects. Once again, the results are intriguing: a 1,000-GRP shift causes a 0.05 point change in the 2000 vote and a 0.20 point change in the 2004 vote. For 2000, such a shift in Miami (Florida), Albuquerque (New Mexico), Portland (Oregon), or Milwaukee (Wisconsin) would have swung those states. For 2004, a shift on this order in Cleveland, Cincinnati, or Columbus would have drawn Kerry close enough for a legal challenge of the Ohio statewide result (and the presidential election itself). Of course, the prospects for an across-the-board alteration in the distribution of television advertising along these lines are faint. Shifts of this magnitude in singular states or markets, however, are quite plausible.

Turning to candidate appearances, the effects are almost all in the expected direction (so far, so good) and occasionally have a statistically and substantively impressive influence. For example, appearances by Al Gore in 2000, holding all other factors constant, drove his support up by almost half a percentage point at the state level. At the media market level, the effect was a whopping 1.5 points. Similarly, an appearance by Joe Lieberman in a media market improved Gore's numbers by 1.9 points. This finding is consistent with previous research (Franklin 2001; Johnston, Jamieson, and Hagen 2004), as well as with anecdotal evidence suggesting Lieberman received enormously favorable press (especially local press) in 2000. But most appearance coefficients do not meet conventional levels of statistical significance. Republican candidates, in particular, did not affect statistically significant shifts in the vote with their personal appearances.

The level of analysis may be an issue here. It is notable that candidate appearances seem to be more correlated with movement in the media markets than in the states. A Bush appearance was worth only 0.02 points at the state level in 2004 but increased his media market vote share an estimated 0.96 points. Meanwhile, a Cheney appearance produced a slightly negative shift in the ticket's statewide numbers but improved its vote share by almost 1.3 points in the media market of the visit. This tendency holds for the Democrats as well.

The vote-share models also allow us to shed a ray of light on the curious possibility that the GOP ticket was hurt by Cheney's appearances. We see that there is a negative (i.e., pro-Kerry) coefficient associated with

Cheney's statewide appearances in 2004. This finding fits with some analyses of 2000 alluded to earlier, which questioned Cheney's contribution as a stump speech, on-the-hustings candidate. If one segments the 2000 and 2004 data into before and after the vice presidential debate, however, it is clear that Cheney was a second-half candidate. That is, his influence on GOP vote share was negative (though insignificant) in September of 2000 and 2004 but turned positive and significant in October. In fact, from October 12, 2000, until Election Day, no candidate had a stronger, more positive effect on the vote than Cheney.[18] By contrast, Joe Lieberman's appearances were hugely effective through the first three weeks of September. From September 21 on, however, Lieberman's appearances were not especially influential—in fact, they were mildly counterproductive after October 12. There was almost no temporal effect associated with any of the remaining candidates.

Given the influence of the campaigning measures, it is perhaps surprising that the interaction terms produce minimal effects. This is not, I hasten to add, evidence that mobilization and persuasion did not occur. To the contrary, the control for deviation from historical average is the single most significant predictor in each of the four estimations, while the percentage undecided stands out as a strong explanation for pro-Bush movement in 2000 and pro-Kerry movement (at the state level) in 2004. But these mobilization and persuasion effects do not seem to hinge on either TV ad differences or individual candidate appearances. As such, they have been dropped from the models presented in table 5.5.

More peripherally, but worth mentioning, support for Ralph Nader is not correlated with a directional shift in the two-party vote distribution, nor were any of the cross-sectional (state/market) or time series (weeks) control variables. The Nader variable is thus omitted from the final model specifications, although the cross-sectional and time series controls are retained (but not presented) for methodological reasons.

The main result to be gleaned from the multivariate models is that candidate activities affected candidate support in the predicted direction, but the effects tended to be on the order of tenths of percentage points. Thus, building truly significant campaign effects required sustained weekly advantages or overwhelming advantages in a single week. While neither is easy to attain, the former is a more realistic possibility. In addition, campaign effects are clearly more likely in areas where (1) a candidate was significantly underperforming given party voting averages from recent elections and/or (2) there was a relatively high percentage of undecided voters. There is little evidence, however, that TV ads or candidate appearances are critical trigger mechanisms for mobilization or persuasion.

Although elections are ultimately about votes, a simple observation is in order: it is not easy to convince someone to vote for you (or for your candidate). More to the point, a campaign must get voters to feel good (or at least less bad) about its candidate before it can credibly ask for their votes. Table 5.6 presents four models of shifts in candidate favorability. These models parallel the vote choice models of table 5.5, differing only in that the dependent measure is the net difference in the candidates' relative favorabilities over the preceding week. The results are similar yet sharper than those for the vote choice models. The overall predictive power of the models, for example, is greater (see the adjusted R^2 statistics, which can be interpreted as the proportion of total variance explained by the models).

TABLE 5.6   Estimations of Relationship between Candidate Favorability Change and Campaign Activities (Weekly)

DEP. VAR. = THIS WEEK'S (BUSH NET FAV. − KERRY NET FAV.) − LAST WEEK'S (BUSH NET FAV. − KERRY NET FAV.)	2000		2004	
	STATES	DMAS	STATES	DMAS
Television Advertising				
Television advertising differentials	0.328*	0.374	0.234	0.902
log(Rep. TV lagged one week) − log(Dem. TV lagged one week)	(0.149)	(0.794)	(1.067)	(1.362)
Candidate Appearances				
Bush	0.186	0.961	0.110	0.464
	(0.185)	(2.245)	(0.872)	(0.372)
Gore/Kerry	−0.230	−0.254	−0.565	−0.550***
	(0.140)	(0.257)	(1.393)	(0.038)
Cheney	0.219	0.295	0.368	0.782
	(0.207)	(0.314)	(1.226)	(0.442)
Lieberman/Edwards	−0.360*	−0.218	−0.197	−0.177
	(0.178)	(0.244)	(0.103)	(0.339)
Control Variables				
% undecided in Sept. polls (lagged one week)	−0.332	0.322	−2.833**	−2.327**
	(0.343)	(0.343)	(1.014)	(0.759)
Deviation from hist. avg. in Sept. polls (lagged one week)	1.178***	0.312***	0.400***	.198***
	(0.292)	(0.019)	(0.066)	(0.016)
Intercept	2.156	1.545***	1.307	1.230***
	(5.494)	(0.105)	(4.278)	(0.343)
N	73	276	74	239
Standard error	10.915	20.860	9.737	23.514
Adjusted R^2	0.222	0.503	0.309	0.415

Note: Cell entries represent the results of least squares recession equations (standard errors in parentheses). The models are of pooled time series data, with states or DMAs serving as cross sections and weeks serving as units of time. Dummy variables for the states/DMAs and the weeks were included in the estimations but are omitted from the table for presentational clarity. Regression coefficients are calculated using a least squares estimator. Standard errors are actually panel-corrected standard errors (see Beck and Katz 1997). Most of the complications associated with time series analysis (e.g., serial autocorrelation, random walks, etc) are ameliorated by the use of a differenced dependent variable. Television advertising is measured in hundreds of gross rating points (GRPs).
*$p < .05$ **$p < .01$ ***$p < .001$

Furthermore, there are almost no unexpected results. Only the direction of the effect associated with percentage undecided for the 2000 election—negative at the state level, positive at the media market level—stands out as surprising.

Perhaps more germane to the core of the study, candidate appearances are more consistently correlated with improved favorability ratings. All sixteen candidate appearance coefficients are in the expected direction, and two are statistically significant at the 0.05 level (three more are significant at the 0.10 level). On average, and holding all other factors constant, a four-appearance swing through a battleground state would have netted an improvement ranging from 1 to 4 points in the candidate's relative favorability rating. A simple regression of net favorability on the vote tells us that for every 5 points on the favorability scale, a candidate would have received an extra percentage point of the two-party vote, suggesting that the aforementioned four-appearance campaign trip would have been worth about an extra point at the polls.

The effects of TV advertising differentials on candidate favorability are in line with those uncovered in the vote choice models, if somewhat smaller. Only one of the four TV ad differential coefficients is statistically significant at the .05 level, but all are in the predicted direction, and the effects (especially at the DMA level) increase over the course of the campaign. While it is, of course, perilous to extrapolate substantive effects based on coefficients with relatively large standard errors, I believe there is still value gained here in using the models to estimate substantive effects, especially if the results are interpreted cautiously. For example, an increase of 1,000 GRPs for five weeks would, all other factors held constant, have improved a candidate's relative favorability rating in a state by about 0.5 points. TV ads had the most dramatic influence at the media market level in 2004; here an increase of 1,000 GRPs per week in the TV ad differential over five weeks would have produced a 1-point shift in a candidate's relative favorability. Even noting the statistical concerns mentioned before, I would argue that these estimates are conservative: the use of the difference of logged TV advertising and the assumption of heavy advertising limits the predicted influence.[19] In nonbattleground states, where campaign activity is less extensive, the potential effect on favorability for a candidate gaining an edge in TV advertising is considerable.

As with the vote choice models, I find that deviations from historical vote share greatly affect shifts in relative favorability. Voters warm to candidates who have heretofore underachieved. I also find that states or media markets with higher percentages of undecided voters viewed Kerry more favorably than Bush on a week-to-week basis in 2004. The impact of undecided voters is less clear in 2000, although if one isolates the October data, one finds that Bush tended to do better when there were higher percentages of undecided voters in the preceding week's electorate (less so in states than in media markets). Once again, these mobilization and persuasion effects are inconsistently tied to TV advertising differentials or candidate appearances, leading me to drop these interaction terms from the final models.

The remaining control variables—for Nader's vote share and for the cross sections and time units—were uniformly unimpressive. As with the vote choice models, I drop the Nader vote variable but keep the other controls (omitting them, though, from the presentation in table 5.6).

FURTHER DISCUSSION

The multivariate models of vote choice and candidate favorability differentials afford an opportunity to more directly consider the research hypotheses posed earlier. Initially, a comparison of the regression coefficients in tables 5.5 and 5.6 does not allow us to reject the hypothesis that campaign activities affect favorability ratings more dramatically than vote choice. In fact, the hypothesis is quite consistent with the estimated effects associated with candidate appearances. For television advertising differentials, the hypothesis cannot be falsified, although the effect differences are less distinct across the different models.

I also hypothesized that campaign effects on both vote choice and candidate favorability are likeliest at the media market level. This notion is clearly true for candidate appearances but is less impressively so for television advertising differences. Again, the data certainly do not allow us to discount the hypotheses with respect to TV advertising; they are simply less obviously supportive.

The one hypothesis that garners unqualified affirmation is that week-by-week data are much more likely to yield insight into campaign effects than are cross-sectional data. The cross-sectional data from 2000 and 2004, in fact, tell us that candidate activity produced insignificant (at best) or negative (at worst) effects on vote share. The time series data, in contrast, show candidate activities had a positive and often significant impact on both vote share and candidate favorability.

Beyond the particular research hypotheses, there are a number of issues, some narrow and some broad, that merit discussion in light of the data and analyses introduced in this chapter. The narrower issues concern methodology and explanations for the findings. Let me address them first.

Initially, there is the question of endogeneity. That is, do campaigns simply target states where they know they can move the numbers, leading to misspecification errors and biased estimates of campaign effects? At this point, it is almost axiomatic that campaigns target the most promising battleground states, but it is also true that every campaign has to amass 270 electoral votes to win. This fact typically leads the underdog campaign to target states that it (realistically) has little to no chance of winning. Following this logic, endogeneity therefore appears to be more of an issue for close elections such as 2000 and 2004, in which both campaigns *can* choose states where there is a realistic chance of moving voters. But this does not jibe with even a cursory overview of the Bush campaign's major offensive forays in 2000. Bush aggressively campaigned in California, to little or no effect. Illinois received attention also, with no payoff.

A second concern is the possibility of spatial autocorrelation among the states or media markets. Spatial autocorrelation occurs when geographic units are close together and move similarly in response to proximate stimuli. For example, voters in Wisconsin and Minnesota might move toward Gore after a campaign stop in Madison due to the pervasiveness of news coverage and the underlying similarity of these statewide electorates. This problem can be gauged with simple tests, however, none of which indicate serious problems with the current data sets. More broadly, the idea of regional effects is viewed with increasing suspicion by campaign operatives. If anything, the trend seems to be moving in the opposite direction, toward the balkanization of voters.

Third, as is evident from the pooled time series data, campaigns appear to limit campaign effects by matching the opposition's TV advertising and appearances. This practice is known as *bracketing,* and it was employed by the Republican and Democratic presidential campaigns in 2000 and 2004. The pooled time series data allow us to get at this factor to some degree, but measuring the true impact of bracketing requires daily data on candidate standing (which I have, albeit with substantial error terms), candidate appearances (which I also have), and TV ads (which I do *not* have). These daily data would be especially interesting over the last seventy-two hours of the race, where TV ads and appearances are more difficult to match.

Fourth, candidate appearances might have been less effective in 2000 and 2004 because of local news media coverage. This observation follows from Dowd's notion that the local news media—which convey information about candidate events to the broader audience within the media market and, ultimately, the state—did not routinely present the positive images and photo opportunities provided by the campaigns during appearances. Instead, they may have opted to follow the patterns set by the national news media, focusing on the horse race, gaffes, scandals, and inconsistencies. Fully exploring and testing this argument is beyond the purview of this study, but most people who work in campaigns will tell you that the local media are no longer thrilled just to have the candidate in their neck of the woods. Bush found that out on November 4, 1999, when Andy Hiller of WHDH-TV in Boston turned a routine sit-down interview into a pop quiz on world leaders. In short, this sort of coverage may have been common in 2000 and 2004 and would certainly have affected the pooled time series estimates presented in tables 5.5 and 5.6.

Fifth and finally, the exclusion of nonbattleground states in several of my analyses may affect my estimates of campaign effects. As stated earlier, I omitted states when there were no reliable polling data. I am also of the opinion that it is reasonable to focus campaign analyses on venues in which there was actually a campaign. Of course, this perspective is debatable. One could plausibly argue that we want to know how candidate support shifts in the absence of a campaign. Based on my analyses of data from 1988 through 1996, such an inclusion should *increase* the estimated impact of campaigning (zero campaigning equals zero movement in the polls), but this is only an educated guess for 2000 and 2004.

Beyond these methodological issues are other matters of broad and obvious import. In particular, the big questions arising from this analysis are whether presidential campaign activities can influence voters and thereby improve a candidate's prospects for victory, and (more narrowly) whether Bush's campaigns won these elections by outmaneuvering their Democratic counterparts. Let us first consider the common perception that Gore ran a poor campaign in 2000, dissipating the goodwill of voters engendered by eight years of peace and prosperity under the Clinton administration. Is there evidence that Gore ran a poor campaign or, conversely, that Bush ran a great campaign in 2000? In this chapter (and in this book) I concentrate on volume rather than quality. In this context, what catches the eye is the enormous Republican advantage in the allocation of television advertising and, to a lesser extent, candidate appearances. As was suggested earlier, much of this differential was due to the Democrats' decision to spend money in the summer and focus a relatively large portion of their extant financial resources on get-out-the-vote efforts. Although I cannot gauge the effectiveness of this summer spending or the Election Day mobilization efforts, it is clear that the Republicans' cash advantage allowed them to target a range of states that might have otherwise been out of reach. Some of these efforts were of little consequence, such as in California and Illinois. Others were significant, such as in West Virginia, Tennessee, and even Minnesota. The fact that the campaigns would pursue different tactics and strategies—if only for a week or two—encourages us to reconsider some of our assumptions about presidential campaigns.

On the other side of the ledger, the multivariate models give us little indication that the Republicans were more effective than the Democrats. Coefficients for Gore's appearances are usually larger than Bush's, and coefficients for Lieberman's appearances are usually larger than Cheney's. These coefficients do not, of course, take into account some of the factors discussed earlier that may influence the effectiveness of appearances. But regardless of the reasons, there appears to be scant difference in the effectiveness of the candidates' appearances in 2000.

The story is similar for television. In the interest of parsimony, and to limit the strains on some of the lower-N data sets, my analyses rely on difference measures to estimate the effectiveness of television. But if one separates TV advertising into those sponsored by Bush, Gore, RNC, and DNC, one sees few significant differences between the parties or, for that matter, between candidates and parties. There is some evidence that the RNC's ads were slightly more effective than those of the other players, but this finding is neither robust nor consistent enough to be definitive.

In 2004, the Bush and Kerry campaigns also appear to have been comparably effective. Unlike 2000, in 2004 there were almost no differences in television advertising levels between the Republicans and Democrats. But like 2000, candidate appearances were roughly equivalent. Interestingly, the estimated effects of this campaigning are more favorable toward the Republicans, although the magnitude of these advantages is not overwhelming. This finding is especially true at the local level; Bush and Cheney appearances produce more striking reactions than appearances by Kerry and Edwards in battleground media markets. It is also worth mentioning that while separate analyses of TV advertising by special interest groups demonstrate that they had a lesser impact than candidate advertising on vote choice, their impact on candidate favorabilities is indistinguishable from the candidates' ads. The implication is that Kerry was not necessarily handicapped by relying on left-leaning 527 groups to supplement his paid advertising campaign.

In sum, the data at hand do not allow me to conclude that Gore or Kerry ran particularly poor races while Bush ran particularly excellent ones. They do suggest, however, that Bush enjoyed a volume advantage in 2000 and perhaps a very slight quality advantage in 2004. Clearly, these same data provide compelling reasons to believe presidential campaigning can move voters even if net advantages are small. More specifically, they show that accounting for the dynamic character of presidential campaigns is critical to understanding effects.

CONCLUSION

The smorgasbord of data and analyses presented here tell a number of important stories for practitioners and political scientists. The first points scored are for skeptics of presidential campaign effects. Simple cross-tabs of campaign activity and support movement across battleground states and media markets show little campaign influence. Furthermore, the pooled time series analyses provide little evidence for the sorts of interactive effects—mobilization and persuasion—that I found for 1988 through 1996.

Conversely, the pooled time series estimates go a long way toward redeeming the campaign effects argument and clarifying the difficulty in discerning these effects in the first place. Campaign activities, most notably differences in television advertising volume and some of the candidates' personal appearances, were correlated with changes in both favorability toward the candidates and vote choice. These effects are clearest when examining weekly data from battleground media markets and controlling for a host of additional explanatory variables. The obvious implication is that campaign advantages drive shifts in voters' preferences but that these shifts are difficult to achieve and even more difficult to sustain. Again, the broader implication is that future studies of campaigning, and particularly presidential campaigning, must take into account their dynamic character.

6

LEARNING FROM OUR MISTAKES

In the previous three chapters, I make the case that the 2000 and 2004 presidential campaigns developed rational and strategic plans to win 270 electoral votes by targeting specific states and media markets, that they by and large followed the plans when allocating TV advertising dollars and candidate appearances, and that these efforts affected voters' opinions and preferences. Understanding the campaigns' strategies (chapter 3) and their subsequent allocation patterns (chapter 4) was critical to properly assessing the impact of their efforts (chapter 5). In my view, the most intriguing findings are presented in chapter 5, in which we uncover evidence for the most important of the research hypothesis advanced in chapter 1: that weekly shifts in candidate support and favorability are correlated with changes in the relative distribution of TV ads and candidate appearances. Furthermore, despite the reactive nature of presidential campaigns, these shifts are not necessarily undone by the opposition's counteractivities—small net advantages across a range of battlegrounds *are* possible. This finding implies that campaigns matter for voters and can even influence statewide election outcomes provided the underlying distribution of preferences does not tilt more than a few percentage points one way or the other. This result is consistent with recent work by other political scientists analyzing detailed, time series data on presidential campaigning and public opinion (e.g., Hillygus and Jackman 2003; Holbrook 1996; Johnston, Jamieson, and Hagen 2004; Wlezien and Erikson 2002).

The other three research hypotheses put forth in chapter 1 also fare well. The data show that (1) media markets are more likely than states to reveal campaigning effects, (2) candidate favorability differentials are more sensitive to campaigning differentials than is the vote margin, and (3) campaign effects are much more robust and predictable when examining weekly—as opposed to cross-sectional—data. In short, better theory and data produce a more plausible and coherent conception of presidential campaign effects.

In this final chapter, I think it appropriate to return to another of my central claims: that political scientists and practitioners are beginning to pay attention to (and learn from) each other. During the course of the 2000 and 2004 campaigns, there was some interplay between practitioners and academics. Practitioners and the media were, for example, quite aware of the presidential forecasting models. Indeed, the May 26, 2000, edition of the *Washington Post* dedicated substantial space to the forecasters' predictions of a Gore victory.[1] This story drove news for two days and forced the Bush campaign to distribute a press release critiquing the models. Republican and Democratic campaign officials were also quite aware of the Knowledge Networks Project in 2000, as well as the electoral vote predictions derived from these and other publicly available data (Jackman and Rivers 2001). Furthermore, both the University of Pennsylvania Annenberg School for Communication's rolling cross-sectional survey and the Pew Foundation's Vanishing Voter Project were known and monitored by the campaigns in 2000 and 2004. Still, the campaigns rarely used these data in their own research and tended to view the projects as enterprises that could produce negative publicity. In this sense, they considered them potential "problems."

Political scientists, on the other hand, are interested in these campaigns. This interest is manifest in the number of books on the 2000 and 2004 elections[2] as well as from casual conversations with colleagues both before and after the elections. The academic emphasis has been on measuring and analyzing voters' perceptions during the campaigns, as is apparent in the aforementioned polling projects run by Annenberg, Pew, and Knowledge Networks. There has been less emphasis, however, on obtaining better measures of campaigning as an explanatory variable. Moreover, many of these efforts have done little to advance our knowledge of campaign effects. For example, while several data collection projects focused on television advertising, they were typically done by independent organizations and did not become publicly available until well after the elections. Most prominently, the Brennan Center and the Campaign Media Analysis Group (CMAG) tracked the flow of television advertising money in 2000 and 2004 but for a time charged commercial rates for access to the data. Along these lines, a few scattered studies focused on candidate appearances, mostly adding 2000 and then 2004 data to larger analyses of the effects of visits (e.g., Althaus, Nardulli, and Shaw 2002). No one has yet gathered data on direct mail, phone calls, or in-person contacting. Studies of the effects of these enterprises would thus be forced to rely on self-reported contacting in postelection surveys. Still, scholars have made the most of what they have from the Bush elections, and the quality of the analyses focusing on television and candidate appearance effects is quite high (e.g., Franklin 2001; Goldstein and Freedman 2002a, 2002b).

So if practitioners are still wary of political scientists, and political scientists focus more on measurement and less on campaign stimuli, where is the "coming together"? It appears to be occurring—as it did in 1988, 1992, and 1996—long after Election Day. Both professions look to the other for things they cannot provide nor do themselves. Political scientists look to the campaigns for data. Some of these data have been forthcoming, as seen in this study. When hard data cannot be found, practitioners are contacted to confirm or deny general appraisals or characterizations concerning strategy or execution. Political scientists then offer something for which campaigns have neither the time nor the inclination—complex, controlled analyses of the vote. Aggregate forecasting models are adjusted to account for the newest data. Individual-level models of voting behavior—gauging the effects of party identification, ideology, issues, and candidate traits—are offered in professional conferences and journals, and these models make their way into the collective wisdom of professional campaign consultants.

So far, this process has been somewhat attenuated for 2000 and 2004, largely because the attention of political science was absorbed by the peculiar events in Florida (e.g., Sabato 2001; Wand et al. 2001). Quite a few scholars of voting were drawn to the National Opinion Research Council (NORC) Florida Ballots Project, contributing both original analyses and expert commentary on the estimates of news media consortia recounts. This diversion of researchers' attention has necessarily resulted in fewer analyses of the campaign itself.

Even so, the paucity of critical analyses about the effectiveness of the Bush and Gore campaigns (and, to a lesser degree, the Bush and Kerry campaigns) is unusual. Critical analyses were a prominent part of the post-1988 campaign studies, and were important for (1) setting the record straight with respect to what candidates did right or wrong in their bids for the White House and (2) offering substantively meaningful advice for future campaigns. Not all of these studies came to the same conclusion: some excoriated the Dukakis campaign for allowing Bush to use negative TV ads to define the Democrat's candidacy, while others argued that Bush's comeback was inevitable given the state of the economy and general approval of Reagan's job performance. But they had a collective impact on professional understanding of that election. These sorts of analyses were somewhat less common after 1992 and 1996, although this reduction in scholarly interest seemed to be a function of comfortable victory margins. For 2000 and 2004, political science has been surprisingly willing to parrot the conventional wisdom about certain events in those races—the significance of the debates, Gore's alleged exaggerations, Kerry's alleged flip-flopping, and Bush's forays onto Democratic turf—without offering much additional analysis.

This final chapter proceeds on three broad fronts. First, I offer a modest overview of the supposed mistakes of the 2000 and 2004 presidential election campaigns. I do not confine the analysis to the campaigns, however. I also consider the performance of political science. The object here is to further our understanding of campaigns and campaign effects by specifically evaluating certain activities, decisions, and analyses. I employ a combination of qualitative and quantitative data to consider these so-called mistakes. Second, I expand the consideration of the interplay between political science and presidential campaigns by forecasting which political science concepts are likely to be of value to future campaigns and which campaign practices or concepts are likely to be of value to future studies in political science. It is an exercise based largely on intuition, albeit intuition informed by professional experience on both fronts. Third, I use my experiences in 2000 and 2004 to suggest future trends in the conduct and study of presidential campaigns. This final discussion builds on several of the findings from the earlier chapters, especially the campaign effects estimates of chapter 5.

FIVE MISTAKES OF RECENT DEMOCRATIC PRESIDENTIAL CAMPAIGNS

DOWNPLAYING TIES TO CLINTON, 2000

I begin by considering the most common and intense criticism of Gore's campaign. The essence of the critique is that Gore failed to identify with (and defend the record of) the Clinton administration. Political scientists have been particularly harsh on Gore's strategy to distance himself from Clinton. They cite economic growth figures and presidential job approval numbers that are typically associated with landslide wins for the in-party. Indeed, many of those responsible for erroneous forecasts of the vote cite Gore's failure to "prime" voters' retrospective evaluations of the economy and approval of Clinton's job handling as *the* primary reason for Gore's loss and their own mispredictions (see especially Holbrook 2001; Wlezien 2001).

But Gore's consultants make two important counterarguments. Initially, they contend that Gore needed to establish his own identity and demonstrate an independent vision. Part of doing so required distancing their candidate from the president. Gore's speech at the Democratic National Convention explicitly mentioned "standing as my own man," a statement of political and ethical independence reinforced by the memorable and quasi-disturbing public kiss Gore gave his wife, Tipper. The implicit assumption of the Gore campaign was that voters are forward-thinking and are not prone to reward past performances, particularly if the candidate seeking reward was not the one in charge.

The Gore team's second argument is that Clinton was personally unpopular in critical areas of battleground states. More specifically, Clinton's unfavorable ratings were unusually high in collar (suburban) counties surrounding battleground metropoles. For example, Clinton's favorable-to-unfavorable ratio averaged 1:3 in places such as Bucks and Montgomery counties outside Philadelphia, and Macomb and Oakland counties outside of Detroit. Democratic pollster Stanley Greenberg made this point at the bipartisan Campaign 2000 conference at the Annenberg School, and Bush's polling numbers showed much the same thing. This finding meant that using Clinton or embracing his legacy would ultimately be an albatross for Gore in these areas. Better to focus on Gore's vision for the future.

Still, Gore's consultants did shift their campaign focus to the economy in the last three weeks of the campaign. Media consultant Bill Knapp and others bristle at the notion that they "found" the economy in the closing days of the campaign. Knapp contends it was always the campaign's plan to "build up" to the economic argument and that the race would not have closed as much as it did had the Democrats not greased the tracks with arguments bolstering Gore's credentials and attacking Bush's credibility. In short, the Gore team denies that it ignored his connection to the successes of the Clinton years and defends its decision not to use Clinton himself more extensively.

I am not convinced by Knapp's argument that the Gore campaign laid the groundwork for its economic appeal throughout the fall and then successfully made its specific case in the closing days. Having said so, I am also not convinced by the criticism that a more concentrated economic appeal would have worked. Polling data from 2000 consistently showed the economic boom of the 1990s was not attributed to the policies of the federal government in general or the Clinton administration in particular. The entrepreneurship of the American people and the high-tech boom were consistently preferred as explanations by voters. As for the argument that Clinton was a liability in critical areas, the data convince me that this perspective is defensible.

Another criticism of Gore's team is a bit subtler and merits consideration. This one contends that Gore's particular manner of establishing his own identity—attacking powerful interests and claiming that he (Gore) was on "your side"—not only failed to capitalize on the successes of the Clinton administration but represented an antiquated, populist appeal that lacked credibility. In other words, distancing himself from Clinton may have been advisable, but the means by which he did so was a disaster. I disagree with this assessment. Greenberg's data indicate that a populist presentation of Gore's policies scored approximately 5 percentage points better than a more straightforward presentation. Furthermore, an underappreciated justification of this approach is that the "fighting Al" persona allowed Gore to undo the straightjacket of the vice presidency, a notably emasculating job, without directly attacking the likable Bush.

LEAVING $17 MILLION IN CAMPAIGN FUNDS UNSPENT, 2004

After the 2004 campaign, reports surfaced that Kerry failed to spend almost $17 million of the $74.6 million in general election public funds he received as the Democratic Party's presidential nominee. This amount was on top of the $45 million in primary money he left on the table. Since Kerry could not transfer the primary money to his general election campaign fund and extensive summer campaigning is considered wasteful, the unspent primary funds are somewhat excusable.[3] But to not spend more than 20 percent of your campaign budget in an election you ultimately lose by 2 points is unpardonable.

Or is it? There are two reasons to downplay the significance of this mistake. First, there was almost no television time available in the battleground media markets between October 24 and November 1. Even if Kerry had wanted to spend the money, his ads would have aired during off hours and on low-rated shows. Cable advertising slots would have been available, but there is little evidence cable TV ads have any effect on presidential elections.[4] Second, the Kerry campaign, in conjunction with the Democratic National Committee (DNC) and Democratic-leaning 527 groups, matched or exceeded Bush and the Republicans in almost every state over the final ten days of the campaign. Put a different way, there is no reason to believe the Democrats were outgunned in the closing days of the race.

The problem, of course, is that saying Kerry achieved parity and did not lose ground at the end misses the point: he should have had an advantage. By my estimates, an extra three million dollars over the last two weeks in New Mexico and Iowa could have tipped those states, and an extra ten million dollars in Ohio would have produced a virtual tie in the Buckeye State. And if television time was not available, Kerry could have extended his get-out-the-vote (GOTV) operation. Or enhanced his Hispanic outreach efforts. Or helped Democratic Senate and House candidates. In short, failing to use those funds seems to have been a disastrous mistake.

LOSING TENNESSEE, 2000

Had Al Gore been able to carry his home state, Florida would have been an afterthought. The Volunteer State was worth eleven electoral votes and had gone for Clinton-Gore in 1992 and 1996, despite an increasingly Republican tilt in statewide races. In 2000, however, Bush carried the state by 4 percentage points, putting an exclamation point on a day in which he carried every state of the old Confederacy. Moreover, Gore's loss was not simply an Electoral College issue. One of the most common statements I heard in the aftermath of the Supreme Court's decision in *Bush v. Gore* was (and I am paraphrasing), "I can't feel sorry for the guy—he didn't even carry his home state." Whatever the merits of this perspective, it was common, and the psychology of the electorate was clearly important as the campaigns plotted strategy during the Florida recount.[5]

The specific criticism I consider here is that Gore waited too long to mount a serious challenge to Bush's aggressive television advertising campaign in Tennessee. It is important to note that the aggregate campaigning numbers, both in terms of television and appearances, were not particularly skewed toward Bush. Still, they mask the fact that Bush began a substantial television advertising campaign at the beginning of October, to which Gore took at least one week to respond. Bush's tracking polls indicate that he was able to turn an even race into a 5-to-8-point lead during this time. In addition, the same scenario unfolded in West Virginia and Minnesota (though the consequences were less pernicious in the latter).

My sense is that the Gore campaign could have taken efforts to shore up Tennessee earlier in the campaign. It didn't for one simple reason: Gore's team was reluctant to spend resources on *any* lean Democratic states unless it was under attack from the Bush campaign. Bush did not target Tennessee with significant resources in September, so the Democrats spent elsewhere. When Bush launched his initiative in Tennessee, Gore's campaign responded and stopped the movement toward Bush. In fact, Gore's appearances in late October closed the gap to 2 percentage points and rallied African American voters in record numbers. There are also those who contend that the state's increasingly Republican tendencies were bound to be manifest in the vote, regardless of how much Gore campaigned there.

While defensible, the loss of support during the week in which Bush campaigned unopposed on the airwaves clearly put Gore in a hole from which he never emerged.[6] Given the relatively static nature of candidate support during the weeks in which campaigning was roughly equal, it is probable that Gore's belated response cost him the state.

GIVING UP ON THE SOUTH, 2004

Gore, a native southerner, vigorously contested Arkansas, Florida, Missouri, and Tennessee in 2000. In addition, he spent money and time in Louisiana and Kentucky. In contrast, Kerry made no serious effort in any southern state except Florida. This omission created an ominous electoral map, one that required him to virtually run the table in the Pacific Northwest, Middle Atlantic, and New England states (which he did), as well as the upper Midwest states (which he did not). Furthermore, Kerry had inviting southern targets in Virginia (with its growing and liberal population in the northern reaches of the state) and Missouri (which has seen razor-thin margins in every presidential, Senate, and gubernatorial election since 2000). And he had John Edwards, born in South Carolina and a former senator for North Carolina, as his vice presidential nominee.

At its core, however, the nonsouthern strategy is defensible. If Gore couldn't carry these states, how could Kerry—a liberal Yankee running against a wartime president? Besides, compensatory electoral targets loomed in the Rocky Mountain West: Arizona, Colorado, Nevada, and New Mexico. The difficulty, as the Democrats knew all too well, was that Kerry had little affinity for their burgeoning Latino populations. Nor did he have a strong record on the particular environmental and growth issues that animate localized debates in these states. Still, the demography and broader ideological bent of the Rocky Mountain West looked more hospitable than the South.

The choice facing the Democrats in 2004 thus seems to have been identifying the lesser of two evils. Although Kerry lost Arizona, Colorado, Nevada, and New Mexico, it is doubtful that he could have carried the

Carolinas, Virginia, or even Missouri. The error, if any existed, might have been in failing to mount an exploratory campaign in one or two southern states simply to avoid the rash of negative news stories that accompanied the abandonment of the South. These accounts may have reinforced perceptions of Kerry as a candidate of limited appeal and the Democrats as a party too liberal to compete in Dixie.

WAITING TOO LONG TO RESPOND TO
REPUBLICAN ATTACKS, 2000 AND 2004

This is the only criticism of the Democrats that was equally common in 2000 and 2004. The cognoscenti have more frequently articulated it, but political scientists have mentioned it as well. In 2000, the logic behind the criticism is that Bush managed to gain traction in late September and early October with two specific attacks; first, that Gore was a chronic exaggerator who would say anything to get elected; and second, that Gore's health-care proposals forced seniors into a "government-run HMO." The criticism itself is that the Gore campaign never effectively responded to Bush's attacks on Gore's character, and that its health-care response took three weeks to make clear that the "government-run HMO" in question was, in fact, Medicare.

This is perhaps the most difficult criticism of Gore's campaign to evaluate. Judging the effect of a hypothetical occurrence is, at best, treacherous work. Still, some evidence on the matter can be brought to bear. At the Annenberg conference, both Bob Shrum and Bill Knapp admitted to being extremely frustrated by the effectiveness of Bush's attacks on Gore's health-care policy and suggested that their inability to find a response allowed Bush to sustain his early October momentum. Stanley Greenberg did not offer confirmatory evidence in his discussion of polling, however. Bush's polling showed that the Medicare attacks were effective at blunting Gore's advantage on the issue but had little direct impact on vote choice.

While the health-care response may be too "inside baseball" to constitute a critical mistake, few observers would deny that the issue of Gore's veracity crippled his campaign (perhaps fatally). According to Bush's internal polls, evaluations of Gore's truthfulness nose-dived after the late-September and early October stories about his exaggerations. The pertinent question, then, is whether the Gore team could have dealt with these stories more effectively. I think the Gore campaign underestimated the news media's interest in stories that fit their thumbnail sketch of Gore's strengths and weaknesses. Questions had lingered since 1988 about Gore's willingness to claim credit for things he had little or nothing to do with. In truth, many of these episodes were taken out of context or simply wrong. But there was a sufficient kernel of truth in each allegation to convince the media that there was a weakness, and the Gore campaign did not appear to grasp this. Perhaps more important, the Gore team failed to follow the Clinton template: when confronted with a media feeding frenzy, attack the media's own practices. The news media are as interested in discussing themselves and their profession as anything else, and an offensive strategy questioning the media's news gathering and editorial discretion might well have worked in the fall of 2000.

The failure of a Democratic candidate to respond to GOP attacks was even more of an issue in the Kerry-Bush race. In 2004, pundits and academics were astounded by Kerry's belated response to television advertisements by the Swift Boat Veterans for Truth. The "Swifties" were an anti-Kerry 527 group, formed on March 23, 2004, by retired Rear Admiral Roy Hoffman and Vietnam veteran John O'Neill. Their specific gripes against Kerry were that he allegedly had (1) substantially exaggerated his service record and heroism in Vietnam and (2) falsely maligned the actions of his comrades and hurt the morale of the troops with his antiwar activities—especially his testimony to the U.S. Senate—upon returning home. They wanted to publicize their claims and undermine Kerry's presidential bid.

Initially, they organized a media conference at the National Press Club and issued an open letter to Kerry. But the response was disappointing. As one observer wrote, "The National Press Club (5/4/04) was a big failure. They scheduled it too early in the morning, it was way too long and mostly a mess. But more than that, their open letter to John Kerry was a big flop. Back then, the media's position was a very clear disdain for their story. Mainly the medias [sic] told them that they do not want to run stories about the Vietnam War."[7] The Swifties decided to move in a different direction: they would produce and air their own political advertisements. Furthermore, in the first ad, they would highlight the most sensational of the allegations against Kerry—that he had lied about his war record. The ads themselves—two, in total—were rolled out in early August and received little attention from the mainstream media.

The Kerry team, up in the national polls by 3 to 5 percentage points and seeking to build on the momentum of the party's Boston convention, decided to ignore the allegations. The marginality of the group, the failure of the May press conference, the posture of the elite news media, and the timing of the attacks (in August, just before the Olympics and with most Americans enjoying summer vacation) seemed to justify the Kerry team's judgment. But two factors gave the Swift Boat charges life. First, cable news outlets devoted significant time and attention to the allegations. Fox

News, in particular, considered and reconsidered the substance and significance of the ads. Second, Internet bloggers[8] fixated on the charges, disseminating them to a surprisingly large audience throughout the wired world. Ironically, by repeatedly emphasizing his service in Vietnam during the Democratic National Convention, Kerry seemed to legitimize the deconstruction of that episode of his life. The result was a public relations disaster: increasingly unfavorable views of Kerry and a drop in the polls even before the Republican convention. Kerry belatedly but aggressively answered the allegations nearly three weeks after the first ads hit.

Was the failure to immediately address the charges a mistake? Undoubtedly. Was it a mistake that could have been avoided at the time, given available information? The answer to this question is less obvious. Surely the Kerry campaign understood the need to reply to negative allegations within the same news cycle. This lesson has been part of the Campaign 101 curriculum since the Dukakis campaign. The complication was the initial reaction of the mainstream news media; if they did not intend to cover the story, why respond to cable TV inquiries and perhaps encourage wider scrutiny? Campaign manager Mary Beth Cahill and Shrum both argued not to dignify the charges with a response. But there were those who strongly suspected *at the time* that the Kerry campaign's reaction was a mistake. GOP operatives and former Clinton campaign officials openly opined that the Kerry team was making an error. More crucially, Kerry pollster Mark Mellman, communications director Stephanie Cutter, and former campaign manager Jim Jordan all saw the damage being done within the first week and pushed for a direct response. Even the vice presidential candidate was off the reservation—Edwards had wanted to start an August 5 speech with a condemnation of the Swift Boat ad but was overruled by Cahill and Shrum.

Kerry himself was soon chomping at the bit to answer the charges and was set to blister the Swift Boat Veterans for Truth in a speech to the Veterans of Foreign Wars on August 18. But his handlers on the road were ordered to restrain the candidate because the campaign brain trust was afraid he would come across as too bitter and angry. Kerry's inherent ambivalence also appears to have complicated matters even further. Evan Thomas of *Newsweek* observes,

> Kerry wanted the truth to come out, but he wanted to get it out in his own careful, deliberate way. The former prosecutor wanted to marshal the evidence, to build a case that would hold up. But that took time, and in the world of bloggers and 24/7 talking heads on cable, every day spent fact checking was a day lost. . . . The Kerry campaign did work closely with the major dailies, feeding

documents to *The New York Times*, *The Washington Post* and *The Boston Globe* to debunk the Swift Boat Vets. The articles were mostly (though not entirely) supportive of Kerry, but it was too late. The old media may have been more responsible than the new media, but they were also irrelevant. (Thomas and Staff of *Newsweek* 2004, 120)

The damage was done. By the end of August, Kerry's lead was gone and Bush had momentum heading into his New York convention. Would Bush have been ahead on Labor Day if not for the Swift Boat Veterans? It is difficult to say. Bush probably would have entered New York City behind in the polls and the bar would have been set higher. As it is, there is little doubt that the mistakes of August forced Kerry to play from behind for an entire month, with all of the negative horse race coverage that comes with being an underdog.

FIVE MISTAKES OF RECENT REPUBLICAN CAMPAIGNS

DEBATE NEGOTIATIONS AND PREPARATIONS, 2000 AND 2004

The popular perception is that George W. Bush lowers expectations heading into his public debates and then often exceeds those expectations, garnering favorable media attention and increased public support. This perception is not wholly unfounded. But planning and preparing for the presidential debates caused trouble for the Bush campaigns in both elections. In 2000, the Bush campaign misjudged news media and public reaction to debate negotiations. In 2004, it was criticized for its position on the sequencing of the debates and for apparently allowing its candidate to enter the first debate unprepared. Both times the campaign was able to recover, but the criticisms linger.

Let us first examine the debate controversy of 2000. Almost as soon as they were issued in early September, the Bush camp rejected the Commission on Presidential Debates' recommendations on the number, dates, and formats of the debates. The campaign then issued a series of debating challenges to Gore. The thinking was that the Bush team could put Gore on the defense by holding him to his earlier pledge to meet the Texas governor "anywhere, anytime" to debate the issues.

This strategy assumed that voters and the news media would not see the Commission on Presidential Debates' recommendations as carrying any particular weight or legitimacy. This assumption had some basis in fact and history. Prior to 1992, the campaigns had negotiated the terms of the debates between themselves. In 1992, the Commission on Presidential Debates, a bipartisan organization constituted to make the debate process more consistent and more efficacious for the public, offered a series of debate recommendations that were immediately agreed to by the Clinton campaign. The George H. W. Bush campaign held out for one-on-one negotiations but soon appeared to be ducking debates. This problem was exacerbated by the appearance at numerous Bush rallies of a Clinton supporter dressed like a chicken, highlighting the Democratic message that Bush was too "chicken" to debate the Arkansas governor. Bush added to this problem by verbally sparring with the chicken at his own rallies.[9] At any rate, the campaigns eventually met and hammered out a debate schedule, as they would do in 1996.

The mistake made by the Bush campaign in 2000 was that it failed to fully comprehend that the Commission on Presidential Debates had become an institutionalized part of the debate process and (more important) was seen as credible by the national news media. Thus, rejecting the commission's proposals became *the* story and took much of the steam out of Bush's subsequent challenge to meet Gore early and often in a series of televised debates. Compounding the error was the campaign's decision to air advertisements on the matter, which were arguably the worst (and least effective) of the fall cycle. All in all, the strategy cost the campaign time, credibility, and votes.

By early October 2004, two criticisms of the Bush team and its handling of the debates emerged. The first questioned allowing foreign policy to be the subject of the first debate. The second questioned the preparation of Bush himself, partly in terms of substance but mostly in terms of style. The first of these criticisms seems obvious only with the benefit of hindsight. The Bush campaign believed that interest and attention would be greatest for the first debate, and they wanted the most favorable terrain for the president. They presumed Kerry would be uncomfortable talking about the war on terror and clarifying his position on Iraq. He might, they reasoned, revert to his tendency of speaking in rambling "Senate-ese." Meanwhile, the president could use the rhetoric that had been so effective at the Republican convention. Despite their confidence in the president's mastery of the subject matter, the Bush staffers also figured that a gaffe was most likely on foreign policy, and they liked the idea of having three subsequent debates—a vice presidential and two presidential—to undo any damage. It seems to me that there is not much to fault in this line of thinking, even knowing that Bush underperformed in the first debate.

The second criticism is that the Bush team did not adequately prepare the president for Kerry, whose coolly detached yet aggressive demeanor seemed to get under Bush's skin. The notion that the campaign devoted neither sufficient time nor attention to the debate is incorrect. In the six months before the first encounter with Kerry, Bush had participated in at least four mock debates. Meanwhile, the Republican National Committee (RNC) had compiled an exhaustive portfolio on Kerry's past debates, policy statements, likely attacks, body language, and speaking tendencies. Its conclusion was that Kerry had been a remarkably consistent debate performer, rarely hitting a home run but almost never striking out. Bush and the campaign were also briefed by former Massachusetts governor Bill Weld, whom Kerry had vanquished in a 1996 senate race. Weld testified that Kerry "had the nerves of a burglar" and "would say almost anything" without flinching (Thomas and Staff of *Newsweek* 2004). Finally, the campaign had Senator Judd Gregg of New Hampshire play Kerry in Bush's debate preparation, during which he attempted to affect Kerry's air of superiority.

In spite of this groundwork, there appears to have been little sense of urgency in the lead-up to the debate. Indeed, several accounts of the morning walk-through prior to the University of Miami debate noted the casual and confident mood of Bush's advisers. Moreover, even if some supporters were nervous about Kerry coming at Bush, few in the Bush camp were willing and able to candidly warn the president to avoid the defensive and somewhat peevish posture he had assumed in his April 2004 press conference. Bush was a wartime president with a no-nonsense, CEO management style who was coming off a successful convention and held a small but steady lead in the polls. Only Rove and perhaps Karen Hughes had the standing to issue a warning, but neither seemed to think it necessary. The mistake may therefore have been that those closest to the president had simply become accustomed to an aspect of his personality that voters found unattractive.

Bush's lead went from 5 percentage points to a single point in the days after the first debate. It is thus tempting to conclude that his performance—and the campaign's failure to have him at his best—allowed Kerry to climb back into the race. I think the debate was surely the stimulus for this development, but it is also probable that Kerry would have closed on Bush anyway. Recall from chapter 5 that Bush's support was remarkably stable throughout early October, whereas Kerry expanded his vote from 44 percent to 48 percent. Looking beneath the surface, it is also clear that those who moved to Kerry following the debate were strongly predisposed to support him—by large majorities, they disapproved of Bush's handling of his job and believed the Iraq War was a mistake. In short, in the first debate Kerry provided a reassuring option for voters who were looking to vote against Bush. The suddenness of the movement created a buzz that drove news media coverage for a few days, however, which might have cost Bush additional support.

TAKING FLORIDA (2000) AND OHIO (2004) FOR GRANTED

The argument that Bush could have done more in Florida in 2000 is correct, but the story is more complex than most people realize. Contrary to some accounts, Bush did campaign aggressively in Florida. From chapter 4 we know that Bush significantly outspent Gore on TV advertising in Florida and came close to matching Gore's stump activity in the state. It is true, however, that Bush's early activities in the state were primarily designed to raise money and did not emphasize energizing the Republican organization or establishing a favorable political reputation. Rove made exactly this point in reviewing the 2000 campaign at the Annenberg conference. The result was that Bush never pulled ahead of Gore by more than 5 percentage points or so in the early polls, practically daring Gore to make a significant play for the state. Gore did so, and Bush lacked the head start and infrastructure he needed to put the state out of reach.

The case of Ohio in 2004 revolves around a scheduling mystery: Bush did not make an appearance in Ohio for nineteen days, from October 3 through 21. On October 22, he made an appearance in Canton but then left the state again. The contrast with Kerry, who made four appearances during that time, was striking. An October 22 report on National Public Radio's *Day to Day* program noted that Ohio Democrats were using words such as *inexplicable* and *bizarre* to describe Bush's absence. Speculation was running rampant that Bush either (1) thought he had the state won, or (2) was conceding. No one was sure which was true.

The truth here is less interesting than the speculation. Bush's schedule, tight to begin with, tightened even more after his poorly received performance in the first debate. The campaign decided not to add any Ohio stops because the state was being blanketed with surrogates during this period of time—including Cheney, California governor Arnold Schwarzenegger, and Secretary of State Condoleeza Rice—and Bush was slated to return several times in the last two weeks. Bush's tracking polls did not show any discernible movement in the race during this time (except for a slight dip at the very end), reinforcing the decision and reducing the clamor for an additional visit. Despite some bad press, there appears to be no empirical reason to think the "nineteen missing days" affected the outcome.

NOT ADMITTING MISTAKES, 2004

Some voters and many reporters were concerned about Bush's apparent lack of interest in critically reviewing his actions as president. In a prime-time news conference on April 13, 2004, Bush was asked repeatedly by reporters whether he had made any mistakes in interpreting intelligence information before the terrorist attacks of 9/11 or in handling the Iraq War. Bush demurred. This response prompted a rash of stories, some implying that Bush's "refusal" to admit mistakes demonstrated ignorance and arrogance. Even some of Bush's supporters cringed. Why couldn't the president offer up one or two instances in which he had made a mistake by, for example, trusting certain people? (The name George Tenet, director of the CIA, came up consistently in conversations with these supporters.) Doing so would defuse the issue without reflecting badly on the president.

The "mistake" issue cropped up again in the fall campaign. A young woman posed the following question in the final minutes of the second presidential debate, held on October 8 in St. Louis: "Please give three instances in which you came to realize you had made a wrong decision, and what you did to correct it." Bush suggested that the question was really about Iraq and went on to defend his positions and his approach to making decisions. The next day, he was once again criticized for his response by newspaper reporters and morning talk show hosts.

This was an instance in which the campaign was subservient to the candidate. In particular, there were two factors driving Bush's response to the "mistake" question. First, and most important, Bush seems to genuinely disdain what he has called "Monday morning quarterbacking." He appears to believe extensive retrospection undermines your willingness to make a decision in the first place. From Bush's frame of mind, current problems require one to focus on what to do next, not what could have been done earlier. Second, Bush believed that identifying a "mistake" would have produced a front-page, above-the-fold story in the New York Times (not to mention all the other elite news media outlets). This belief, in fact, led to a self-fulfilling prophecy: the more reluctant Bush was to admit a mistake, the more likely such an admission, were it to be made, would be a huge news story.

But did the lack of an admission cost Bush votes? On the one hand, Bush's "leadership" and "intelligence" ratings were largely unaffected by the April 13 press conference and the October 8 debate. Furthermore, in response to the National Election Study's open-ended question "What do you dislike about George W. Bush?" almost no one cited his reluctance to admit a mistake. On the other hand, public polls showed that Bush scored much lower than Kerry on "willing to admit a mistake" items and that the two were about even on who was more "forthright" (a somewhat vague measure that Bush had typically scored very well on). In addition, Bush's advantage over Kerry on measures of "who is a better leader" was slightly reduced by the October 8 debate. In sum, Bush's lack of introspection and the subsequent media reaction probably cost him votes.

WASTING TIME AND MONEY IN CALIFORNIA, 2000

This is perhaps the most common criticism of Bush's 2000 campaign. In my opinion, it is also enormously overblown. Let me elaborate on why I think this criticism is a red herring. For starters, of the roughly six million dollars spent by the GOP in California, five million came from the RNC. Some appreciable portion of it was promised to California Victory 2000, the organizational manifestation of the national party in California, when Bush was fund-raising in 1999 and early 2000.[10] Bush's campaign made this commitment because California donors feared that Bush, like his father, would raise a large war chest in California and then forget the state during the fall campaign, leaving other GOP candidates to fend for themselves without a presence at the top of the ticket.

Ultimately, the Bush campaign, having committed the party to spending in California, decided to package the opening of the television advertising assault as a sign of Bush's national strength and willingness to take the offensive. Indeed, California constituted the second week of a three-week initiative (Tennessee was week one, while Minnesota was week three). This strategy generated a fair amount of positive free media coverage, although much of the local coverage in California played up the strategic side, insisting that Bush was not serious and that this effort was primarily an attempt to get Gore to commit resources in the Golden State (which was basically correct).

It is true that the Bush team spent approximately one million dollars of its own money in the final week of the campaign. This expenditure was made because (1) some polls showed that Bush had closed to within 6 percentage points in California and (2) there were few other targets with available TV advertising slots. Was it a mistake? Undoubtedly. Did it cost Bush a chance to push for votes in Florida, Wisconsin, Iowa, Oregon, or New Mexico? Perhaps, although it is difficult to say, since there was little or no network commercial time available in these states' media markets. The more trenchant criticism, as with Kerry in 2004, is that these funds might have been more effectively used to supplement GOTV efforts.

COASTING IN THE LAST 72 HOURS, 2000

During the final three weeks of the fall campaign, Bush continued to have downtime each day and was off the trail for some appreciable portion of one day each week. This pattern had been established early in the campaign, and Bush and his wife grew protective of their time away from the hustings. The argument in favor of continuing this practice during the homestretch was that the candidate needed this time to keep fresh and avoid the kind of fatigue-induced gaffes that could feed news cycles and prove deadly in such a close race. The argument for expanding the schedule and limiting downtime was that Bush needed to hit as many battleground states and markets as possible and that any letup could be taken as a sign of the candidate's cockiness.

What Bush actually did in the last seventy-two hours was slightly inconsistent with the popular rendition of reality. Bush did, as was reported, keep some of his schedule clear. That was a mistake. The number of events was increased, however, and visits to a host of untouched states were added. The bigger mistake, I think, was in the particular pattern of visitation. Seeking to shore up GOP congressional candidates, Bush made an East Coast swing—including a stop in New Jersey—before visiting the border South battlegrounds and Florida. The schedule was not substantially altered in spite of Thursday-night tracking polls showing the race narrowing in midwestern states such as Wisconsin and Iowa. In retrospect, a Midwest swing followed by a swing through Tennessee and Arkansas and a final stop in Florida would have made much more sense.

FIVE MISTAKES OF POLITICAL SCIENCE

Having taken a look at the "mistakes" of the campaigns, it is appropriate to critically review the alleged mistakes made by political scientists in their interpretations of the 2000 and 2004 presidential elections.

FAILING TO UNDERSTAND THE ECONOMY'S LIMITED INFLUENCE ON SUPPORT FOR THE IN-PARTY'S CANDIDATE, 2000

The most pervasive belief among academics about the 2000 election was that the race was Gore's to lose because voters, ceteris paribus, will reward the party presiding over a strong economy. Although the definition of a "strong economy" has changed over the years as data and analyses have become more sophisticated, this argument remains close to those espoused in the original works of Tufte (1978) and Fair (1978), who claimed that robust growth and/or low unemployment is the in-party's recipe for electoral victory. But the economy did not propel Gore to victory. So what happened?

Some scholars claim that Gore blew the race by not emphasizing the economy enough (Holbrook 2001; Lewis-Beck and Tien 2001; Wlezien 2001). Their models were correct, it's just that the candidate and his campaign failed to do what any reasonable, competent campaign would have done. I have already gone on record stating that I think the Gore campaign's decisions with respect to Clinton and the economy were reasonable, if controversial. More generally, I think the notion that voters would have flocked to Gore had he only primed them on economic prosperity is mistaken.

Other scholars have argued that the models were wrong, but only insofar as they overrated the health of the economy. Bartels and Zaller (2001) contend that the economy was not especially strong in the third quarter of 2000 and that a more sophisticated estimation technique based on a range of economic data accurately predicts a very close race. But voters consistently rated the economy as "excellent" or "good" during the fall of 2000. The argument that macroeconomic indicators showed the economy in decline is meaningless unless voters were aware of and understood this reality, and there is no good evidence that they did. Bartels and Zaller's contention is thus that voters told survey interviewers the economy was good but somehow perceived it as relatively weak when evaluating the choice between Bush and Gore.

It seems more likely that voters simply did not ascribe much credit to the sitting vice president when they took stock of the economy. This could be a new development, driven by voter perceptions of the nature of the dot-com economy. Or it could be a perception for which there is some distant historical precedent but little empirical data. Or it could be a combination of factors cited earlier—that the Gore campaign failed to frame the more complicated nature of the economic boom of the 1990s and did not draw connections between economic growth and governmental policies. Whatever the explanation, political science needs to reconsider the relationship between the macroeconomy and voting behavior in presidential elections.

FAILING TO UNDERSTAND PRESIDENTIAL JOB APPROVAL'S LIMITED INFLUENCE ON SUPPORT FOR THE IN-PARTY'S CANDIDATE, 2000

Like the first criticism, this one is also derived from the mispredictions of election forecasters. If, as we often hear, presidential approval explains such a large portion of the variance in voting, how did Gore end up in a dead-heat with Bush while President Clinton's approval hovered above 60 percent?

Again, one explanation is that Gore distanced himself from Clinton, severing the connection that would have allowed him to benefit from presidential approval. In other words, Gore's campaign is to blame for the models' failures. However, without revisiting the debate about Clinton's role in the campaign, it is worth pointing out that Gore *never* seemed to benefit from his association with Clinton, even before his coming-out party at the Democratic convention. In the fall of 1999, Bush led Gore by at least a dozen points in the national polls, while most hypothetical trial ballots between Bush and Clinton showed a neck and neck race and several had Clinton ahead. Of course, Gore could have bear-hugged Clinton to force the connection, but Gore had done so (literally and figuratively) following Clinton's impeachment, and Gore's favorability ratings dipped more than Clinton's.

The more likely explanation is that the impact of presidential job approval on the vote is more complicated than the models would have us believe. Two specific complications existed in 2000. Initially, although Clinton's job approval numbers were quite strong, his personal favorability numbers were poor. It is plausible that Clinton would have underperformed were he running as a candidate in 2000 because voters believed him to be unethical. Second, Gore was only the heir to the throne, not the king. Our understanding of the transferability of presidential job approval numbers relies on the elections of 1960, 1968, and 1988. This is hardly a large enough sample to conclude that sitting vice presidents either do or do not accrue credit for their boss's performance.

FAILING TO UNDERSTAND 9 / 11, THE WAR ON TERROR, AND RALLY EFFECTS, 2004

There is a large body of research describing and explaining what is popularly known as the *rally effect* (see, e.g., Mueller 1970, 1973, 1994; Brody 1984, 1991). The basic contours of the phenomenon are simple: Americans are more supportive of the president after the country or its troops have been attacked or after the president makes a decision to commit the U.S. military to an armed conflict. The psychology of the rally effect is similarly straightforward. People feel a heightened sense of identity as Americans, a heightened sense of the president as the leader of the United States, and a heightened tendency to support his policies and view him favorably. After the terrorist attacks of September 11, 2001, this template described the mood of the country and Bush's robust approval ratings.

But while the reaction to 9/11 was consistent with the rally effects template, the magnitude of the attacks and their impact on the American public appear to have been unique. The loss of American life on 9/11 (2,986 dead) was greater than Pearl Harbor (2,403) and constituted the worst single-day violent death toll since World War II. This loss, combined with the shock of the attacks—on American soil, aimed at symbols of American strength—produced a sense of anger and outrage disproportionate even to the staggering body count.

This interpretation is manifest in both the size of the increase in Bush's approval rating after 9/11 and its durability. Bush's job approval rating rose to 90 percent for the polling period of September 21–22, 2001; it was the highest rating ever recorded by Gallup, eclipsing the marks of George H. W. Bush after the Persian Gulf War and Franklin Roosevelt after Pearl Harbor. Given the inherent tensions in American politics, and the particularly prickly state of affairs between the Republicans and Democrats since the mid-1990s, this number was extraordinary. More extraordinary, however, was the persistence of the rally effect. For January 25–27, 2002, Bush's job approval rating was 84 percent. By May 28–29, 2002, it was 77 percent. A full year after 9/11, for the period of September 13–16, 2002, an estimated 70 percent of the American public still approved of Bush's performance as president. As Bush laid out his case for going to war with Iraq, his approval rating finally dipped below 60 percent, but a second rally in the opening stages of the Iraq War pushed his rating back to 71 percent in April 2003. In fact, it was not until September 2003 that Bush's job approval numbers dropped below 60 percent, where they stayed for the duration of his first term. All told, Bush stayed well above 60 percent approval *for two years*. Neither Clinton nor Reagan had ratings that high during their first terms. Nixon, Carter, and Ford were never really close. The most comparable predecessor is George H. W. Bush, but the elder Bush's rally effect lasted only ten months—from about January to October 1991.

The implication of all this is that 9/11 and the subsequent war on terror did more than temporarily transform attitudes about the sitting president. They transformed the issue and trait calculus voters use to evaluate leaders. The issues of security and defense, largely dormant since the end of the cold war, reemerged in a distinct form. The fear of nuclear annihilation was replaced by a fear of a random and personal attack. And how does this fear affect the psychology of voters? A recent article by David Glenn in *The Chronicle of Higher Education* (Glenn 2004) pulls together a number of studies to suggest that 9/11 has had a transforming effect on voters but that the candidates and parties have yet to fully come to grips with it. Glenn argues that research by social psychologists shows that if people are haunted by concerns about their own mortality, they act very differently than do otherwise similar people who have not been prompted to think about death. At the political level, those concerned about death are more likely to prefer "charismatic" (as opposed to "relationship oriented" or "task oriented") leaders. And in studies in which people were asked about real-world candidates, the mortality-conscious participants were much more likely than their peers to prefer George W. Bush to John Kerry.

Glenn points out, however, that despite the consistency of the experimental results and the stunning agreement among social psychologists about the effects of mortality anxiety on political behavior, political scientists are intrigued but skeptical. This timidity seems misplaced. Although some skepticism is warranted—we do not know how laboratory experiments translate into the real world of voting—the research coming out of social psychology is much more interesting than the rehashing of the rally effects literature presently occurring in political science. If we are to help elites and ordinary citizens make sense of politics, our tasks are to (1) theoretically and empirically document the changes in issue agendas and trait considerations that occurred as a result of the attacks of 9/11, and (2) gauge the extent to which either the Republicans or the Democrats have been more effective in adjusting to this new climate. If we tackle the first task and find that nothing has changed, then we can conclude that the impact of 9/11 is akin to a singular rally effect. Otherwise, more appropriate explanations and theories ought to be developed and tested.

FAILING TO PUBLICLY SCRUTINIZE PUNDIT-DRIVEN CONVENTIONAL WISDOMS, 2004

Ideally, political scientists are most valuable when they bring theoretical and empirical rigor to otherwise ad hoc debates on topics such as democratization, revolutions, and (yes) voting. Unfortunately, the discipline was almost completely absent in 2004 as a number of contentious observations garnered an enormous amount of attention on cable television, political Internet sites, and even the more "respectable" Sunday morning talk shows. Part of the trouble is that political scientists are not often asked to weigh in on elections because we tend not to speak in sound bites or see things as black or white. Part of the trouble is that we can also be unresponsive to the topics of the day, as our research often takes months (not days) and focuses on larger issues that may not be immediately relevant for the 24/7 news crowd. But that does not excuse our performance in 2004, as the news media *did* ask us about a number of issues on which there *is* relevant political science research.

For example, after the debates, pundits began to state that Bush was going to lose the election unless he garnered at least 50 percent in the trial ballot questions on public opinion surveys. The argument was that incumbent vote shares always fall within a point or two of their poll numbers because they are well known and unlikely to attract the support of undecided voters or those leaning toward the challenger. This contention was coupled with the related argument that undecided voters always break for the challenger. The contentious extension of these arguments was that Kerry should be treated as the front-runner and Bush should be viewed as the candidate "in trouble" because Bush's average lead in the polls was "only" 48 percent to 46 percent.

Setting aside the implications for handicapping the race, there is scant empirical evidence for the "50 percent rule" for incumbent presidents. Most of those espousing this rule simply asserted that it is well known among consultants and holds in legislative races. The extrapolation to presidential elections was purely a matter of faith, since we had never had an incumbent polling so close to 50 percent so late in the campaign. (During the modern polling era, 2004 is unique. Previously, we only had landslide victories—Eisenhower, Johnson, Nixon, Reagan, and Clinton—and landslide defeats—Carter and George H. W. Bush. Ford was the sitting president but not an incumbent seeking reelection.)

Given this, I examined National Election Study (NES) data to gauge the accuracy of the claim that undecided voters always break for the challenger. In fact, since 1948, those undecided in the preelection wave of the NES have voted only 48 percent to 44 percent for the challenger. If one narrows the frame to those who say they did not decide until the last week, the challenger's edge is only 47 percent to 44 percent. It was therefore not surprising to me when late deciders split about evenly in 2004. Yet many fell into the trap of believing the punditry's assertions. Even the Gallup Poll fell prey, allocating more than 80 percent of undecided voters in its final preelection poll to Kerry and turning a Bush lead of 49 percent to 47 percent into a tie.

Perhaps an even more prominent claim was that "security moms" drove Bush's lead in the polls. News reports intimated that suburban, socially moderate women had moved toward Bush because of their fears about terrorism in the aftermath of 9/11. The story was very attractive. Supposedly, it even had empirical support. The problem was that none of this empirical support was made public. Nor did the basic idea comport with recent evidence from political science (most notably, Kaufmann and Petrocik 1999) that the so-called gender gap is largely attributable to the movement of men away from the Democratic Party.

Where was political science on these and other such matters? Unfortunately, when asked about them, we rarely called for (let alone provided) empirical tests. To be fair, reporters often have a story line when they call academics and sometimes are not above pulling the most "useful" quote out of an extensive conversation. But when talking to reporters, I believe we political scientists are also prone to lapsing into a kind of "shop talk" that emphasizes short-term, atheoretical intuitions—exactly what we guard against in our professional research. The remedy is to emphasize, and better communicate, the broader theoretical concepts and specific empirical studies that ought to interest any political audience. In other words, we ought to trust both reporters and consumers to prefer first-rate social science to second-rate punditry.

THINKING OF CAMPAIGNS AS DETERMINISTIC, 2000 AND 2004

One critical assumption behind all of the forecasting models is that campaigns are the vehicles through which voters become aware of factors that will ultimately lead them to support one candidate over the other. A less-obvious but nonetheless critical second assumption is that external context severely circumscribes the abilities of the campaigns to effect additional movement (Gelman and King 1993). In other words, voters need only a nominal push from the campaign to get where they "ought to be," but it is almost impossible to get more support than reality suggests you are entitled to. Campaigns are assumed to be competent, and the only way for the models to produce inaccurate results is for a campaign to be incompetent. (Supercompetence is not, from this perspective, rewarded.) To be accurate, it is both context and the activities of the other campaign that limit the potential for support beyond these circumscribed levels. Still, the notion is that campaigns easily get the electorate to a certain point but struggle mightily to push support beyond this level.

Two problems exist with this perspective. First, although it is quite plausible that campaigns are equally competent in some aggregate sense, it is decidedly less plausible that they are equal in a given year. I doubt that Democrats or Republicans are inherently better at campaigning, but I am dubious that there are no differences in a given election cycle. Put another way, the volume of campaigning may be roughly equal (although we have seen that discrepancies can and do occur), but the quality of the TV ads, issue appeals, and free media strategies may not be. A second problem is the indifference this perspective shows toward how campaigns effect "predicted" movement. The reality is that some appeals work, while others do not. Moreover, the nature of successful appeals is important—it tells candidates something about the preferences of voters and makes candidates accountable to voters.

BORROWING CONCEPTS

While I admit to occasionally enjoying recriminations for their own sake, I genuinely believe that critical overviews are essential to improved performance on the part of both practitioners and political scientists. Continued cross-fertilization between political backrooms and the ivory tower should also be mutually beneficial. In this vein, and thinking ahead to the next few election cycles, what can each side offer the other?

FROM POLITICAL SCIENCE, WITH LOVE

Given questions about the Bush administration's plans to reform Social Security and the Democrats' thoughts on national security and defense, campaigns would be well advised to read John Petrocik's theory of "issue ownership" (Petrocik 1996). As mentioned in chapter 2, Petrocik argues that parties tend to spend a disproportionate amount of time talking and thinking about issues that are critical to building and maintaining their electoral coalitions. They build credibility on these issues and do well when voters consider them important. More concretely, the Democrats "own" issues such as health care, the environment, Social Security and Medicare, and civil rights, while Republicans "own" issues such as national defense, taxes, and crime.

But Petrocik's critical point for consultants is that campaigns tend to succeed when they concentrate on raising the salience of issues that they own. Conversely, when they focus on the other party's issues, they face a disadvantageous distribution of opinion and run the risk of being "outbid" in policy terms. For example, a Republican initiative on Medicare is almost sure to be met by a more ambitious Democratic proposal, putting the GOP candidate in a position of opposing the more "serious" policy.

Interestingly, while George H. W. Bush followed this recipe religiously in 1988—Lee Atwater was, in fact, an early and fervent convert to Petrocik's idea—both Clinton in 1996 and Bush in 2000 appeared to have strayed from the theory. Clinton focused on crime in 1996, boasting of his plan to put one hundred thousand new cops on the street. In the wake of school shootings, he also repeatedly emphasized his support for gun control legislation. George W. Bush took a page out of Clinton's playbook when he made education one of his core issues for 2000. Bush often talked about programs he had introduced or backed in Texas and how these programs could inform the federal government's education policy. Bush made particular points about the need for standardized tests, greater accountability, and an end to "social promotion."[11]

The common denominator between Clinton and Bush is that both faced issues that could not be ignored, and both attempted to reframe the issues in a way that was relatively advantageous. When discussing crime, Clinton focused on funding police services, and Democrats traditionally fare better with the public than Republicans do when it comes to spending initiatives. He also focused on gun control, perhaps the only aspect of the crime issue where Democrats have a natural public opinion advantage over Republicans. Bush turned the debate on education from one of funding, where GOP candidates usually face a losing battle, to one of accountability and standards. The lesson for the future is that it may be possible to issue trespass, but only if you can successfully reframe the issue in a way that negates a disadvantageous distribution of opinion (see Sides 2003 for a more detailed critique of issue ownership).

A second concept that campaigns ought to borrow from political science concerns research design: the field experiment. Field experiments offer a means to realistically gauge the likely success of campaign activities. For example, one of the central questions facing future presidential campaigns is how resources ought to be allocated. The traditional approach has been to emphasize television advertising. But this approach may be on the way out. As I touched on earlier, labor unions and other interest groups made a concerted decision in the mid-1990s to direct their resources towards in-person, face-to-face contacts. The Republicans, in fact, were so concerned with the prospect of falling behind the Democrats in this capacity that they commissioned a 72-Hour Plan to develop and test the impact of more aggressive fieldwork. But how do you measure the success of these activities? Is the conventional wisdom about the success of the labor unions' activities correct? Was the Republicans' 72-Hour Plan a major part of GOP success in 2002 and 2004? And how are we to evaluate the success of other innovative campaign initiatives? If this study shows anything, it is the difficulty any researcher has in attempting to isolate the effects of a specific campaign stimulus. Field experiments in which different campaign efforts (or *treatments*) are randomly assigned to counties, towns, or precincts could be employed to estimate the relative success of outreach plans.

Field experiments have, of course, been around a long time. But we do not have many applications gauging the effects of large-scale campaign activities. Among the best is the work of Alan Gerber and Donald Green (2000) on the effects of direct mail and phone calls in an Oregon statewide initiative election (also see Gerber and Green's 2001 study of mobilization contacting in New Haven, Connecticut). Many consultants are familiar with this study, though no one has fully exploited the template outlined therein. Some tentative forays in this direction have been made, however. The Republicans used the 2001 Virginia gubernatorial election and a handful of special elections to test the effects of their proposed 72-Hour Plan. They applied various contacting plans in certain precincts and then compared results with those for control precincts that received no comparable activity.[12] In addition, the 2006 reelection campaign of Texas governor Rick Perry consulted with Gerber and Green to use field experiments to test fund-raising outreach, candidate appearances, and television advertising messages. As we move beyond the 2000 and 2004 campaigns, it appears that the parties will conduct extensive tests of voter contacting programs and that the natural design for these tests is the field experiment.

The third political science concept that might be usefully adopted by practitioners is a methodological innovation. In political science, a number of studies were conducted during the late 1990s that envisioned fully informed electorates (see, e.g., Althaus 1998; Bartels 1996). The methodology is reasonably simple: take voters with the highest levels of political knowledge and information and use them to impute the preferences of unsophisticated voters who otherwise look like them. Researchers can then recalculate the distribution of candidate support under conditions of full information. Interestingly, the aforementioned Bartels and Althaus studies reached somewhat different conclusions on the partisan implications of a fully informed electorate, mostly because Althaus included nonvoters in his analysis and Bartels did not. But the main implication for practitioners is that one can anticipate the distribution of opinion and preferences under different information conditions. Furthermore, one can adjust the candidate's strategy accordingly, an attractive possibility for consultants.

LOOTING AND PILLAGING THE REMNANTS
OF PRESIDENTIAL CAMPAIGNS

If political science has a few conceptual insights that might benefit campaigns, campaigns also have some ideas that might usefully advance the understanding of voting and elections in political science.

First, the concept of swing voting is something that has miraculously escaped the empirical scrutiny of scholars. I have attended conferences and seminars where the term *swing voters* was tossed around as loosely as on any cable TV news show. The difference is that political science is supposed to demand definitional precision and conceptual clarity. And it is not that we find the notion trivial. Political science has focused extensively on political independents, moderates, undecided voters, ticket-splitters, and "floating voters." We are clearly enamored with the idea that certain voters are more persuadable and therefore disproportionately important for our understanding of close elections. Furthermore, the notion of swing voters has become more interesting since 1992 because, in the wonderful phrase coined by Michael Barone, we are currently a "49 percent nation" (Barone 2001). With national elections so closely contested, swing voters are (almost by definition) the decisive segment of the electorate. But we are not quite sure what we want to say on the matter.

The news media, by contrast, know exactly what they want to say. In 1994, the media took the marketing phrase "angry white males" and used it repeatedly in its analyses of the Gingrich-led GOP takeover of Congress. In 1996, 1998, and 2002, the media offered us "soccer moms," "waitress moms," and "office park dads," respectively. Clearly, the news media understand the value of a clever label and a quick and easy answer to the electoral question, "why?"

But what should not be lost in the news media's tendency to oversimplify is that campaign professionals do, in fact, have a clear and concise understanding of swing voters. Swing voting is actually an aggregate-level phenomenon, defined as the difference between the maximum and minimum party vote for a particular office over a defined set of elections. So, for example, it is easy to compute the swing voting rates for California counties for presidential elections from 1980 through 2000. In all likelihood, you would be taking Reagan's 1984 percentage (presumably the GOP high) and subtracting Bush's 1992 percentage (the low).

The individual-level analogue would be to determine an individual's voting history for a particular type of election across some subset of years. Voters who do not have a strong tendency to support candidates from one side would be classified as swing voters. Unfortunately, this kind of study requires panel data, something we rarely have in political science. What we could do, however, is model the vote for a number of presidential elections and use these models to interpolate the votes of survey respondents for other elections.[13] The result would allow political science to add to the otherwise anecdotal debate on swing voting and swing voting groups.

A second area in which campaigns could help political science has to do with voter lists. I have yet to be involved in a campaign where someone, at some time, did not bemoan the condition of the voter list. What are voter lists? As the name implies, they are lists of registered voters, complete with demographic information, some vote history, campaign contribution history (if any), and perhaps even a listing of important memberships (such as to a gun club, labor union, or sportsmen's association). Good voter lists are updated frequently, taking into account new information, especially the entrance and exit of eligible voters. These lists are used to identify voters to be persuaded and/or mobilized during the campaign.

Voter lists could also be invaluable to political scientists for two reasons. First, they give us information on whom the campaigns targeted. If we want to gauge the effects of direct mail, phone, and person-to-person contacting, we need to know who was exposed to this campaigning; voter lists would facilitate this knowledge. Second, these lists can be coupled with aggregate-level data on campaign resource allocations to create a precise sense of the geographical spread (or concentration) of campaigning. Gimpel (2003) has pioneered this research in many ways, and the idea that location matters in politics has great attraction.

Third, campaigns routinely use *dial groups* (or "perception analyzers") to augment their qualitative analyses of voters' perceptions. Dial groups would be a useful addition to the experimental and focus group designs that have been incorporated into political science research since the early 1990s. A dial group is, in some ways, an enhanced focus group. Dial groups involve from ten to forty people, recruited by mall intercepts, with little or no attempt to achieve any kind of random representation. Instead, these groups are intentionally stacked with people who meet, or claim to meet, a certain profile. Most commonly, campaigns recruit uncommitted voters, intentionally seeking to gauge their reactions to a variety of aspects of electioneering. Campaigns routinely test television ads, stump speeches, debate performances, and other visual stimuli with these groups. Their distinctive feature is that participants turn *dials*, knobs calibrated on a scale from 0 to 100, to register their reaction to whatever it is that they are seeing. Those conducting the dial group thus get a continuous measure of voter response to particular appeals, comparisons, and attacks.

If an academic study were to employ this technology, it could be used to estimate the impact of specific campaign events or appeals on key voting groups. To meet the standards of social science, the question of representativeness would have to be squarely addressed. Perhaps more people, selected through a more rigorous, random process, could be recruited. This modification would at least partially deal with the difficulty of inferring results to the population. There is also the question of the durability of effects, which could be addressed by follow-up surveys. But the possibility for more precise measurements of voters' responses to particular statements, images, or appeals is enormously enticing.

PREDICTING FUTURE DEVELOPMENTS IN PRESIDENTIAL CAMPAIGNS

Much of this chapter has considered weaknesses, and the potential for improvement, in the study of presidential campaigns. If there is an overriding theme, it is that the story is more complicated than previously appreciated. Or it may be that the story *has become* more complicated than earlier explanations suggested. This means that we will need better theory, additional data, and more innovative designs to assess the role of presidential campaigns in the future. One downside to pursuing this approach is that it suggests breaking down and complicating elegant theories of elections and voting.

As for predicting what we will see, the trouble with prognostications in the area of elections and election studies is that neither campaigns nor political science can be counted on to behave predictably. My emphasis, therefore, has been on *likely* or even *possible* areas where one side will acknowledge the useful work of the other. But I think both political scientists and political practitioners would also agree that presidential campaigns and those who study them *should* do certain things in the next few elections.[14] I forthwith present a number of trends that are likely to continue or even accelerate, in no particular order.

A DECREASED EMPHASIS ON TELEVISION ADVERTISING

Mark McKinnon, Bush's media adviser, and Matthew Dowd, Bush's campaign strategist, predict that TV advertisements will be less important in the 2008 presidential election than they were in 2000 or 2004. Democratic media adviser Bill Knapp agrees. The reasons are multiple. First, it is increasingly difficult to reach voters given the proliferation of cable TV channel options. Second, these same options allow voters to avoid commercials, as do technological innovations such as digital video recorders (DVRs) and TiVo. Third, saturation advertising on network shows has probably had deleterious consequences for voters' tolerance of political advertising. Fourth, other outlets for political communication have recently become—or are seen as—more viable. Most notably, there are newer vehicles such as e-mail and blogs, and older vehicles such as door-to-door contacting. Speaking of which, we should also see . . .

AN INCREASED EMPHASIS ON PERSONAL CONTACTING

This prediction is an extension of the discussion of the strategic shifts of the labor unions and the Republican Party's development of its 72-Hour Plan. Perhaps the core concept is that mobilization is *the* critical component to contemporary elections and that mobilization is best accomplished through personal contacting. Equally important are the assumptions that (1) television advertising has become decreasingly effective at reaching and affecting voters, and (2) the costs of personal contacting have decreased with the development of targeting and data collection technologies. Democratic precinct walkers, for example, are easily recruited from college campuses and labor unions and are routinely given Palm Pilots so they can enter data on households they visit. For the Republicans, the costs are higher because they have fewer supporters willing to walk precincts. Furthermore, their supporters tend to be less geographically concentrated than the Democrats, who are often clustered in urban locales. Still, the GOP recruited 1.4 million volunteers for the 2004 election and continues to invest heavily in this old-school form of campaigning.[15]

AN INCREASED EMPHASIS ON UNDERSTANDING
THE CONNECTION BETWEEN CANDIDATES
OR CAMPAIGNS AND THE NEWS MEDIA

Here is a trend that ought to be manifest in both academic and practitioner research. There is a general consensus that candidates help drive the issue agenda of the news media. Content analyses of the elite news media have borne this point out consistently since 1988 (Hayes 2005; Lichter and Farnsworth 2003; Lichter and Noyes 1996; Patterson 1993). But candidates and campaigns have not had universal success in advancing their issue agendas. Certain issue initiatives do not gain widespread coverage or do so in a way that emphasizes the strategic (rather than the substantive) rationale behind them. In 2000, Bush repeatedly focused attention on his plan to "rebuild" the military and bolster national defense, but this issue rarely appeared on the front page of the nation's elite newspapers. Why? What tactics are more or less successful in advancing a candidate's issue agenda? Or are agendas constrained by external reality in a way that minimizes what the campaign can do? What frames are most appealing? We know a great deal about the news media, but little attention has been focused on how candidates effectively advance and frame their agendas. Both campaigns and political science ought to focus on this dynamic.

OBTAINMENT OF BETTER DATA ON A
WIDE VARIETY OF CAMPAIGNING

This trend is already occurring and should only accelerate. We now routinely gather data on television advertising and candidate appearances, matching them with public opinion data (e.g., Althaus, Nardulli, and Shaw 2002; Goldstein and Freedman 2002a, 2002b; Shaw 1999a). We also collect and code all of the candidates' speeches and public utterances, giving us the opportunity to analyze their content and compare them with contemporaneous and subsequent press coverage.

But as campaigns begin to take advantage of new technologies and older proven practices, the range of data ought to improve. We should begin to see data collection on phone calls, direct mail, personal contacting, e-mail contacting, and possibly other campaign efforts. The limitations here are (1) the campaign's willingness to collect and preserve this information, and (2) political scientists' ability to put together the resources to track this information flow. The former strikes me as more daunting, as it now appears probable that academics will be able to track the dollars allocated for these activities and conduct preliminary analyses of impact. Research of this sort would almost assuredly enhance our understanding of the influence of political information on opinion and behavior.

OBTAINMENT OF BETTER DATA ON
OPINIONS ACROSS THE CAMPAIGN

Again, this trend is already occurring and is likely to accelerate. Data are now being acquired from the campaigns, as well as from academic sources apart from the NES. I have already described the efforts by researchers at Annenberg, Stanford (Knowledge Networks), and Pew, and my thoughts on the merits of their studies should be obvious.

At the aggregate level, James Stimson (1995, 2004) has developed a smoothed time series model of vote choice based on publicly available, national polling data. Similarly, Erikson and Wlezien (1999) have developed time series estimates of candidate support that allow them to measure the effects of specific campaign events. These efforts take advantage of the proliferation of public polls and sophisticated time series methodologies to construct more precise estimates of daily fluctuations in popular opinion, which, in turn, aid our attempts to model the influence of campaigning.

The irony is that these projects have come as the grandfather of election surveys, the National Election Study, has been scaled back. Of course, this is not necessarily a bad thing for the study of campaigns. The NES, which is at least partly responsible for the behavioral revolution in political science and continues to serve as a popular reservoir of data, has in some ways encouraged the neglect of presidential campaigns. The empirical findings of voting behavior that draw on the NES, some based on problematic recall measures, have led us to focus on other explanatory variables when examining presidential elections. The budget crises of 1991–1992 and 2002–2003 have somewhat clouded the future of the NES, however, while encouraging voting behavior entrepreneurs to explore other measures of vox populi.[16]

MORE SYSTEMATIC ATTEMPTS TO MEASURE THE QUALITY (NOT THE QUANTITY) OF CAMPAIGNS

It would probably surprise people to learn that political scientists are reluctant to judge the quality of campaign activities, but we are. Practitioners are less reluctant, but their judgments are often tainted by self-interest. Everyone would agree, however, that campaign analyses need a measuring stick of quality that goes beyond whether or not you win. A TV ad might be excellent and yet not move voters because of situational factors. Similarly, a poor TV ad might move voters simply because they were predisposed to move. The problem, of course, is the question of endogeneity: how do you assess the quality of campaigning *if not* by looking for favorable movement in the polls?

Three possibilities occur. First, one could use poll movement as the dependent variable but concentrate on more effective measurement of the different *types* of TV ads, candidate appearances, and contextual variables. Estimates of the consequent variance in effects could be quite instructive. Second, experiments (or field experiments) could be conducted on particular ads or speeches to isolate their effects. The complication is that doing so would require random assignment of voters to control and treatment groups—and (presumably) plenty of advance warning. Third, subjective assessments of TV ad or speech quality could be made by scholars and entered as explanatory variables in multivariate models of effects. There are downsides to each of these approaches, but the importance of campaign quality to our understanding of influence and the dearth of data on the subject are such that these sorts of studies would be welcome.

DISTINCTIONS BETWEEN CANDIDATES AND THEIR CAMPAIGNS

A small but important point raised earlier is that campaigns (and their effects) are not the same as candidates. The candidate is the chief resource of the campaign and is the vehicle through which campaign appeals are made. But elections are about people, and the personal qualities of the candidate influence how voters decide. The campaign is responsible for putting the candidate in a position to succeed, but candidates can fail (or succeed) in spite of the best efforts of the campaign.

This point is sometimes lost by consultants and academics. Contrary to the received wisdom, for example, I think the Gore 2000 campaign was good but that Al Gore was a poor candidate. Conversely, George W. Bush has not received enough credit for the success of his candidacy. This general observation is even more obvious for past candidates: Bill Clinton and Ronald Reagan were so skilled that they made their campaigns look good even when the campaigns' decisions were dubious.

✳ ✳ ✳

In sum, I believe there is a good chance that all of these developments will be realized to some degree over the next few election cycles. Most have already begun to come true, and all are driven by a core set of professional realities that exist for both political science and political consulting. Political scientists are driven not only by the search for truth but also by publishing opportunities within the discipline. Admittedly, these "market incentives" are muted compared to those in other professions. Still, university publishers and the top journals are always interested in analyses of political behavior, and the role of campaigns in shaping behavior remains an understudied area. Political consultants, by comparison, are even easier to peg; they want to land clients and win elections. The developments predicted here thus stand a good chance of realization since all are consistent with more efficient, effective campaigns.

It is this confluence of incentives that has produced some of the increased interaction between the practical work of campaign professionals and the broader studies of political scientists. Although the trail can be traced to 1988, the 2000 and 2004 elections represent important points for such collaboration. The exchange of data and ideas both during and after these elections was largely informal and often uneasy, but my strong sense is that academics and professionals are now positioned to systematically monitor the outputs of each other. This is a good thing and can only enhance our understanding of presidential campaigns and other electoral processes.

APPENDIX 1

TELEVISION ADVERTISING BY MEDIA
MARKETS, 2000 AND 2004

STATE/DMA	BUSH/RNC	GORE/DNC	CUM. GRP DIFF. (REP. − DEM.)	BUSH/RNC	KERRY/DNC	REP. SPECIAL INT.	DEM. SPECIAL INT.	CUM. REP.	CUM. DEM.	CUM. GRP DIFF. (REP. − DEM.)
Arizona										
Phoenix	0	0	0	1,379	0	0	0	1,379	0	1,379
Tucson	0	0	0	1,378	0	0	0	1,378	0	1,378
Yuma	0	0	0	0	0	0	0	0	0	0
Statewide average	0	0	0	1,320	0	0	0	1,320	0	1,320
Arkansas										
Jonesboro	16,451	11,637	4,814	633	0	0	600	633	600	33
Fort Smith–Fayetteville–Springdale–Rogers	24,270	20,019	4,250	750	0	875	1,150	1,625	1,150	475
Little Rock–Pine Bluff	24,175	23,348	827	751	0	650	1,200	1,401	1,200	201
Shreveport, LA	0	0	0	0	0	0	0	0	0	0
Memphis, TN	0	0	0	0	0	0	0	0	0	0
Springfield, MO	0	0	0	0	0	0	0	0	0	0
Monroe–El Dorado	0	0	0	0	0	0	0	0	0	0
Greenwood-Greenville	0	0	0	0	0	0	0	0	0	0
Statewide average	18,106	16,582	1,524	582	0	509	887	1,091	887	204
California										
Los Angeles	5,520	0	5,520	0	0	0	0	0	0	0
Sacramento-Stockton-Modesto	1,049	0	1,049	0	0	0	0	0	0	0
San Diego	773	0	773	0	0	0	0	0	0	0
San Francisco–Oakland–San Jose	606	0	606	0	0	0	0	0	0	0
Santa Barbara–San Marcos–San Luis Obispo	0	0	0	0	0	0	0	0	0	0
Fresno-Visalia	0	0	0	0	0	0	0	0	0	0
Monterey-Salinas	0	0	0	0	0	0	0	0	0	0
Chico-Redding	0	0	0	0	0	0	0	0	0	0
Bakersfield	0	0	0	0	0	0	0	0	0	0
Palm Springs	0	0	0	0	0	0	0	0	0	0
Eureka	0	0	0	0	0	0	0	0	0	0
Reno, NV	0	0	0	0	0	0	0	0	0	0
Medford, OR–Klamath Falls, OR	0	0	0	0	0	0	0	0	0	0

Yuma, AZ–El Centro	0	0	0	0	0	0	0	0	0	0
Phoenix, AZ	0	0	0	0	0	0	0	0	0	0
Statewide average	2,715	2,715	0	0	0	0	0	0	0	0
Colorado										
Denver	0	0	0	10,207	6,350	900	2,775	11,107	9,125	1,982
Colorado Springs	0	0	0	10,271	7,300	3,250	3,600	13,521	10,900	2,621
Grand Junction	0	0	0	8,582	3,550	500	3,950	9,082	7,500	1,582
Statewide average	0	0	0	10,089	6,375	1,304	2,948	11,393	9,323	2,070
Delaware										
Salisbury	13,759	12,974	785	0	0	0	0	0	0	0
Philadelphia, PA	0	0	0	0	0	0	0	0	0	0
Statewide average	2,614	2,465	149	0	0	0	0	0	0	0
Florida										
Fort Myers–Naples	19,124	2,375	16,748	12,988	7,250	2,750	7,075	15,738	14,325	1,413
Jacksonville–Brunswick, GA	16,145	2,177	13,968	13,193	7,600	3,200	7,900	16,393	15,500	893
Mobile, AL–Pensacola	26,465	12,595	13,870	9,686	2,025	2,275	2,700	11,961	4,725	7,236
Panama City	20,996	7,520	13,476	11,816	3,600	3,350	7,490	15,166	11,090	4,076
Gainesville	16,103	7,613	8,490	11,808	5,250	2,600	4,625	14,408	9,875	4,533
Miami–Fort Lauderdale	13,785	5,846	7,939	10,770	7,225	1,375	7,275	12,145	14,500	-2,355
Orlando–Daytona Beach–Melbourne	18,175	10,668	7,507	13,427	10,875	2,650	6,925	16,077	17,800	-1,723
West Palm Beach–Fort Pierce	15,159	9,695	5,463	13,814	9,920	1,125	5,525	14,939	15,445	-506
Tampa–St. Petersburg–Sarasota	14,749	10,410	4,339	13,530	11,750	2,575	8,500	16,105	20,250	-4,145
Tallahassee–Thomasville, GA	11,532	9,896	1,636	12,965	7,500	2,500	7,250	15,465	14,750	715
Statewide average	16,096	8,249	7,847	12,646	9,045	2,229	7,155	14,875	16,200	-1,325
Illinois										
Peoria-Bloomington	7,557	2,742	4,815	0	0	0	0	0	0	0
Rockford	6,161	3,454	2,706	0	0	0	0	0	0	0
Champaign-Springfield-Decatur	7,348	4,747	2,601	0	0	0	0	0	0	0
Chicago	3,960	2,199	1,762	0	0	0	0	0	0	0
Evansville, IN	843	0	843	0	0	0	0	0	0	0
Davenport, IA–Rock Island–Moline	0	0	0	0	0	0	0	0	0	0

continued

STATE / DMA	2000 BUSH / RNC	2000 GORE / DNC	2000 CUM. GRP DIFF. (REP. – DEM.)	2004 BUSH / RNC	2004 KERRY / DNC	2004 REP. SPECIAL INT.	2004 DEM. SPECIAL INT.	2004 CUM. REP.	2004 CUM. DEM.	2004 CUM. GRP DIFF. (REP. – DEM.)
Paducah, KY–Cape Girardeau, MO–Harrisberg–Mount Vernon	0	0	0	0	0	0	0	0	0	0
Quincy–Hannibal, MO–Keokuk, IA	0	0	0	0	0	0	0	0	0	0
Terre Haute, IN	0	0	0	0	0	0	0	0	0	0
St. Louis, MO	0	0	0	0	0	0	0	0	0	0
Statewide average	3,770	2,065	1,605	0	0	0	0	0	0	0
Iowa										
Davenport–Rock Island, IL–Moline, IL	33,747	28,227	5,520	11,107	7,950	7,588	7,000	18,695	14,950	3,745
Sioux City	19,624	16,073	3,550	10,974	8,425	6,038	5,740	17,012	14,165	2,847
Omaha, NE	2,782	1,008	1,773	1,801	0	0	1,950	1,801	1,950	–149
Des Moines–Ames	26,637	25,432	1,205	11,406	10,100	8,815	7,850	20,221	17,950	2,271
Ottumwa–Kirksville, MO	13,070	12,538	533	7,892	1,500	6,373	5,880	14,265	7,380	6,885
Cedar Rapids–Waterloo–Dubuque	15,682	15,587	95	11,357	8,675	8,330	8,025	19,687	16,700	2,987
Rochester, MN–Mason City–Austin, MN	5,466	6,060	–594	8,723	3,625	6,400	5,195	15,123	8,820	6,303
Quincy, IL–Hannibal, MO–Keokuk	0	0	0	0	0	0	0	0	0	0
Sioux Falls, SD–Mitchell, SD	0	0	0	0	0	0	0	0	0	0
Mankato, MN	0	0	0	0	0	0	0	0	0	0
Statewide average	20,163	18,636	1,527	9,725	7,765	6,941	6,549	16,666	14,314	2,352
Kentucky										
Lexington	10,648	0	10,648	0	0	0	0	0	0	0
Bowling Green	5,971	0	5,971	0	0	0	0	0	0	0
Cincinnati, OH	0	0	0	0	0	0	0	0	0	0
Evansville, IN	0	0	0	0	0	0	0	0	0	0
Charleston, WV–Huntington, WV	0	0	0	0	0	0	0	0	0	0

Paducah–Cape Girardeau, MO–Harrisberg, IL–Mount Vernon, IL	0	0	0	0	0	0	0	0	0	0
Louisville	7,596	1,648	5,948	0	0	0	0	0	0	0
Nashville, TN	0	0	0	0	0	0	0	0	0	0
Knoxville, TN	0	0	0	0	0	0	0	0	0	0
Statewide average	5,244	468	4,776	0	0	0	0	0	0	0
Louisiana										
Shreveport	20,445	16,199	4,246	0	0	0	0	0	0	0
Lake Charles	13,306	9,240	4,066	0	0	0	0	0	0	0
Alexandria	12,055	8,755	3,300	0	0	0	0	0	0	0
New Orleans	14,189	11,287	2,902	0	0	0	0	0	0	0
Baton Rouge	16,530	13,904	2,626	0	0	0	0	0	0	0
Monroe–El Dorado, AR	10,783	9,037	1,746	0	0	0	0	0	0	0
Lafayette	11,000	9,460	1,540	0	0	0	0	0	0	0
Statewide average	14,384	11,600	2,784	0	0	0	0	0	0	0
Maine										
Presque Isle	15,993	7,509	8,484	7,110	2,500	0	3,200	7,110	5,700	1,410
Portland–Auburn	20,361	12,709	7,652	9,084	6,200	0	4,850	9,084	11,050	-1,966
Bangor	16,700	11,123	5,578	9,677	4,575	0	7,150	9,677	11,725	-2,048
Statewide average	19,111	11,969	7,142	9,138	5,573	0	5,365	9,138	10,938	-1,800
Michigan										
Alpena	11,529	2,460	9,069	6,930	0	0	3,500	6,930	3,500	3,430
South Bend, IN–Elkhart, IN	8,796	1,332	7,464	0	0	0	0	0	0	0
Detroit	23,027	18,943	4,084	9,720	4,285	750	3,400	10,470	7,685	2,785
Marquette	29,736	26,961	2,775	10,394	3,950	0	4,100	10,394	8,050	2,344
Flint–Saginaw Bay	25,220	23,279	1,942	11,112	6,075	0	6,025	11,112	12,100	-988
Traverse City–Cadillac	31,001	30,701	301	10,543	4,200	750	5,500	11,293	9,700	1,593
Lansing	34,554	34,493	60	10,038	3,700	1,100	5,550	11,138	9,250	1,888
Toledo OH	0	0	0	0	0	0	0	0	0	0
Grand Rapids–Kalamazoo–Battle Creek	22,098	22,260	-162	10,184	6,475	750	4,750	10,934	11,225	-291
Green Bay–Appleton	0	0	0	0	0	0	0	0	0	0

continued

STATE/DMA	BUSH/RNC	GORE/DNC	CUM. GRP DIFF. (REP. – DEM.)	BUSH/RNC	KERRY/DNC	REP. SPECIAL INT.	DEM. SPECIAL INT.	CUM. REP.	CUM. DEM.	CUM. GRP DIFF. (REP. – DEM.)
Duluth, MN–Superior, WI	0	0	0	0	0	0	0	0	0	0
Statewide average	23,931	21,402	2,529	9,693	4,727	636	4,188	10,329	8,915	1,414
Minnesota										
Minneapolis	7,014	3,661	3,353	10,944	6,550	2,450	6,450	13,394	13,000	394
Duluth–Superior, WI	0	0	0	9,606	6,475	6,410	6,650	16,016	13,125	2,891
Rochester–Mason City, IA	0	0	0	8,725	3,625	6,400	5,195	15,123	8,820	6,303
Mankato	0	0	0	7,988	1,225	1,450	1,950	9,438	3,175	6,263
La Crosse, WI–Eau Claire, WI	0	0	0	11,457	6,650	8,050	11,500	19,507	18,150	1,357
Sioux Falls, SD–Mitchell, SD	0	0	0	0	0	0	0	0	0	0
Fargo, ND	1,226	0	1,226	9,100	500	400	40	9,500	580	8,920
Statewide average	5,430	2,834	2,596	10,139	5,722	2,424	5,570	12,563	11,292	1,271
Missouri										
St. Louis	24,940	19,224	5,716	1,580	0	2,300	1,500	3,880	1,500	2,380
Paducah, KY–Cape Girardeau–Harrisburg, IL–Mount Vernon, IL	22,133	17,804	4,329	1,580	0	1,600	800	3,180	800	2,380
Kansas City	14,446	10,533	3,914	1,581	0	3,200	1,050	4,781	1,050	3,731
St. Joseph	18,341	15,992	2,349	1,585	0	1,800	550	3,385	550	2,835
Quincy, IL–Hannibal–Keokuk, IA	22,188	20,286	1,901	1,578	0	2,000	900	3,578	900	2,678
Springfield	17,198	16,226	972	1,578	0	2,000	900	3,778	900	2,878
Joplin–Pittsburg, KS	18,568	17,138	830	1,580	0	2,200	900	3,780	900	2,880
Columbia–Jefferson City	24,900	25,833	-932	1,579	0	2,200	950	3,779	950	2,829
Ottumwa, IA–Kirksville	0	0	0	0	0	0	0	0	0	0
Memphis, TN	0	0	0	0	0	0	0	0	0	0
Jonesboro, AK	0	0	0	0	0	0	0	0	0	0
Omaha, NE	0	0	0	0	0	0	0	0	0	0
Des Moines, IA–Ames, IA	0	0	0	0	0	0	0	0	0	0
Statewide average	20,198	16,680	3,518	1,552	0	2,383	1,141	3,935	1,141	2,794

Nevada										
Reno	16,259	7,676	8,583	11,800	5,625	3,885	8,850	15,685	14,475	1,210
Las Vegas	15,425	5,140	7,285	12,861	8,025	4,975	11,025	17,836	19,050	-1,214
Salt Lake City, UT	0	0	0	0	0	0	0	0	0	0
Denver, CO	0	0	0	0	0	0	0	0	0	0
Statewide average	13,368	5,856	7,512	12,279	7,213	4,574	10,199	16,853	17,412	-559
New Hampshire										
Boston, MA	3,050	659	2,391	7,470	4,730	0	3,735	7,470	8,465	-995
Portland, ME–Auburn, ME	0	0	0	9,084	6,200	0	0	9,084	6,200	2,884
Burlington, VT–Plattsburgh, NY	878	113	765	7,962	250	0	1,750	7,962	2,000	5,962
Statewide average	2,617	558	2,059	7,020	3,956	0	3,282	7,020	7,238	-218
New Mexico										
Albuquerque–Santa Fe	19,881	16,452	3,368	12,358	13,650	8,725	7,350	21,083	21,000	83
El Paso, TX	0	0	0	0	0	0	0	0	0	0
Amarillo, TX	0	0	0	0	0	0	0	0	0	0
Odessa, TX–Midland, TX	0	0	0	0	0	0	0	0	0	0
Statewide average	17,284	14,346	2,938	11,054	12,065	7,573	6,445	18,627	18,510	117
North Carolina										
Charlotte	0	0	0	0	0	0	0	0	0	0
Greensboro–High Point–Winston-Salem	0	0	0	0	0	500	0	500	0	500
Atlanta, GA	0	0	0	0	0	0	0	0	0	0
Norfolk, VA–Portsmout, VA–Newport News, VA	0	0	0	0	0	0	0	0	0	0
Greenville–New Bern–Washington	0	0	0	0	0	500	0	500	0	500
Wilmington	0	0	0	0	0	150	0	150	0	150
Statewide average	0	0	0	0	0	200	0	200	0	200
Ohio										
Lima	12,886	3,490	9,396	9,918	5,900	2,450	2,595	12,368	8,495	3,873
Zanesville	12,161	2,930	9,231	7,510	3,750	1,650	2,325	9,160	6,075	3,085
Cincinnati	15,737	11,222	4,515	13,009	6,625	6,300	11,600	19,309	18,225	1,084

continued

STATE/DMA	BUSH/RNC	GORE/DNC	CUM. GRP DIFF. (REP. – DEM.)	BUSH/RNC	KERRY/DNC	REP. SPECIAL INT.	DEM. SPECIAL INT.	CUM. REP.	CUM. DEM.	CUM. GRP DIFF. (REP. – DEM.)
Youngstown	14,508	12,242	2,266	12,334	8,575	6,275	7,800	18,609	16,375	2,234
Toledo	14,993	13,307	1,686	13,452	7,350	6,160	9,265	19,612	16,615	2,997
Cleveland	12,860	11,645	1,216	13,283	8,725	4,985	8,685	18,268	17,410	858
Charleston, WV–Huntington, WV	0	0	0	11,812	6,200	0	0	11,812	6,200	5,612
Columbus	11,850	11,267	583	13,512	10,700	4,925	8,125	18,437	18,825	-388
Wheeling, WV–Steubenville	11,571	11,408	163	11,710	6,925	0	0	11,710	6,925	4,785
Dayton	10,709	11,768	-1,059	13,653	10,900	5,085	8,525	18,738	19,425	-687
Parkersburg, WV	0	0	0	0	0	0	0	0	0	0
Fort Wayne, In	0	0	0	0	0	0	0	0	0	0
Statewide average	12,624	11,132	1,492	12,493	8,354	5,018	8,392	17,511	16,746	765
Oregon										
Medford–Klamath Falls	33,448	20,215	13,233	7,122	3,175	0	2,550	7,122	5,725	1,397
Bend	29,846	18,999	10,847	6,594	450	0	1,750	6,594	2,200	4,394
Eugene	26,536	22,016	4,520	6,228	2,900	0	2,400	6,228	5,300	928
Portland	19,520	17,114	2,405	8,004	6,825	0	1,450	8,004	8,275	-271
Yakima, WA–Pasco, WA–Richland, WA–Kennewick, WA	0	0	0	0	0	0	0	0	0	0
Boise, ID	0	0	0	0	0	0	0	0	0	0
Spokane, WA	0	0	0	0	0	0	0	0	0	0
Statewide average	21,959	17,832	4,127	7,318	5,332	0	1,694	7,318	7,026	292
Pennsylvania										
Philadelphia	18,129	14,292	3,836	12,812	6,725	3,475	8,050	16,287	14,775	1,512
Harrisburg-Lancaster-Lebanon-York	16,900	13,686	3,214	11,278	8,700	5,550	4,900	16,828	13,600	3,228
Erie	28,043	25,502	2,541	12,241	4,450	4,375	7,065	16,616	11,515	5,101
Johnstown-Altoona	18,578	17,566	1,012	12,254	7,600	4,050	5,200	16,304	12,800	3,504
Wilkes-Barre–Scranton	21,854	21,465	389	12,757	8,800	5,450	8,275	18,207	17,075	1,132
Pittsburgh	15,210	14,920	291	12,868	12,200	6,175	8,130	19,043	20,330	-1,287
Youngstown, OH	0	0	0	0	0	0	0	0	0	0

Washington, DC	0	0	0	0	0	0	0	0	0	0
Buffalo, NY	0	0	0	0	0	0	0	0	0	0
Elmira, NY	0	0	0	0	0	0	0	0	0	0
New York City	0	0	0	0	0	0	0	0	0	0
Statewide average	17,518	15,310	2,208	12,127	8,267	4,570	7,191	16,697	15,458	1,239
Tennessee										
Chattanooga	6,886	4,408	2,478	0	0	0	0	0	0	0
Jackson	4,959	2,601	2,358	0	0	0	0	0	0	0
Kroxville	7,671	5,860	1,810	0	0	0	0	0	0	0
Nashville	6,474	5,519	955	0	0	0	0	0	0	0
Tri-Cities, TN-VA	5,248	5,403	-155	0	0	0	0	0	0	0
Memphis	6,356	6,670	-313	0	0	0	0	0	0	0
Pacucah, KY-Cape Girardeau, MO-Harrisburg, IL-Mount Vernon, IL	0	0	0	0	0	0	0	0	0	0
Huntsville-Decatur-Florence	0	0	0	0	0	0	0	0	0	0
Statewide average	6,456	5,536	920	0	0	0	0	0	0	0
Washington										
Yakima-Pasco-Richland-Kennewick	37,841	21,456	16,385	1,681	3,800	0	2,100	1,681	5,900	-4,219
Spokane	34,439	25,116	9,323	1,682	1,450	0	3,750	1,682	5,200	-3,518
Seattle-Tacoma	24,378	17,052	7,326	1,684	2,325	0	2,550	1,684	4,875	-3,191
Portland, OR	0	0	0	0	0	0	0	0	0	0
Statewide average	24,880	17,155	7,725	1,554	2,157	0	2,457	1,554	4,614	-3,060
West Virginia										
Pittsburgh, PA	0	0	0	0	0	0	0	0	0	0
Washington, DC	0	0	0	0	0	0	0	0	0	0
Wheeing-Steubenville, OH	0	0	0	0	0	0	0	0	0	0
Charleston-Huntington	24,167	10,973	13,194	11,812	6,200	980	6,900	12,792	13,100	-308
Clarksburg-Weston	14,299	4,214	10,085	9,192	2,950	1,090	5,100	10,282	8,050	2,232
Harrisonburg	0	0	0	0	0	0	0	0	0	0
Roanoke-Lynchburg, TN	0	0	0	0	0	0	0	0	0	0
Bluefield-Beckley-Oak Hill	18,395	10,349	8,046	8,967	2,750	1,625	6,200	10,592	8,950	1,642
Parkersburg	3,786	989	2,797	6,665	2,475	0	2,900	6,665	5,375	1,290

continued

| | 2000 | | | 2004 | | | | | | |
STATE/DMA	BUSH/RNC	GORE/DNC	CUM. GRP DIFF. (REP. − DEM.)	BUSH/RNC	KERRY/DNC	REP. SPECIAL INT.	DEM. SPECIAL INT.	CUM. REP.	CUM. DEM.	CUM. GRP DIFF. (REP. − DEM.)
Hagerstown, MD	1,793	846	947	0	0	0	0	0	0	0
Statewide average	14,362	6,445	7,917	8,514	3,878	948	4,860	9,462	8,738	724
Wisconsin										
Madison	44,704	31,988	12,716	11,423	6,000	7,050	8,300	18,473	14,300	4,173
Duluth, MN–Superior	8,665	3,686	4,979	9,606	6,475	6,410	6,650	16,016	13,125	2,891
Milwaukee	15,261	14,214	1,047	11,759	10,700	6,400	9,250	18,159	19,950	-1,791
Wausau–Rhinelander	26,281	25,951	330	11,452	6,300	8,800	8,850	20,252	15,150	5,102
Green Bay–Appleton	24,165	25,329	-1,164	12,583	12,200	6,850	12,000	19,433	24,200	-4,767
Minneapolis–St. Paul, MN	0	0	0	10,944	6,550	2,450	6,450	13,394	13,000	394
La Crosse–Eau Claire	28,913	31,507	-2,595	11,457	6,650	8,050	11,500	19,507	18,150	1,357
Waterloo, IA–Dubuque, IA	0	0	0	0	0	0	0	0	0	0
Marquette, MI	0	0	0	0	0	0	0	0	0	0
Statewide average	22,963	20,730	2,233	11,000	8,765	6,492	9,138	17,903	-411	-411
Average in battleground markets	12,799	9,486	3,313	6,416	3,660	2,089	3,654	8,403	7,167	1,235

Note: Figures represent gross rating points (GRPs).
Source: Television advertising figures are provided by the Bush-Cheney campaign and reflect purchases between August 20 and November 6, 2000, and between September 3 and November 1, 2004.

APPENDIX 2

CANDIDATE APPEARANCES BY
MEDIA MARKETS, 2000 AND 2004

STATE / DMA	2000					2004				
	BUSH	GORE	CHENEY	LIEBERMAN	APPEAR. DIFF. (REP. – DEM.)	BUSH	KERRY	CHENEY	EDWARDS	APPEAR. DIFF. (REP. – DEM.)
Arizona										
Phoenix	1	0	0	0	1	2	3	0	0	−1
Tucson–Nogales	0	0	0	0	0	0	0	0	1	−1
Yuma–El Centro	0	0	0	0	0	0	0	0	0	0
Albuquerque–Santa Fe	0	0	0	0	0	0	3	0	0	−2
State total	1	0	0	0	1	2	3	0	1	−2
Arkansas										
Little Rock–Pine Bluff	2	1	1	3	−1	0	0	0	0	0
Fort Smith–Fayetteville–Springdale–Rogers	0	0	2	1	1	0	0	0	0	0
Jonesboro	0	0	0	0	0	0	0	0	0	0
Shreveport, LA	1	0	0	0	1	0	0	0	0	0
Memphis, TN	0	0	0	0	0	0	0	0	0	0
Springfield, MO	0	0	0	0	0	0	0	0	0	0
Monroe–El Dorado	0	0	0	0	0	0	0	0	0	0
Greenwood–Greenville	0	0	0	0	0	0	0	0	0	0
State total	3	1	3	4	1	0	0	0	0	0
California										
Los Angeles	7	2	2	3	4	0	0	0	1	−1
San Francisco–Oakland–San Jose	2	1	0	1	0	0	0	0	1	−1
San Diego	2	0	0	2	0	0	0	0	0	0
Sacramento–Stockton–Modesto	1	0	1	0	2	0	0	0	0	0
Santa Barbara–San Marcos–San Luis Obispo	2	0	1	0	3	0	0	0	0	0
Fresno–Visalia	1	0	1	1	1	0	0	0	0	0
Monterey–Salinas	1	0	0	0	1	0	0	0	0	0
Chico–Redding	0	0	0	0	0	0	0	0	0	0
Bakersfield	1	0	2	0	3	0	0	0	0	0
Palm Springs	0	0	0	0	0	0	0	0	0	0
Eureka	0	0	0	0	0	0	0	0	0	0
Reno, NV	0	0	0	0	0	0	0	0	0	0
Medford, OR–Klamath Falls, OR	0	0	0	0	0	0	0	0	0	0
Yuma, AZ–El Centro	0	0	0	0	0	0	0	0	0	0

Phoenix, AZ	0	0	0	0	0	0	0	0	0	0
State total	17	3	7	7	14	0	0	0	2	-2
Colorado										
Denver	0	0	1	0	1	3	2	1	2	0
Colorado Springs–Pueblo	0	0	0	0	0	1	1	1	0	1
Grand Junction–Montrose	0	0	0	0	0	0	0	1	0	1
Albuquerque, NM–Santa Fe, NM	0	0	0	0	0	0	0	0	0	0
State total	0	0	1	0	1	4	3	3	2	2
Delaware										
Philadelphia, PA	0	0	1	1	0	0	0	0	0	0
Salisbury	0	0	0	0	0	0	0	0	0	0
State total	0	0	1	1	0	0	0	0	0	0
Florida										
Tampa–St. Petersburg–Sarasota	3	6	2	1	-2	6	3	2	5	0
Miami–Fort Lauderdale	3	2	1	6	-4	4	8	1	4	-7
Orlando–Daytona Beach–Melbourne	2	3	1	4	-4	4	5	2	6	-5
West Palm Beach–Fort Pierce	2	0	2	3	1	3	4	1	3	-3
Fort Myers–Naples	1	0	0	0	1	1	0	2	2	1
Jacksonville–Brunswick, GA	0	0	1	0	2	1	1	3	2	1
Mobile, AL–Pensacola	0	0	0	0	1	1	0	2	1	2
Tallahassee–Thomasville, GA	0	1	1	0	0	0	0	1	1	0
Panama City	0	0	0	0	0	1	0	1	0	1
Gainesville	0	0	0	0	0	1	0	2	1	2
State total	11	12	10	14	-5	22	21	16	25	-8
Georgia										
Atlanta	0	1	1	0	0	0	0	0	0	0
Savannah	0	0	0	0	0	0	0	0	0	0
Macon	0	0	0	0	0	0	0	0	0	0
Albany	0	0	0	0	0	0	0	0	0	0
Augusta	0	0	0	0	0	0	0	0	0	0
Chattanooga, TN	0	0	0	0	0	0	0	0	0	0
Columbus	0	0	0	0	0	0	0	0	0	0

continued

STATE/DMA	BUSH	GORE	CHENEY	LIEBERMAN	APPEAR. DIFF. (REP. − DEM.)	BUSH	KERRY	CHENEY	EDWARDS	APPEAR. DIFF. (REP. − DEM.)
Tallahassee, FL–Thomasville	0	1	0	0	−1	0	0	0	0	0
Greenville, NC–Spartanburg, NC–Asheville, NC–Anderson	0	0	0	0	0	0	0	0	0	0
Jacksonville, FL–Brunswick	0	0	0	0	0	0	0	0	0	0
Dothan	0	0	0	0	0	0	0	0	0	0
State total	0	2	1	0	−1	0	0	0	0	0
Hawaii										
Honolulu	0	0	0	0	0	0	0	1	0	1
State total	0	0	0	0	0	0	0	1	0	1
Illinois										
Chicago	6	3	4	3	4	0	0	1	0	1
Champaign-Springfield-Decatur	1	0	0	0	1	0	0	0	0	0
St. Louis	0	1	0	0	−1	0	0	0	0	0
Peoria-Bloomington	2	0	1	1	2	0	0	0	1	−1
Davenport, IA–Rock Island–Moline	1	1	1	1	0	0	0	0	0	0
Rockford	0	0	0	0	0	0	0	0	0	0
Paducah, KY–Cape Girardeau, MO–Harrisburg–Mount Vernon	1	0	0	0	1	0	0	0	0	0
Quincy–Hannibal, MO–Keokuk, IA	0	1	0	1	−2	0	0	0	0	0
Terre Haute, IN	0	0	0	0	0	0	0	0	0	0
Evansville, IN	0	0	0	0	0	0	0	0	1	0
State total	11	6	6	6	5	0	0	1	1	0
Iowa										
Cedar Rapids–Waterloo–Dubuque	2	4	3	1	0	3	5	2	2	−2
Des Moines–Ames	3	3	0	0	0	2	3	3	4	−2
Davenport–Rock Island, IL–Moline, IL	1	3	0	1	−3	1	0	3	2	2
Sioux City	0	0	0	0	0	1	1	1	2	−1
Rochester, MN–Mason City–Mankato, MN	0	0	0	0	0	0	0	0	0	0
Omaha, NE	0	0	1	0	0	1	0	0	1	0
Ottumwa–Kirksville, MO	0	0	0	0	0	0	0	1	0	1
Quincy, IL–Hannibal, MO–Keokuk	0	1	0	1	−2	0	0	0	0	0

Sioux Falls, SD–Mitchell, SD	0	0	0	0	0	0	0	1	0	-1
Mankato, MN	0	0	0	0	0	0	0	0	0	0
State total	6	11	4	3	-4	8	9	11	13	-3
Kentucky										
Louisville	1	1	0	0	0	0	0	0	1	-1
Lexington	1	0	2	4	-1	0	0	0	0	0
Cincinnati, OH	0	0	0	0	0	0	0	0	0	0
Evansville, IN	0	0	0	0	0	0	0	0	0	0
Charleston, WV–Huntington, WV	0	0	0	0	0	0	0	0	0	0
Puducah–Cape Girardeau, MO–Harrisburg, IL–Mount Vernon, IL	0	0	1	0	1	0	0	0	0	0
Bowling Green	0	0	0	0	0	0	0	0	0	0
Nashville, TN	0	0	0	0	0	0	0	0	0	0
Knoxville, TN	0	0	0	0	0	0	0	0	0	0
Tri-Cities, TN–VA	0	0	0	0	0	0	0	0	0	0
State total	2	1	3	4	0	0	0	0	1	-1
Louisiana										
New Orleans	1	2	1	0	0	0	1	0	0	-1
Lafayette	1	0	0	0	1	0	0	1	0	1
Shreveport	0	1	1	0	0	0	0	0	0	0
Baton Rouge	0	1	1	0	1	0	0	0	0	0
Monroe–El Dorado, AK	0	0	0	0	0	0	0	0	0	0
Alexandria	0	0	0	0	0	0	0	0	0	0
Lake Charles	0	0	0	0	0	0	0	0	0	0
State total	2	3	3	3	2	0	1	1	0	0
Maine										
Portland–Auburn	1	2	1	1	1	0	0	0	0	0
Bangor	1	0	3	3	-2	1	0	0	2	-1
Presque Isle	0	0	0	0	0	0	0	0	0	0
State total	2	1	2	4	-1	1	0	0	2	-1
Maryland										
Annapolis	0	0	0	0	0	0	0	0	1	-1
State total	0	0	0	0	0	0	0	0	1	-1

continued

STATE/DMA	BUSH	GORE	CHENEY	LIEBERMAN	APPEAR. DIFF. (REP. – DEM.)	BUSH	KERRY	CHENEY	EDWARDS	APPEAR. DIFF. (REP. – DEM.)
Michigan										
Detroit	8	2	2	3	5	2	3	2	4	-3
Grand Rapids–Kalamazoo–Battle Creek	6	2	3	0	7	4	0	2	1	5
Flint–Saginaw–Bay City	3	4	1	1	-1	1	0	1	1	1
Lansing	1	0	1	0	2	0	0	2	0	2
Traverse City–Cadillac	0	0	2	0	2	0	0	1	0	1
South Bend, IN–Elkhart, IN	0	0	0	0	0	0	0	1	0	1
Marquette	0	0	0	0	0	0	0	0	0	0
Toledo, OH	0	0	0	0	0	0	0	0	0	0
Alpena	0	0	0	0	0	0	0	0	0	0
Green Bay, WI–Appleton, WI	0	0	0	0	0	0	0	0	0	0
Duluth, MN–Superior, WI	0	0	0	0	0	0	0	0	0	0
State total	18	8	9	4	15	7	3	9	6	7
Minnesota										
Minneapolis–St. Paul	1	0	1	3	-1	4	1	2	3	2
Duluth–Superior, WI	0	0	0	0	0	0	0	2	2	0
Rochester–Mason City, IA	0	0	0	0	0	3	2	1	0	2
Mankato	0	0	0	0	0	0	0	0	0	0
Fargo	1	0	1	3	0	0	0	1	0	1
State total	1	0	1	3	-1	7	3	6	5	5
Missouri										
St. Louis	5	5	2	2	0	1	2	1	0	0
Kansas City	2	3	2	1	0	1	0	0	1	0
Springfield	1	0	1	1	1	0	0	0	0	0
Columbia–Jefferson City	0	1	1	0	0	2	0	0	0	2
Paducah, KY–Cape Girardeau–Harrisburg, IL–Mount Vernon, IL	0	0	1	0	1	0	0	0	0	0
Joplin–Pittsburg, KS	0	0	0	0	0	0	0	0	0	0
St. Joseph	0	0	0	0	0	0	0	1	0	1
Quincy, IL–Hannibal–Keokuk, IA	0	1	0	1	-2	0	0	0	0	0
Ottumwa, IA–Kirksville	0	0	0	0	0	0	0	0	0	0
Memphis, TN	0	0	0	0	0	0	0	0	0	0

Jonesboro, AK	0	0	0	0	0	0	0	0	0	0
Omaha, NE	0	0	0	0	0	0	0	0	0	0
Des Moines, IA–Ames, IA	0	0	0	0	0	0	0	0	0	0
State total	8	10	7	5	0	4	2	2	1	3
Nevada										
Las Vegas	0	1	3	1	0	2	2	1	0	0
Reno	0	0	1	0	0	1	3	2	1	2
Salt Lake City, UT	0	0	0	0	0	0	0	0	0	0
Denver, CO	0	0	0	0	0	0	0	0	0	0
State total	0	1	4	1	2	3	3	3	1	2
New Hampshire										
Boston, MA	2	1	2	2	1	2	4	1	3	-4
Burlington, VT–Plattsburgh, NY	0	0	0	0	0	0	0	0	0	0
Portland, ME–Auburn, ME	0	0	0	0	0	0	0	0	0	0
State total	2	1	2	2	1	2	4	1	3	-4
New Jersey										
New York City	0	1	0	2	-3	3	2	0	2	-1
Philadelphia, PA	0	1	0	2	-3	1	0	1	3	-1
State total	0	2	0	4	-6	4	2	1	5	-2
New Mexico										
Albuquerque–Santa Fe	2	2	3	2	1	3	5	3	1	0
El Paso, TX	1	1	1	0	1	0	1	0	0	-1
Amarillo, TX	0	0	0	0	0	0	0	0	0	0
Odessa, TX–Midland, TX	0	0	0	0	0	0	0	0	1	0
State total	3	3	4	2	2	3	5	3	1	-1
North Carolina										
Charlotte	0	0	1	1	1	1	0	0	0	1
Greensboro–High Point–Winston-Salem	2	1	0	0	1	0	1	0	1	-2
Atlanta, GA	0	0	0	0	1	0	0	0	0	0
Norfolk, VA–Portsmouth, VA–Newport News, VA	0	0	0	0	0	0	0	0	0	0

continued

STATE/DMA	2000					2004				
	BUSH	GORE	CHENEY	LIEBERMAN	APPEAR. DIFF. (REP. – DEM.)	BUSH	KERRY	CHENEY	EDWARDS	APPEAR. DIFF. (REP. – DEM.)
Greenville–New Bern–Washington	0	0	0	0	0	0	0	0	0	0
Raleigh-Durham	0	0	0	0	0	0	0	0	2	-2
Greenville, NC–Spartanburg, NC–Asheville, NC–Anderson, GA	0	0	0	0	0	0	0	0	0	0
Wilmington	0	0	0	0	0	0	0	0	0	0
Florence, SC–Myrtle Beach, SC	0	0	0	0	0	0	0	0	0	0
Chattanooga, TN	0	0	0	0	0	0	0	0	0	0
State total	2	1	1	0	2	1	1	0	3	-3
Ohio										
Cleveland	2	1	2	1	2	4	1	1	5	-1
Columbus	1	1	3	1	2	5	6	3	2	0
Cincinnati	0	1	1	1	-1	3	1	4	3	3
Dayton	1	1	1	1	0	2	3	1	2	-2
Toledo	2	0	1	1	2	2	4	3	3	-2
Youngstown	1	1	1	0	1	1	2	0	0	-1
Charleston, WV–Huntington, WV	0	0	0	0	0	0	0	0	0	0
Wheeling, WV–Steubenville	0	0	0	0	0	0	0	0	0	0
Zanesville	0	0	0	0	0	0	0	1	0	1
Lima	0	0	1	0	1	0	0	0	1	-1
Parkersburg, WV	0	0	0	0	0	0	0	0	0	0
Fort Wayne, IN	0	0	0	0	0	0	0	0	0	0
State total	7	5	10	5	7	17	17	13	16	-3
Oregon										
Portland	3	3	4	2	2	0	0	1	2	-1
Eugene	0	1	1	0	0	0	0	1	1	0
Medford–Klamath Falls	0	0	1	0	1	1	0	0	1	0
Bend	0	0	1	0	1	0	0	0	0	0
Yakima, WA–Pasco, WA–Richland, WA–Kennewick, WA	0	0	0	0	0	0	0	0	0	0
Boise, ID	0	0	0	0	0	0	0	0	0	0
Spokane, WA	0	0	0	0	0	0	0	0	0	0
State total	3	4	7	2	4	1	0	2	4	-1

Pennsylvania										
Philadelphia	3	2	3	1	3	5	4	1	3	−1
Pittsburgh	5	3	3	3	2	2	1	3	2	2
Harrisburg-Lancaster-Lebanon-York	0	0	1	0	1	2	0	2	0	4
Wilkes-Barre-Scranton	2	3	4	0	3	2	1	1	2	0
Johnstown-Altoona	0	0	1	0	1	2	0	0	1	1
Erie	2	0	0	0	2	2	0	1	1	0
Ycungstown, OH	0	0	0	0	0	0	0	0	0	0
Washington, DC	0	0	0	0	0	0	0	0	0	0
Buffalo, NY	0	0	0	0	0	0	0	0	0	0
Elmira, NY	0	0	0	0	0	0	0	0	0	0
New York City	0	0	0	0	0	0	0	0	0	0
State total	12	8	12	4	12	13	6	8	9	6
Rhode Island										
Providence	0	0	0	0	0	0	0	0	1	−1
State total	0	0	0	0	0	0	0	0	1	−1
South Carolina										
Columbia	0	0	0	0	0	0	0	0	1	−1
State total	0	0	0	0	0	0	0	0	1	−1
Tennessee										
Nashville	1	2	1	2	−2	0	0	0	0	0
Knoxville	1	1	0	0	0	0	0	0	0	0
Memphis	1	1	2	1	1	0	0	0	0	0
Chattanooga	2	0	0	0	2	0	0	0	0	0
Tri-Cities, TN–VA	1	0	0	0	1	0	0	0	0	0
Jackson	0	1	0	1	−2	0	0	0	0	0
Paducah, KY–Cape Girardeau, MO–Harrisburg, IL–Mount Vernon, IL	0	0	0	0	0	0	0	0	0	0
Hintsville-Decatur-Florence	0	0	0	0	0	0	0	0	0	0
State total	6	5	3	4	0	0	0	0	0	0
Texas										
Dallas	0	0	0	0	0	1	0	0	0	1
Houston	0	0	0	0	0	0	0	0	1	−1

continued

STATE/DMA	BUSH	GORE	CHENEY	LIEBERMAN	APPEAR. DIFF. (REP. − DEM.)	BUSH	KERRY	CHENEY	EDWARDS	APPEAR. DIFF. (REP. − DEM.)
Waco	0	0	0	0	0	6	0	0	0	6
State total	0	0	0	0	0	7	0	0	1	6
Washington										
Seattle-Tacoma	4	3	1	3	−1	0	0	0	0	0
Spokane	1	1	1	0	1	0	0	0	0	0
Yakima-Pasco-Richland-Kennewick	0	0	3	0	3	0	0	0	0	0
Portland, OR	0	0	0	1	−1	0	0	0	0	0
State total	5	4	5	4	2	0	0	0	0	0
West Virginia										
Pittsburgh, PA	1	0	0	0	1	0	0	0	0	0
Washington, DC	0	0	0	0	0	0	0	0	0	0
Wheeling-Steubenville, OH	0	0	1	0	1	0	0	0	2	−2
Bluefield-Beckley-Oak Hill	0	0	0	0	0	0	0	1	0	1
Charleston-Huntington	1	1	0	0	0	1	0	1	1	1
Harrisonburg	0	0	0	0	0	0	0	0	0	0
Roanoke-Lynchburg, TN	0	0	0	0	0	0	0	0	0	0
Parkersburg	0	0	0	0	0	0	0	0	2	−2
Clarksburg-Weston	0	0	1	0	1	0	0	1	1	0
State total	2	1	2	0	3	1	0	3	6	−2

Wisconsin										
Milwaukee	4	3	0	4	−2	2	5	6	3	0
Green Bay–Appleton	4	1	1	1	3	2	4	3	0	1
Madison	0	2	1	1	−2	3	5	0	0	−2
Wausau-Rhinelander	0	0	1	1	−1	1	0	0	0	1
La Crosse–Eau Claire	1	1	1	1	−3	1	1	2	2	0
Minneapolis–St. Paul, MN	0	0	0	3	0	0	0	0	0	0
Duluth, MN–Superior	0	0	0	0	0	0	0	0	0	0
Cedar Rapids, IA–Waterloo, IA–Dubuque, IA	0	0	0	0	0	0	0	0	0	0
Marquette, MI	0	0	0	0	0	0	0	0	0	0
State total	9	7	4	11	−5	9	15	11	5	0
Average in battleground markets	0.70	0.48	0.61	0.50	0.34	0.82	0.73	0.70	0.77	0.02

Note: Figures represent public appearances made by candidates in the media market. Private fund-raising events and vacation days are excluded, as are working days in Washington, DC.

Source: Appearance figures are provided by the Bush-Cheney campaign and are validated by the *New York Times* and the *Hotline*. They encompass appearances between August 20 and November 6, 2000, and between September 3 and November 1, 2004.

APPENDIX 3

MEDIA MARKETS USED IN POOLED
TIME SERIES ANALYSES, 2000 AND 2004

2000		2004	
STATE	MEDIA MARKET	STATE	MEDIA MARKET
Arizona	Phoenix	*Arizona*	Phoenix
	Tucson		Tucson
Arkansas	Fort Smith		
	Fayetteville		
	Jonesboro		
	Little Rock–Pine Bluff		
		Colorado	Colorado Springs
			Denver
Florida	Jacksonville	*Florida*	Jacksonville
	Tampa–St. Petersburg		Tampa–St. Petersburg
	Miami–Fort Lauderdale		Miami–Fort Lauderdale
	Orlando–Daytona Beach		Orlando–Daytona Beach
	West Palm Beach		West Palm Beach
			Fort Myers–Naples
Illinois	Champaign–Springfield		
	Chicago		
Iowa	Cedar Rapids	*Iowa*	Cedar Rapids
	Davenport		Davenport
	Des Moines		Des Moines
	Omaha, NE		Omaha, NE
	Sioux City		Sioux City
			Ottumwa
Maine	Bangor	*Maine*	Bangor
	Portland		Portland
Michigan	Detroit	*Michigan*	Detroit
	Flint-Saginaw		Flint-Saginaw
	Grand Rapids–Kalamazoo		Grand Rapids–Kalamazoo
	Traverse City		
		Minnesota	Duluth–Superior, WI
			Minneapolis–St. Paul
Missouri	Springfield	*Missouri*	Springfield
	Columbia–Jefferson City		Columbia–Jefferson City
	Kansas City		Kansas City
	St. Louis		St. Louis
		Nevada	Las Vegas
			Reno
		New Hampshire	Boston, MA
			Burlington, VT
New Mexico	Albuquerque–Santa Fe	*New Mexico*	Albuquerque–Santa Fe
		Ohio	Cincinnati
			Cleveland
			Columbus
			Dayton
			Toledo
Oregon	Portland	*Oregon*	Portland
	Eugene		Eugene
	Medford–Klamath Falls		Medford–Klamath Falls

MEDIA MARKETS USED IN POOLED TIME SERIES ANALYSES

2000		2004	
STATE	MEDIA MARKET	STATE	MEDIA MARKET
Pennsylvania	Harrisburg	*Pennsylvania*	Harrisburg
	Philadelphia		Philadelphia
	Pittsburgh		Pittsburgh
	Wilkes-Barre		Wilkes-Barre
			Johnstown
Tennessee	Chattanooga	*Tennessee*	Chattanooga
	Knoxville		Knoxville
	Memphis		Memphis
	Nashville		Nashville
Washington	Seattle	*Washington*	Seattle
	Spokane		Spokane
	Yakima		Yakima
West Virginia	Bluefield-Beckley	*West Virginia*	Bluefield-Beckley
	Charleston-Huntington		Charleston-Huntington
	Clarksburg-Weston		Clarksburg-Weston
			Washington, DC
			Wheeling–Steubenville, OH
Wisconsin	Green Bay	*Wisconsin*	Green Bay
	La Crosse–Eau Claire		La Crosse–Eau Claire
	Madison		Madison
	Wausau-Rhinelander		Wausau-Rhinelander
	Milwaukee		Milwaukee

Source: Media markets identified from tracking polls provided by Voter Consumer Research for 2000 and 2004 and by Market Strategies Inc. for 2000 for the Bush-Cheney campaigns.

NOTES

CHAPTER ONE

1. A Democratic pollster later confirmed this quote.

2. Most social scientists who have participated in recent presidential campaigns have done so by advising on public-policy matters. Scholars such as Cornel West and Ann Norton served as advisers to Bill Bradley's presidential campaign in 2000, while Marvin Olasky and John Dilulio are widely credited with laying the theoretical groundwork and devising the practical political application of George W. Bush's "compassionate conservatism." This sort of interaction has a long history and is probably no more common in recent years. My interest, however, is in political scientists who aid in the development of electoral and public opinion stratagems. While I know of half a dozen such individuals who worked in either the 2000 or the 2004 race, I am reluctant to "out" people to a professional audience still slightly uncomfortable with the notion that one can take off one's party hat (and put on a tweed jacket with leather elbow patches) after Election Day. Not naming names makes it difficult to sustain my assertion that this activity is any more common than it has been in the past, but the relative youth of those involved in the 2000 and 2004 campaigns makes me think this sort of interchange is on the upswing.

3. Many political scientists are currently of the opinion that the "Do campaigns matter?" debate is either hackneyed or a straw man. I discuss this debate in detail in chapter 2.

4. On top of these tasks, I eventually produced precinct-level analyses and general election targets for the battleground states, as well as overseeing a content analysis of political coverage for more than one dozen newspapers and the top three broadcast media outlets.

5. White himself wrote two more editions for the 1964 and 1972 campaigns (White 1965; 1973), as well as *America in Search of Itself* (1982), all of which remain vital historical documents on campaigns and the press.

6. Jack Germond quoted on ABCNews.com, February 2, 2001, http://abcnews.go .com/sections/us/DailyNews/chat_jackgermond991109.html.

7. The Annenberg School for Communication hosted an important conference on Campaign 2000 on February 10, 2001, at the University of Pennsylvania. Members of the Gore campaign present included senior advisers Robert Shrum and Carter Eskew, national pollster Stanley Greenberg, and media adviser Bill Knapp. Members of the Bush campaign present included senior adviser Karl Rove, pollster Fred Steeper, polling director Matthew Dowd, and media advisers Mark McKinnon, Alex Castellanos, and Lionel Sosa. For 2004, I rely primarily on contemporaneous journalistic accounts—including the *Newsweek* book on the 2004 campaign—and informal presentations and published interviews from Kerry strategist Tad Devine and pollster Greenberg.

8. I find it interesting that many observers have characterized 2000 as a boring campaign that ended with a great election. This interpretation is, of course, not baseless. Neither Bush nor Gore caught the imagination of the public as some of their predecessors had. Still, with the passing of time, I think it might well be considered an exceptional and memorable campaign. The closest analogy I can think of is the Super Bowl—close games, even those not expertly played, are the games we remember. Moreover, some of the indifference about the 2000 campaign is undoubtedly due to its unusual aftermath. The Florida recount and court battles were gripping, and this exciting saga has produced a lack of attention to (and respect for) the campaign itself.

9. There was movement in voters' preferences, as I show in chapter 5. But this movement is not exceptional compared to other recent elections.

10. For present purposes, a *battleground* is defined as a state that is (1) publicly identified by both campaigns as a target and (2) receives television advertising or presidential or vice presidential candidate appearances from both campaigns. This issue is treated more systematically in chapter 3.

11. I would put 1824, 1876, and 1888 on this list as well.

12. On October 12, however, James Campbell's forecasting model pegged Bush's share of the 2004 presidential vote at 51.4 percent.

CHAPTER TWO

1. The conference was the annual meeting of the Midwest Political Science Association, Chicago, April 19–22, 2001.

2. An entire issue of *PS: Politics & Political Science* (March 2001) was dedicated to the modelers' explanations of the 2000 presidential election. The October 2004 issue offered their forecasts for the Bush-Kerry contest.

3. Bartels and Zaller (2001) question the reputed failure of objective economic factors, focusing on the economic downturn during fall 2000 and positing that it portended a much closer race than other economic models had predicted. Taking third-quarter growth figures as well as a variety of other economic indicators, they use Bayesian Model Averaging (BMA) to generate estimates and offer a much more accurate prediction for 2000. However, Erikson, Bafumi,

and Wilson (2001) point out that this process ignores the other critical variable used in most forecasting models: presidential approval. Entering presidential approval estimates and expanding on the BMA process outlined by Bartels and Zaller, Erikson and his colleagues find that Gore's predicted vote share increases to about where the original models had it.

4. McCombs and Evatt (1995) consider "priming" an instance of what they call "second-level agenda setting."

5. The Bush campaign did not produce or air an advertisement mentioning Willie Horton. An independent, conservative group produced the ad in question, which aired a single time in one New England media market. The news media picked up on the flap over the ad and rebroadcast it in reporting on the controversy so that the ad eventually was seen in whole or in part in most markets.

6. It is not clear why Election Day seems to have this magical, "enlightening" quality.

7. But see Dalager 1996 for a dissenting view on Senate elections.

8. See also Ansolabehere et al. 1994. In addition, L. L. Kaid also deserves credit for pioneering research in the area of negative campaigning (Kaid and Boydson 1987; Kaid and Johnston 1991; Kaid, Leland, and Whitney 1992), as does Richard Lau for his work on negativity and political perception (Lau 1982).

9. While Holbrook uses three categories to classify campaign events (conventions, debates, other events), I use eleven. These findings are thus properly viewed as "further explorations" rather than challenges to Holbrook's work.

10. For an alternative view, see Patterson and McClure 1976.

11. On the subject of race/ethnicity and voting, there is also the work of Bobo and Gilliam (1990) on the positive effect of black candidates on black turnout, as well as the work of Shaw, de la Garza, and Lee (2000) on the positive effect of in-group contacting (Latino groups contacting Latino registrants) on Latino turnout.

12. More recently, the top one hundred media markets.

13. Elite newspapers include the *New York Times* and the *Washington Post*.

CHAPTER THREE

1. One additional and somewhat obvious point to note is that my focus is on George W. Bush's 2000 and 2004 campaigns. I also consider the strategies of Al Gore and John Kerry in order to complement the analysis of Bush and to check its portability.

2. The elections literature, in general, offers a number of theoretical and empirical analyses of how candidates allocate their resources. These analyses tend to focus on "targeting," which is the process of identifying persuadable voters and gaining their support (see, for example, J. Campbell 2003; Herrnson 2002; Jacobson 1990; Salmore and Salmore 1992; Shea and Burton 2001). The difficulty is that this literature is largely silent on the precision with which voters are targeted and the extent to which targeting plans drive resource allocation. It is also the case that most studies of targeting focus on congressional elections and do not address the peculiarities endemic to presidential elections and the Electoral College. Targeting is relatively easy in a single district; it is infinitely more complicated when you have to simultaneously contest multiple states whose values are, in effect, weighted by their populations.

3. It should be noted that some of the most interesting ideas about Electoral College effects on strategy and resource allocation come from studies of presidential primaries—another multistate, differentially weighted series of contests. In particular, there is Aldrich's work (1980) on the influence of population size and competitiveness on allocation strategies and Bartels's analysis (1988) of the diminishing returns of resource allocations.

4. In 1992, the Clinton campaign referred to their states as "sure bet," "must have," "play hard," "worth watching," and "rough road" (Matalin, Carville, and Knobler 1994; Goldman et al. 1994). These correspond to categories 5 through 1, respectively, of my list.

5. The Democrats had their own troubles in Oregon, where there was a well-known rift between the Democratic governor John Kitzhaber and the Clinton administration.

6. This was a source of some amusement for those of us in the Strategy Department, as reporters assumed we were waging holy wars in states such as Illinois and New Jersey that were never part of the core strategy.

7. The prominence of Oregon and Washington in battleground lists from 2000 indicates an underrated effect of Ralph Nader's candidacy: Nader's support in the Pacific Northwest and in some of the upper Midwest states kept Gore's margins down and made them attractive targets. The data in chapter 4 also suggest these states received substantial attention that otherwise might have gone elsewhere. This "Nader effect" appears less significant in 2004. There is no evidence that Patrick Buchanan's candidacy in 2000 caused any alteration of Electoral College strategies.

8. Torricelli withdrew from his race for reelection in 2002 due to corruption charges. McGreevey resigned the governorship in response to questions arising from his homosexual relationship with a former aide.

9. I do not know whether the campaigns of George H. W. Bush or Robert Dole rank-ordered media markets, although it is entirely possible that they did.

10. For nonpresidential elections, a range of statewide races can be used to generate a more precise estimate of the swing or persuadable vote. In presidential races, however, campaigns use presidential results because one wants to make comparisons between and among states, and presidential elections are the only races that span all fifty states and all 210 media markets.

11. Note that "swing" or "persuadable" vote estimates here are not the same as "ticket-splitters." The latter are voters who vote for Republican and Democratic candidates in the same election. Swing or persuadable voters vote for one party's presidential candidate in one election year but vote for the opposite party's presidential candidate in another year (Mayer 2002; Shaw and Underwood 2005).

12. Estimates of persuadable voters in a market can also be derived from voter identification calls, which campaigns undertake to provide useful political information on registered voters. Costs and missing data sometimes undermine these projects, though.

13. As explained in chapter 4, one hundred *gross rating points* (also known as *GRPs* or *points*) is the amount of television advertising necessary to reach, on average, every person in a market one time. The cost per point (or cost per one hundred points) is thus the typical number used in the calculation of market efficiency.

14. My favorite media market from 2000 was unquestionably Paducah–Cape Girardeau–Harrisburg–Mount Vernon, which covered at least three (and by some counts four) battleground states: Kentucky, Missouri, Tennessee, and Arkansas.

15. One thousand points is an arbitrary but realistic example of such an exercise. Media consultants typically estimate that a 1,200-point buy is necessary to move voters.

16. Speaking off the record, two members of the Gore campaign offered these indications in separate conversations with the author.

17. For example, see Barone 2002. For a slightly different perspective, see Judis and Teixeira 2002 and Abramowitz, Alexander, and Gunning 2006.

CHAPTER FOUR

1. While this idea is counterintuitive for students of American politics, it is much less so for those who follow other democracies. European candidates, for example, are often beholden to their political parties, and parties are sometimes more interested in representing groups and advancing ideologies than in winning office. In the United States, however, it seems bizarre that a campaign would not behave in a way that maximized its prospects for winning elective office.

2. Craig Gilbert, "Electoral Vote Battle Being Played Out in Swing States," *Milwaukee Journal Sentinel*, September 17, 2000.

3. The Bush campaign was an example of the precarious position that all nonincumbent presidential campaigns occupy. On the one hand, you are attractive to many voters because you are outside of the current power structure. There are, to be sure, exceptions (Bob Dole in 1996, for example, was a challenger who was also firmly entrenched in the existing power structure). But mostly a nonincumbent campaign constitutes a promise of a new order. On the other hand, you are a threat to the party's internal power structure; a threat to the position that senators and governors have in the out-party. Put plainly, a successful campaign means that you will dominate the party for at least four years. The power structures within and across the various states therefore have a strong tendency to carp and kvetch about the "controlling" nature of your campaign. Unfortunately for the campaign, you need these people to successfully contest a fifty-state election. Consequently, you tend to take their criticisms and smile. This certainly happened with the Bush campaign—every setback was attributed to Austin while there were lines around the block to take credit for "saving" Bush whenever he gained momentum.

4. The endogeneity of campaign allocations makes modeling their effects a difficult proposition. An alternative approach would be to assume, as I did in chapter 3, that plans are developed from available polling, historical voting patterns, current issue and organizational factors, and the costs of campaigning and to model the campaigns' strategic plans as a function of these variables. The expected values derived from these models can then be posed as one of several variables predicting resource allocation. In the words of the political scientist, one would assume a two-stage process, where the electoral plan constitutes stage one and resource allocation constitutes stage two, and estimate the pro-

cess accordingly (see Shaw 1999b). A two-stage approach yields estimates only slightly different in substantive terms than those presented here.

5. The television advertising expectations are based on cumulative exposure to candidate and party advertisements.

6. Abramowitz, Alexander, and Gunning (2006) point out that the absence of California, New York, and Texas from the list of battleground states in 2000 and 2004 reduces the scope of the playing field compared to other recent, close presidential elections (e.g., 1976 and 1960). In part, this argument turns on the definition of the term *battleground,* which is subjective and perhaps even endogenous. It is endogenous in that (1) a campaign needs to reach an Electoral College majority and therefore identifies a set of battleground states in each election irrespective of their "true" competitiveness, and (2) campaigning vigorously could affect competitiveness. Throughout my analyses, I rely on the strategic plans of the campaigns to define battleground states. I also believe it is important to note that the decline of national TV advertising in presidential elections has decreased the percentage of Americans exposed to the campaign.

7. I do not have weekly figures for interest group spending.

8. Television advertisements are tracked through satellite technology, which identifies ads by scanning the bar codes of transmissions. It is virtually impossible to put something on the public airwaves in any U.S. market without leaving a clearly identifiable record. Even cable buys can be tracked this way, although it is a more complicated endeavor.

9. This conversion is based on the RNC's estimates of the cost of 100 GRPs for each of the Nielsen markets for 2000 and 2004.

10. It is worth pointing out that cost discrepancies are not simply a function of population differences. TV ad costs are affected by the size *and affluence* of the audience, which is why San Francisco is even more expensive than one might predict given its relative size. Despite my preference for GRPs as a measure of TV advertising, in table 4.1 I present raw dollar outlays.

11. Many markets span multiple states, which necessitates estimating the number of people within the market that fall within each state's boundaries. I do so by mapping counties into media markets and looking at county-level census and voting data from 2000 and 2004.

12. Interest groups' independent expenditures are relatively minor for 2000, as these groups preferred to donate to the parties. Statewide interest group spending figures for 2000 are from Holman and McLoughlin 2001, 83. In 2004, the Bipartisan Campaign Reform Act's elimination of soft money expenditures by the parties resulted in a striking increase in the independent television advertising expenditures of special interest groups. State and media market figures for 2004 are from the RNC and National Media Inc.

13. The campaigns are the primary source of candidate appearance information because they are more likely to report last-minute additions to the schedule. In addition, they distinguish among official duties, campaign events, and fundraisers. The *Hotline* and the *New York Times* data are used for validation purposes. The *Hotline* is a daily newsletter on national and state politics that draws on print media reports from across the country. It is not published on weekends or holidays.

14. For example, see William Schneider, "Politics: A Popularity Contest," *National Journal*, November 16, 2002; Stephen Dinan, "Democrats Tout Voter Turnout Plan," *Washington Times*, October 31, 2002.

15. Lieberman, of course, faced only token opposition in his Senate reelection campaign back in Connecticut. Bush was governor of Texas, but the Texas Legislature only meets for 140 days in odd-numbered years, so his obligations were minimal.

16. Party and candidate expenditure data are collapsed in 2004, making comparable analyses impossible.

17. I discuss Bush's California strategy in greater detail in chapter 6.

18. Jamieson's research shows that, on the whole, the Republicans had a greater proportion of "advocacy" (as opposed to "contrast" or "attack") ads than the Democrats. Moreover, the Democratic ads were almost exclusively "contrast" or "attack" in the last two weeks of the campaign.

19. Although part of this lack of attention is because eastern New Mexico is called "little Texas" and is one of the most Republican areas of the state, one still would have expected the market to draw more attention given the number of voters within its boundaries.

20. As pointed out earlier, television advertising expenditures actually increased in the first presidential election after the Bipartisan Campaign Reform Act of 2002. However, the GRP figures indicate that there was a decrease in exposure to television advertisements, mostly because (1) TV ad rates went up, (2) the general election campaign was slightly shorter, and (3) GRP buys may have been somewhat less tightly targeted in 2004.

21. An alternate version of the model included the opposing side's actual allocations as a predictor. The results were quite similar. I also estimated models for resource allocation using only electoral votes, historical competitiveness, and their interaction. Adding Electoral College plans increases the explanatory power of the models by between 5 and 12 percentage points.

CHAPTER FIVE

1. Interestingly, the Bush campaign noticed Gore's movement in the polls but was not convinced that the Social Security ads, or any other ads, were responsible for the movement. There was general agreement among Bush's senior staff that Social Security was hurting Bush, but they believed this development was driven by news media coverage of Bush's public statement that "Democrats think Social Security is a federal program." Consequently, rather than change the subject, the Bush campaign actually *increased* the relative frequency of its Social Security ads in the overall mix.

2. I am sure Democrats find this statement ironic given the outcome in 2000.

3. In particular, I am interested in the trial ballot and candidate favorability items. The former takes the following form: "If the election were held today, would you vote for Al Gore, the Democratic nominee, George W. Bush, the Republican nominee, Ralph Nader, the Green Party nominee, or don't you know?" I use Bush's share of the two-party vote (or changes in this measure) as the dependent variable, because the proportion of undecided or third-party voters can otherwise influence candidate standing. The latter item asks: "Would

you say that you feel favorably or unfavorably towards Bush/Gore/Kerry?" A follow-up question asks whether the respondent's feelings are "strong" or "not so strong." I rely on the initial favorability measures, although I experimented with fourfold favorability scales (with little effect on my findings). From the Republican and Democratic candidate favorability scores, I construct a difference measure: (Republican favorability – unfavorability) – (Democratic favorability – unfavorability). This is my dependent variable. Whenever possible, I rely on Bush-Cheney polls to reduce the potential for discrepant results due to variations in question wording, response options, or polling methodology. When I rely on public polls, I use only those with a three-way trial ballot and a likely voter screen.

4. The decision to exclude nonbattleground states is made for practical reasons. Estimating candidate standing in states such as Utah or Rhode Island (let alone the media markets within those states) is difficult due to the paucity of appropriate polling information. The states included in the analysis are Arkansas, California, Delaware, Florida, Georgia, Illinois, Iowa, Kentucky, Louisiana, Maine, Michigan, Minnesota, Missouri, Nevada, New Hampshire, New Mexico, North Carolina, Ohio, Oregon, Pennsylvania, Tennessee, Washington, West Virginia, and Wisconsin (for 2000), and Arizona, Colorado, Florida, Iowa, Maine, Michigan, Minnesota, Missouri, Nevada, New Hampshire, New Mexico, Ohio, Oregon, Pennsylvania, Washington, West Virginia, and Wisconsin (for 2004). California and Illinois are included in the 2000 state-level analysis even though they were not consensus battleground states because they received some attention and were polled extensively. The media markets used in the study are the more populous markets from the most competitive of these battleground states (see appendix 3). More specifically, media markets are included if sample sizes for a given week's tracking polls exceeded forty respondents.

5. For 2000, the historical average is based on the Republican share of the two-party vote in 1988, 1992, and 1996. For 2004, this estimate is 50 percent of the measure, and Bush's share of the two-party vote in 2000 is the other 50 percent.

6. These data come courtesy of Professor James Stimson (http://www.unc.edu/~jstimson/heats.htm). Stimson also has an excellent discussion of presidential campaigns in *Tides of Consent* (2004). On the subject of Labor Day polls, I should note that one *Newsweek* survey showed Gore leading by 10 percentage points heading into the traditional fall campaign. This poll, however, was clearly an outlier and was routinely the subject of high and low (mostly low) satire by members of the Bush campaign's Strategy Department.

7. Gore aides acknowledged that the price the vice president claimed his family was paying for the drug came from a congressional study—not from his own bills.

8. The tune was not written until Gore was twenty-seven. Gore subsequently claimed he was joking when he made the reference during a speech to union members.

9. Gore's facts had come from a September 9 article in a Sarasota newspaper and sparked considerable controversy in the city. Evidently, there was a shortage of chairs in the room, but the principal claimed that it was both temporary and due to administrative issues. Other administrators and several students disputed the principal's version of events.

10. The final vote, averaged across battleground states, is dead even: 48.1 percent for Bush, 48.1 percent for Gore.

11. This aggregation includes all publicly available statewide media polls. Conversations with Republican and Democratic pollsters and independent academic analyses (Jackman and Rivers 2001) corroborate these estimates.

12. Nonbattleground states are allocated based on publicly available statewide media polls. Battleground states are allocated based on the most recent tracking polls conducted by Voter/Consumer Research or Market Strategies Inc.

13. Part of the explanation for the discrepancy between the aggregate cross-sectional and weekly data is that in the cross-sectional analysis, I award a state to the leading candidate irrespective of the magnitude of the margin. By contrast, in the weekly data, I classify states as "even" when the trial ballot results are within margin of error.

14. It is not entirely implausible that a candidate could outspend his opponent and lose ground. It is possible, for example, that the candidate might have lost even more ground had he not spent generously due to unfavorable conditions or events. It is also possible that the candidate spent money on poor TV ads.

15. Because the dependent variables are difference measures, I am less concerned than I might otherwise be about serial autocorrelation and random walks (De-Boef and Granato 1997). For diagnostic purposes, I estimated an alternative model in which Bush's vote share in week t serves as the dependent variable and Bush's vote in week $t-1$ serves as a critical explanatory variable. The results are largely consistent, except that the coefficients are slightly less robust and the percentage of variance explained is, of course, higher (it is always easier to explain a particular vote than differences over time). I also calculate (and present) panel-corrected standard errors (PCSEs) for the regression coefficients in tables 5.5 and 5.6 because the data have more cross sections than time points, rendering traditional estimates of standard errors biased downward (Beck and Katz 1995). Although estimates using PCSEs are very similar to those relying on traditional standard errors, the use of PCSEs makes it more difficult for the campaign variables to produce statistically significant effects.

16. Log values for 0 are set to 1.

17. One important methodological issue involves whether to lag the explanatory variables. There is, of course, some reason to think that campaigning—whether it consists of TV advertising or candidate appearances—will have a delayed (or lagged) impact on voters' preferences and favorability towards the candidates. After trying a variety of specifications, I lag the logged TV advertising variable by one week but allow candidate appearances in the current week to predict candidate support changes. Besides fitting the data, this approach makes theoretical sense. TV advertisements need some amount of accumulation to move an aggregation of voters, whereas visits to a locale cause a more immediate reaction. I also lag the control variables by one week. As a consequence of this decision, the TV advertising interactions also reflect the lagged effect of both the logged TV ad variable and the control variables.

18. A comparable yet distinct dichotomy exists with respect to the level of analysis. In the aggregate, Cheney's appearances seem to be productive at the media market level but a bust at the state level.

19. In estimating effects, I hold all variables at their mean values and calculate

the impact of specific changes in the explanatory variable of interest. Because the mean values for Republican and Democratic TV advertising are high, this method accentuates the affect of the log transformations.

CHAPTER SIX

1. Robert G. Kaiser, "Is This Any Way to Pick a Winner?" *Washington Post*, May 26, 2000.

2. As noted earlier, many of these books have not focused on the campaign per se. Rather, they have concentrated on either the 2000 Florida recount or the general polarization of the electorate during the 2004 election.

3. Of course, Kerry could have allocated these dollars to other federal election campaigns, a point many angry Democrats have raised.

4. The obvious exception is the cable television ads purchased in 2004 by the Swift Boat Veterans for Truth.

5. If Gore had carried Tennessee but lost Wisconsin (both were worth eleven electoral votes in 2000), I believe his position in the Florida recounts would have been stronger. I doubt, however, that his position would have been sufficiently strengthened to have changed the course of events.

6. Bush was actually unopposed for close to ten days, given the pattern of Democratic TV buys in Tennessee.

7. From the Daily Kos, a Web log. Posted on August 28, 2004, at www.william reynolds.com.

8. *Bloggers* is short for *Web loggers,* who write and post their thoughts and activities on their Internet Web sites.

9. Bush, in fact, got a kick out of the chicken, much to the dismay of his consultants.

10. Internal records indicate that Bush raised approximately $13 million for the Republican Party in California.

11. *Social promotion,* loosely defined, is a practice by which students who fail to meet required academic standards are nonetheless promoted to the next grade to avoid "damaging" the student's self-esteem. Social promotion is also done to prevent an accumulation of students in certain grade levels and to avoid making the school appear unproductive.

12. Treatment and control precincts were randomly assigned, although there were some limits on the assignment process that distinguished the GOP design from that of Gerber and Green.

13. These models would have to be built on ascriptive variables, otherwise a given voter's circumstances might change in such a way as to render the model's predictions invalid.

14. See Holbrook and McClurg 2005 for a related discussion.

15. According to the RNC, thirty-one million volunteer phone calls were made in battleground states in 2004, including seventeen million contacts during the final five days of the campaign (RNC news release, May 5, 2005).

16. The long-term budget prospects for NES seem to have improved in the past few years. In addition, NES has recently shown a commitment to more innovative research designs with respect to campaign effects.

REFERENCES

Abramowitz, Alan, Brad Alexander, and Matthew Gunning. 2006. "Incumbency, Redistricting, and the Decline of Competition in U.S. House Elections." *Journal of Politics* 68 (1): 75–88.

Aldrich, John H. 1980. *Before the Convention: Strategies and Choices in Presidential Nominating Campaigns*. Chicago: University of Chicago Press.

Althaus, Scott L. 1998. "Information Effects in Collective Preferences." *American Political Science Review* 3:545–58.

Althus, Scott L., Peter F. Nardulli, and Daron R. Shaw. 2002. "Candidate Appearances in Presidential Elections, 1972–2000." *Political Communication* 19:49–72.

———. 2003. "Campaign Effects on Presidential Voting, 1992–2000." Working paper, University of Illinois, Urbana-Champaign.

Alvarez, R. Michael. 1997. *Information and Elections*. Ann Arbor: University of Michigan Press.

Ansolabehere, Stephen D., and Shanto Iyengar. 1995. *Going Negative: How Political Advertisements Shrink and Polarize the Electorate*. New York: Free Press.

Ansolabehere, Stephen, Shanto Iyengar, Nick Valentino, and Adam Simon. 1994. "Does Negative Advertising Demobilize the Electorate?" American Political Science Review 88 (4): 829–38.

Arterton, F. Christopher. 1984. *Media Politics: The News Strategies of Presidential Campaigns*. Lanham, MD: Lexington Books.

Barone, Michael. 2001. "The 49 Percent Nation." In *The Almanac of American Politics 2002*. Ed. Michael Barone, Richard E. Cohen, and Charles E. Cook Jr. Washington, DC: National Journal Publishing.

Bartels, Larry M. 1985. "Resource Allocation in a Presidential Campaign." *Journal of Politics* 47:928–36.

———. 1988. *Presidential Primaries and the Dynamics of Public Choice.* Princeton, NJ: Princeton University Press.

———. 1993. "Electioneering in the United States." In *Electioneering: A Comparative Study of Continuity and Change.* Ed. David Butler and Austin Ranney, 244–77. Oxford: Clarendon Press.

———. 1996. "Uninformed Votes: Information Effects in Presidential Elections." *American Journal of Political Science* 40 (1): 194–230.

Bartels, Larry M., and John R. Zaller. 2001. "Presidential Vote Models: A Recount." *PS: Politics & Political Science* 34:9–20.

Beck, Nathaniel, and Jonathan Katz. 1995. "What to Do (and Not to Do) with Time Series Cross Section Data in Comparative Politics." *American Political Science Review* 89 (3): 634–47.

Berelson, Bernard, Paul Lazarsfeld, and William McPhee. 1954. *Voting: A Study of Opinion Formation in a Presidential Campaign.* Chicago: University of Chicago Press.

Bianco, William T. 1998. "Different Paths to the Same Result: Rational Choice, Political Psychology, and Impression Formation in Campaigns." *American Journal of Political Science* 42 (4): 1061–81.

Bobo, Lawrence, and Franklin D. Gilliam Jr. 1990. "Race, Sociopolitical Participation, and Black Empowerment." *American Political Science Review* 84:377–93.

Bochel, John M., and David T. Denver. 1971. "Canvassing, Turnout and Party Support: An Experiment." *British Journal of Political Science* 2:257–69.

———. 1972. "The Impact of the Campaign on the Results of Local Government Elections." *British Journal of Political Science* 2:239–43.

Brams, Steven J., and Morton D. Davis. 1974. "The 3/2's Rule in Presidential Campaigning." *American Political Science Review* 68 (1): 113–34.

Brody, Richard. 1984. "International Crises: A Rallying Point for the President?" *Public Opinion* 60 (1): 41–43.

———. 1991. *Assessing the President: The Media, Elite Opinion, and Public Support.* Stanford, CA: Stanford University Press.

Burden, Barry C. 2005. "Ralph Nader's Campaign Strategy in the 2000 U.S. Presidential Election." *American Politics Research* 33:672–99.

Cain, Bruce E., and Ken McCue. 1985. "The Efficacy of Registration Drives." *Journal of Politics* 47 (4): 1221–30.

Campbell, Angus, Phillip Converse, Warren Miller, and Donald Stokes. 1960. *The American Voter.* New York: John Wiley and Sons.

Campbell, James E. 2003. *The American Campaign: U.S. Presidential Campaigns and the National Vote.* College Station: Texas A&M Press.

Campbell, James E., Lynne Cherry, and Kenneth Wink. 1992. "The Convention Bump." *American Politics Quarterly* 20:287–307.

Carmines, Edward G., and James Stimson. 1989. *Issue Evolution: Race and the Transformation of American Politics.* Princeton, NJ: Princeton University Press.

Colantoni, Claude S., Terrence J. Levesque, and Peter C. Ordeshook. 1975. "Campaign Resource Allocation under the Electoral College." *American Political Science Review* 69 (1): 141–54.

Converse, Philip. 1964. "The Nature of Belief Systems in Mass Publics." In *Ideology and its Discontent.* Ed. David Apter. New York: Free Press.

———. 1966. "The Concept of a Normal Vote." In *Elections and the Political Order.* Ed.

A. Campbell, P. E. Converse, W. E. Miller, and D. E. Stokes. New York: John Wiley and Sons.

Corrado, Anthony. 2004. "National Party Fundraising Remains Strong, Despite Ban on Soft Money." Working paper, Brookings Institution, Washington, DC.

Corrado, Anthony, Thomas E. Mann, Daniel R. Ortiz, and Trevor Potter, eds. 2003. *Inside the Campaign Finance Battle: Court Testimony on the New Reforms.* Washington, DC: Brookings Institution Press.

Cramer, Richard Ben. 1992. *What It Takes: The Way to the White House.* New York: Random House.

Crouse, Timothy. 1974. *The Boys on the Bus.* New York: Ballantine Books.

Cutright, P. 1963. "Measuring the Impact of the Local Party Activities on the General Election Vote." *Public Opinion Quarterly* 27:372–86.

Cutright, P., and P. Rossi. 1958. "Grass-Roots Politicians and the Vote." *American Sociological Review* 23:171–79.

Dalager, John K. 1996. "Voters, Issues, and Elections: Are the Candidates' Messages Getting Through?" *Journal of Politics* 58 (2): 486–515.

DeBoef, Suzanna, and James Granato. 1997. "Near-Integrated Data and the Analysis of Political Relationships." *American Journal of Political Science* 41:619–41.

Downs, Anthony. 1957. *An Economic Theory of Democracy.* New York: Harper.

Edwards, George. 2004. *Why the Electoral College is Bad for America.* New Haven, CT: Yale University Press.

Eldersveld, Samuel J. 1956. "Experimental Propaganda Techniques and Voting Behavior." *American Political Science Review* 50 (2): 154–65.

Eldersveld, Samuel J., and Richard W. Dodge. 1954. "Personal Contact or Mail Propaganda? An Experiment in Voting and Attitude Change." In *Public Opinion and Propaganda.* Ed. Daniel Katz, Dorwin Cartwright, Samuel Eldersveld, and Alfred M. Lee. New York: Dryden Press.

Endersby, James, and John R. Petrocik. 2001. "Campaign Spending Influences on Turnout: Mobilization versus Agenda-Setting." Paper presented at the annual meeting of the Southwestern Social Science Association, Fort Worth, TX, March 14–18.

Enelow, James M., and Melvin J. Hinich. 1984. *The Spatial Theory of Voting: An Introduction.* Cambridge, NY: Cambridge Press.

Erikson, Robert S., Joseph Bafumi, and Bret Wilson. 2001. "Was the 2000 Presidential Election Predictable?" *Political Science and Politics* 34 (4): 815–19.

Erikson, Robert S., and Christopher Wlezien. 1999. "Presidential Polls as a Time Series: The Case of 1996." *Public Opinion Quarterly* 63 (Summer): 163–77.

Fackler, Tim, and Tse-min Lin. 1995. "Political Corruption and Presidential Elections, 1929–1992." *Journal of Politics* 57 (4): 971–93.

Fair, Ray. 1978. "The Effect of Economic Events on Votes for President." *Review of Economics and Statistics* 60:159–72.

Finkel, Steven E. 1993. "Re-Examining 'Minimal Effects' Models in Recent Presidential Elections." *Journal of Politics* 55 (1): 1–22.

Finkel, Steven E., and John G. Geer. 1998. "A Spot Check: Casting Doubt on the Demobilizing Effect of Attack Advertising." *American Journal of Political Science* 42 (2): 573–95.

Fiorina, Morris. 1981. *Retrospective Voting in American National Elections.* New Haven, CT: Yale University Press.

Franklin, Charles H. 2001. "Pre-Election Polls in Nation and State: A Dynamic Bayesian Hierarchical Model." Working paper, University of Wisconsin, Madison.

Freedman, Paul, and Kenneth Goldstein. 1999. "Measuring Media Exposure and the Effects of Negative Campaign Ads." *American Journal of Political Science* 43 (4): 1189–1208.

Geer, John G. 1988. "The Effects of Presidential Debates on the Electorate's Preferences for Candidates." *American Politics Quarterly* 16:486–501.

Gelman, Andrew, and Gary King. 1993. "Why Are American Presidential Elections So Variable When Votes Are So Predictable?" *British Journal of Political Science* 23:409–51.

Gerber, Alan S., and Donald P. Green. 2000. "The Effects of Canvassing, Telephone Calls, and Direct Mail on Voter Turnout: A Field Experiment." *American Political Science Review* 94 (3): 653–63.

———. 2001. "Do Phone Calls Increase Voter Turnout?" *Public Opinion Quarterly* 65:75–85.

Germond, Jack W., and Jules Witcover. 1981. *Blue Smoke and Mirrors: How Reagan Won and Why Carter Lost the Election of 1980.* New York: Viking.

———. 1985. *Wake Us When It's Over: Presidential Politics of 1984.* New York: Macmillan.

———. 1989. *Whose Broad Stripes and Bright Stars? The Trivial Pursuit of the Presidency, 1988.* New York: Warner Books.

———. 1993. *Mad as Hell: Revolt at the Ballot Box, 1992.* New York: Warner Books.

Gimpel, James, with Jason E. Schuknecht. 2003. *Patchwork Nation: Sectionalism and Political Change in American Politics.* Ann Arbor: University of Michigan Press.

Glenn, David, 2004. "On Death and Voting." Chronicle of Higher Education. October 8. http://chronicle.com/weekly/v51/i38/38a01201.htm.

Goldman, Peter, Thomas DeFrank, Mark Miller, Andrew Murr, and Tom Mathews. 1989. *The Quest for the Presidency, 1988.* New York: Simon & Schuster.

———. 1994. *The Quest for the Presidency, 1992.* College Station: Texas A&M Press.

Goldman, Peter, Tony Fuller, and Thomas M. DeFrank. 1985. *The Quest for the Presidency, 1984.* New York: Bantam Books.

Goldstein, Kenneth, and Paul Freedman. 2002a. "Campaign Advertising and Voter Turnout: New Evidence for a Stimulation Effect." *Journal of Politics* 64 (3): 721–40.

———. 2002b. "Lessons Learned: Campaign Advertising in the 2000 Elections." *Political Communication* 19:5–28.

Gosnell, Harold F. 1927. *Getting-Out-The-Vote: An Experiment in the Stimulation of Voting.* Chicago: University of Chicago Press.

Greenberg, Stanley B. 1995. *Middle Class Dreams: The Politics and Power of the New American Majority.* New York: Times Books.

Greene, Jay P. 1993. "Forewarned Before the Forecast: Presidential Elections, Forecasting Models, and the 1992 Election." *PS: Politics & Political Science* 26 (1): 17–23.

Hart, Roderick P. 2000. *Campaign Talk: Why Elections Are Good for Us.* Princeton, NJ: Princeton University Press.

Hayes, Daniel. 2005. "Candidate Qualities through a Partisan Lens." *American Journal of Political Science* 49 (4): 908–23.

Herrnson, Paul S. 2002. *Congressional Elections: Campaigning at Home and in Washington.* 3rd ed. Washington, DC: CQ Press.

Hetherington, Marc J. 1996. "The Media's Role in Forming Voters' National Economic Evaluations in 1992." *American Journal of Political Science* 40 (2): 372–95.

Hill, David Lee. 2005. *American Voter Turnout: An Institutional Approach.* Boulder, CO: Westview Press.

Hillygus, D. S. 2005. "Campaign Effects and the Dynamics of Turnout Intentions in Election 2000." *Journal of Politics* 66 (1): 50–68.

Hillygus, D. S., and Simon Jackman. 2003. "Voter Decision-Making in Election 2000: Campaign Effects, Partisan Activation, and the Clinton Legacy." *American Journal of Political Science* 47 (4): 583–96.

Hinich, Melvin, and Michael Munger. 1997. *Analytical Politics.* New York: Cambridge University Press.

Holbrook, Thomas M. 1994. "Campaigns, National Conditions, and U.S. Presidential Elections." *American Journal of Political Science* 38 (4): 973–98.

———. 1996. *Do Campaigns Matter?* Beverley Hills, CA: Sage Publications.

———. 2001. "Forecasting with Mixed Economic Signals: A Cautionary Tale." *PS: Politics & Political Science* 34 (1): 39–44.

———. 2002. "Did the Whistle Stop Campaign Matter?" *PS: Politics & Political Science* 35 (1): 59–66.

Holbrook, Thomas M., and Scott McClurg. 2005. "The Mobilization of Core Supporters: Campaigns, Turnout, and Electoral Composition in United States Presidential Elections." *American Journal of Political Science* 49 (4): 689–703.

Holman, Craig B., and Luke P. McLoughlin. 2001. *Buying Time 2000: Television Advertising in the 2000 Federal Elections.* New York: Brennan Center for Justice Publishing.

Huckfeldt, Robert, Paul Allen Beck, Russell J. Dalton, and Jeffrey Levine. 1995. "Political Environments, Cohesive Social Groups, and the Communication of Public Opinion." *American Journal of Political Science* 39 (4): 1025–54.

Huckfeldt, Robert, and John Sprague. 1992. "Political Parties and Electoral Mobilization: Political Structure, Social Structure, and the Party Canvass." *American Political Science Review* 86 (1): 70–86.

Iyengar, Shanto. 1991. *Is Anyone Responsible?* Chicago: University of Chicago Press.

Iyengar, Shanto, and Donald Kinder. 1987. *News That Matters: Television and American Opinion.* Chicago: University of Chicago Press.

Iyengar, Shanto, and John R. Petrocik. 2000. " 'Basic Rule' Voting: Impact of Campaigns on Party- and Approval-Based Voting." In *Crowded Airwaves: Campaign Advertising in Elections.* Ed. J. A. Thurber, C. J. Nelson, and D. A. Dulio, 113–48. Washington, DC: Brookings Institution Press.

Jackman, Simon, and Douglas Rivers. 2001. "State-Level Election Forecasting during Election 2000 via Dynamic Bayesian Hierarchical Modeling." Paper presented at the annual meeting of the American Political Science Association, San Francisco, CA, August 3–September 2.

Jacobson, Gary C. 1983. *The Politics of Congressional Elections.* New York: Brown.

———. 1990. "The Effects of Campaign Spending in House Elections: New Evidence for Old Arguments." *American Journal of Political Science* 34 (2): 334–63.

Jamieson, Kathleen Hall, with Paul Waldman, eds. 2001. *Electing the President 2000: The Insiders' View.* Philadelphia: University of Pennsylvania Press.

Johnson, Paul E., and Robert Huckfeldt. 2001. "Persuasion and Political Heterogeneity within Networks of Political Communication: Agent-Based Explanations for the

Survival of Disagreement." Paper presented at the annual meeting of the American Political Science Association, San Francisco, CA, August 30–September 2.

Johnston, Richard, Kathleen Hall Jamieson, and Michael G. Hagen. 2004. *The Presidential Campaign of 2000 and the Foundations of Party Politics*. New York: Cambridge University Press.

Judis, John B., and Ruy Teixeira. 2002. *The Emerging Democratic Majority*. New York: Scribner.

Just, Marion R., Ann N. Crigler, Dean E. Alger, and Timothy E. Cook. 1996. Crosstalk: *Citizens, Candidates, and the Media in a Presidential Campaign*. Chicago: University of Chicago Press.

Kahn, Kim F. 1994. "Does Gender Make a Difference? An Experimental Examination of Sex Stereotypes and Press Patterns in Statewide Campaigns." *American Journal of Political Science* 38 (1): 162–95.

Kahn, Kim F., and Patrick J. Kenney. 1997. "A Model of Candidate Evaluations in Senate Elections: The Impact of Campaign Intensity." *Journal of Politics* 59 (4): 1173–1205.

Kaid, L. L., and J. Boydson. 1987. "An Experimental Study of the Effectiveness of Negative Political Advertisements." *Communication Quarterly* 35:193–201.

Kaid, L. L., and A. Johnston. 1991. "Negative versus Positive Television Advertising in U.S. Presidential Campaigns, 1960–1988." *Journal of Communication* 41:53–64.

Kaid, L. L., C. M. Leland, and S. Whitney. 1992. "The Impact of Televised Political Ads: Evoking Viewer Responses in the 1988 Presidential Campaign." *Southern Communication Journal* 57:285–95.

Katz, Daniel, and Samuel J. Eldersveld. 1961. "The Impact of Local Party Activity upon the Electorate." *Public Opinion Quarterly* 25:1–24.

Katz, Elihu, and Paul F. Lazarsfeld. 1955. Personal Influence: The Part Played by People in the Flow of Mass Communications. Glencoe, IL: Free Press.

Kaufmann, Karen M., and John R. Petrocik. 1999. "The Changing Politics of American Men: Understanding the Sources of the Gender Gap." *American Journal of Political Science* 43 (3): 864–87.

Kelley, Stanley. 1961. "The Presidential Campaign." In *The Presidential Election in Transition, 1960–1961*. Ed. Paul T. David. Washington, DC: Brookings Institution.

———. 1966. "The Presidential Campaign." In *The National Election of 1964*. Ed. Milton C. Cummings Jr. Washington, DC: Brookings Institution.

———. 1983. *Interpreting Elections*. Princeton, NJ: Princeton University Press.

Kenny, Chris B. 1992. "Political Participation and Effects from the Social Environment." *American Journal of Political Science* 36 (1): 259–67.

Kerbel, Matthew. 1995. *Remote and Controlled: Media Politics in a Cynical Age*. Boulder, CO: Westview Press.

Kern, Montague. 1989. *30 Second Politics: Political Advertising*. New York: Praeger.

Key, V. O. 1966. *The Responsible Electorate: Rationality in Presidential Voting, 1936–1960*. Cambridge, MA: Harvard University Press, Belknap Press.

Kinder, Donald, and D. Roderick Kiewiet. 1981. "Sociotropic Politics: The American Case." *British Journal of Political Science* 11 (2): 129–61.

King, Gary, Robert O. Keohane, and Sidney Verba. 1994. *Designing Social Inquiry: Scientific Inference in Qualitative Research*. Princeton, NJ: Princeton Press.

Klein, Joe. 1996. *Primary Colors: A Novel of Politics*. New York: Random House.

Knoke, D. 1990. *Political Networks: The Structural Perspective*. New York: Cambridge University Press.

Kramer, Gerald. 1970. "The Effects of Precinct-Level Canvassing on Voter Behavior." *Public Opinion Quarterly* 34:560–72.

Lake, M. 1979. "A New Campaign Resource Allocation Model." In *Applied Game Theory*. Ed. S. J. Brams, A. Schotter, and G. Schwodiauer. Wurzburg, FRG: Physica-Verlag.

Lanoue, David J. 1991. "The'Turning Point': Viewers' Reactions to the Second 1988 Presidential Debate." *American Politics Quarterly* 19:80–95.

Lau, Richard R. 1982. "Negativity in Political Perception." *Political Behavior* 4:353–77.

Lau, Richard R., and David Redlawsk. 1997. "Voting Correctly." *American Political Science Review* 91 (4): 585–98.

Lau, Richard R., Lee Sigelman, Caroline Heldman, and Paul Babbitt. 1999. "The Effects of Negative Political Advertisements: A Meta-Analytic Assessment." *American Political Science Review* 93 (4): 851–75.

Lazarsfeld, Paul, Bernard Berelson, and Helen Gaudet. 1948. *The People's Choice: How the Voter Makes Up His Mind in a Presidential Campaign.* 2nd ed. New York: Columbia University Press.

Leighley, Jan E. 1990. "Social Interaction and Contextual Influences on Political Participation." *American Politics Quarterly* 18 (4): 459–75.

Lewis-Beck, Michael S., and Tim Rice. 1992. *Forecasting Elections.* Washington, DC: CQ Press.

Lewis-Beck, Michael S., and Charles Tien. 2001. "Modeling the Future: Lessons from the Gore Forecast." *PS: Politics & Political Science.* 34:21–23.

Lichter, Robert S., and Stephen J. Fransworth. 2003. *The Nightly News Nightmare: Network Television's Coverage of U.S. Presidential Elections, 1988–2000.* New York: University Press of America.

Lichter, Robert S., and Richard E. Noyes. 1996. *Good Intentions Make Bad News: Why Americans Hate Campaign Journalism.* 2nd ed. Lanham, MD: Rowman & Littlefield.

Lodge, Milton, Kathleen McGraw, and Patrick Stroh. 1989. "An Impression-Driven Model of Candidate Evaluation." *American Political Science Review* 87:399–419.

Lodge, Milton, Marco Steenbergen, and Shawn Brau. 1995. "The Responsive Voter: Campaign Information and the Dynamics of Candidate Evaluation." *American Political Science Review* 89:309–26.

Lodge, Milton, and Patrick Stroh. 1993. "Inside the Mental Voting Booth: An Impression-Driven Model of Candidate Evaluation." In *Explorations in Political Psychology.* Ed. Shanto Iyengar and William J. McGuire. Durham, NC: Duke University Press.

Lupfer, M., and Price, D. E. 1972. "On the Merits of Face-to-Face Campaigning." *Social Science Quarterly* 53:534–43.

Lupia, Arthur, and Mathew D. McCubbins. 1998. *The Democratic Dilemma.* New York: Cambridge University Press.

Magleby, David B., ed. 2003. *The Other Campaign: Soft Money and Issue Advocacy in the 2000 Congressional Elections.* Lanham, MD: Rowman & Littlefield.

Marcus, Gregory B., and Michael Mackuen. 1993. "Anxiety, Enthusiasm, and the Vote." *American Political Science Review* 87:672–85.

Matalin, Mary, and James Carville, with Peter Knobler. 1994. *All's Fair: Love, War, and Running for President.* New York: Random House.

Mayer, William G. 2002. "The Swing Voter in American Presidential Elections: A Preliminary Inquiry." Paper presented at the annual meeting of the American Political Science Association, Boston, MA, August 29–September 1.

Mayhew, David R. 1974. *Congress: The Electoral Connection*. New Haven, CT: Yale University Press.

McClurg, Scott D. 2004. "Indirect Mobilization: The Social Consequences of Party Contacts in an Election Campaign." *American Politics Research* 32 (4): 406–43.

McCombs, Maxwell, and D. Evatt. 1995. "Issues and Attributes: Exploring a New Dimension in Agenda Setting." *Communicacion y Sociedad* 8:7–32.

McCombs, Maxwell, and Donald Shaw. 1972. The Agenda-Setting Function of Mass Media. *Public Opinion Quarterly* 36:176–87.

Mendelberg, Tali. 2001. *The Race Card: Campaign Strategy, Implicit Messages, and the Norm of Equality*. Princeton, NJ: Princeton University Press.

Morris, Dick. 1997. *Behind the Oval Office: Winning the Presidency in the '90s*. New York: Random House.

Mueller, John E. 1970. "Presidential Popularity from Truman to Johnson." *American Political Science Review* 64:18–34.

———. 1973. *War, Presidents and Public Opinion*. New York: John Wiley and Sons.

———. 1994. *Policy and Opinion in the Gulf War*. Chicago: University of Chicago Press.

Mutz, Diana. 2002. "Cross-Cutting Social Networks: Testing Democratic Theory in Practice." *American Political Science Review* 96 (1): 111–26.

Nie, Norman, Sidney Verba, and John Petrocik. 1976. *The Changing American Voter*. Cambridge, MA: Harvard University Press.

Paletz, D. L. 1999. *The Media in American Politics: Contents and Consequences*. New York: Longman.

Patterson, Thomas E. 1980. *The Mass Media Election: How Americans Choose Their President*. New York: Praeger.

———. 1993. *Out of Order*. New York: Knopf.

Patterson, Thomas E., and Robert D. McClure. 1976. *The Unseeing Eye: The Myth of Television Power in National Politics*. New York: Putnam.

Petrocik, John R. 1996. "Issue Ownership in Presidential Elections with a 1980 Case Study." *American Journal of Political Science* 40:825–50.

Popkin, Samuel D. 1991. *The Reasoning Voter: Communication and Persuasion in Presidential Campaigns*. Chicago: University of Chicago Press.

Price, D. E., and M. Lupfer. 1973. "Volunteers for Gore: The Impact of a Precinct Level Canvass in Three Tennessee Cities." *Journal of Politics* 35:410–38.

Putnam, Robert D. 2000. *Bowling Alone: The Collapse and Revival of American Community*. New York: Simon & Schuster.

Rabinowitz, George, and Stuart Elaine MacDonald. 1989. "A Directional Theory of Issue Voting." *American Political Science Review* 83:93–121.

Robinson, Michael J., and Margaret Sheehan. 1983. *Over the Wire and On TV*. New York: Russell Sage.

Rosenstone, Steven J. 1983. *Forecasting Presidential Elections*. New Haven, CT: Yale University Press.

Rosenstone, Steven J., and John Mark Hansen. 1993. *Mobilization, Participation, and Democracy in America*. New York: Macmillan.

Sabato, Larry J. 1993. "Is There an Anti-Republican, Anti-Conservative Media Tilt?" *Campaigns and Elections* 14 (4): 16–20.

———, ed. 2001. *Overtime! The Election 2000 Thriller*. New York: Longman.

Salmore, Barbara, and Stephen Salmore. 1992. *Candidates, Parties, and Campaigns.* 2nd ed. Washington, DC: CQ Press.

Schumaker, Paul D., and Burdett A. Loomis. 2001. *Choosing a President.* New York: Chatham House.

Shaw, Daron R. 1999a. "The Effect of TV Ads and Candidate Appearances On Statewide Presidential Votes, 1988–96." *American Political Science Review* 93 (2): 345–61.

———. 1999b. "The Methods behind the Madness: Presidential Electoral College Strategies, 1988–1996." *Journal of Politics* 61 (4): 893–913.

———. 1999c. "A Study of Presidential Campaign Event Effects from 1952 to 1992." *Journal of Politics* 61 (2): 387–422.

Shaw, Daron R., Rodolfo O. de la Garza, and Jongho Lee. 2000. "Explaining Latino Turnout in 1996: A Three State Validated Survey Approach." *American Journal of Political Science* 44 (2): 338–46.

Shaw, Daron R., and Jeffrey Underwood. 2005. "Swing Voting in U.S. Presidential Elections." Working paper, University of Texas–Austin.

Shea, Daniel M., and Michael J. Burton. 2001. "Campaign Craft." New York: Praeger.

Shelley, Mack C., and Hwang-Du Hwang. 1991. "The Mass Media and Public Opinion Polls in the 1988 Presidential Election." *American Politics Quarterly* 19:59–79.

Sides, John M. 2003. "Mass Opinion and Elite Action in Political Campaigns." PhD diss. University of California–Berkeley.

Sidoti, Liz, and Ron Fournier. 2004. "Kerry Will Buy $45 Million in TV Time in Twenty States." *Associated Press Online*, August 31.

Sigal, Leon V. 1973. *Reporters and Officials.* Lexington, MA: DC Heath.

Stimson, James. 1995. "Regression in Time and Space." *American Journal of Political Science* 29:914–47.

———. 2004. *Tides of Consent.* New York: Cambridge University Press.

Thomas, Evan, and the Staff of *Newsweek.* 2004. *Election 2004: How Bush-Cheney Won and What You Can Expect in the Future.* New York: Public Affairs.

Thompson, Hunter S. 1973. *Fear and Loathing on the Campaign Trail '72.* San Francisco, CA: Straight Arrow Books.

Tufte, Edward R. 1978. *Political Control of the Economy.* Princeton, NJ: Princeton University Press.

Valentino, Nicholas A. 1999. "Who Are We on Election Day? Crime News and the Priming of Racial Attitudes during Evaluations of the President." *Public Opinion Quarterly* 63 (3): 293–320.

Verba, Sidney, Kay Lehman Schlozman, and Henry E. Brady. 1995. *Voice and Equality: Civic Volunteerism in American Politics.* Cambridge, MA: Harvard University Press.

Wand, Jonathan N., Jasjeet S. Sekhon, Walter R. Mebane Jr., Michael C. Herron, and Henry E. Brady. 2001. "The Butterfly Did It: The Aberrant Vote for Buchanan in Palm Beach County, Florida." *American Political Science Review* 95:793–810.

The War Room. 2004. DVD. Directed by Chris Hegedus and D. A. Pennebaker. 1994; Hollywood, CA: MCA Home Video.

Wattenberg, Martin P., and Craig L. Brians. 1999. "Negative Campaign Advertising: Demobilizer or Mobilizer?" *American Political Science Review* 93 (4): 891–99.

West, Darrell M. 1983. "Constituencies and Travel Allocations in the 1980 Presidential Campaign." *American Journal of Political Science* 27:515–29.

————. 1993. *Air Wars: Television Advertising in Election Campaigns, 1952–1992.* Washington, DC: CQ Press.

White, Theodore H. 1961. *The Making of the President, 1960.* New York: Pocket Books.

————. 1965. *The Making of the President, 1964.* New York: New American Library.

————. 1973. *The Making of the President, 1972.* New York: Athenaeum.

————. 1982. *America in Search of Itself: The Making of the President, 1956–1980.* New York: Harper & Row.

Wlezien, Christopher. 2001. "On Forecasting the Presidential Vote." *PS: Politics & Political Science* 34 (1): 25–32.

Wlezien, Christopher, and Robert Erikson. 2002. "The Timeline of Presidential Election Campaigns." *Journal of Politics* 64:969–93.

Zaller, John. 1992. *The Nature and Origins of Mass Opinion.* New York: Cambridge University Press.

INDEX